# GENERAL MUD

OTHER BOOKS BY THE SAME AUTHOR:

*Manpower in the Canadian Army: 1939-1945*

*Between Arab and Israeli*

*Megamurder*

Memoirs of Two World Wars

# GENERAL MUD

BY LT.-GEN. E. L. M. Burns, C.C., D.S.O., O.B.E., M.C.

MAPS BY ANTONY BRADSHAW



CLARKE, IRWIN & COMPANY LIMITED
TORONTO/VANCOUVER/1970

ISBN 0-7720-0475-7
PRINTED IN CANADA

## Acknowledgements

I wish to thank Dr. S.F. Wise, Director of History of the Department of National Defence, and Colonel D.J. Goodspeed, Deputy Director, for supplying me with a copy of my war diary for the period I served in Italy in 1944, and for other historical references. They also kindly read the manuscript, and corrected some slips, as did Colonel G.W.L. Nicholson, author of the two volumes of the Official History of the Canadian Army, *Canadian Expeditionary Force 1914-1919* and *The Canadians in Italy 1943-1945*, which are profusely quoted throughout this book. These military historians do not, of course, bear any responsibility for the opinions on the conduct of war, or any other controversial matters on which I have touched.

I also wish to thank the Public Archives of Canada, and Captain John Swettenham, Historian of the Canadian War Museum for assistance in obtaining the photographs herein.

Miss Ruth DonCarlos and Mrs. Mary Downey, of the editorial staff of the publishers have been most helpful in suggesting ways to make easier reading for those who are not soldiers or military historians.

Finally, many thanks are due to Miss Irene McInroy, who patiently typed and retyped the numerous revisions of the manuscript.

# Contents

# Contents

# Introduction

"This war is so much like the last one, it's not even funny," General Harry Crerar said to me when I reported on taking over command of the 5th Canadian Armoured Division in Italy. Then and there it seemed to be true. It was early in January 1944, and the cold, rainy, snowy, Adriatic winter seemed almost to reproduce the misery of the winters of World War I in France and Flanders. Rain and the churning of the clay soil by feet and the wheels and tracks of vehicles had created the soldier's ancient enemy—mud.

The tough battle in which the 1st Canadian Division had taken Ortona had recently ended. South of the town the wrecked homesteads and hamlets through which the Canadians had advanced recalled the blight and destruction of the western front in the first war.

The 11th Canadian Infantry Brigade, detached from the 5th Canadian Armoured Division, had just had its baptism of fire. After the capture of Ortona it had carried out an attack to the west, intended to extend and strengthen the positions we held. But the green troops had taken no ground, and had not even gained the sort of battle experience likely to improve their confidence. In capturing Ortona, and in the minor operations which followed, there had been numerous casualties—not great, measured against those of the grinding battles of World War I, but serious, compared to Canadian casualties in Italy up to that time.

It did all seem depressingly familiar.

However, for the Canadians, there were really more differences between the war in January 1944 and the war from 1915 to 1918 than there were similarities. First, it was not until July 1943 (nearly four years after the outbreak) that the Canadian Army became engaged in continuous operations. At Hong Kong in 1941 and at Dieppe in 1942 Canadians had fought and sustained heavy losses, but these were isolated and brief actions. In World War I, on the contrary, our men had been at the front within five months, and had fought on until the end. Their successors in World War II did not have to endure the long winters of misery in trenches; and, when they finally entered battle, after their long period of "standing on guard" in England, they did not have to suffer the shattering casualties of the battles on the western front from 1915 to 1917. But the men of 1943-5 were as brave, resourceful and enduring as the men of 1915-18; veterans of the first war recognized this and were duly proud.

When the 1st Canadian Division landed on the Sicilian beaches, the tide of war had turned. The Germans and Italians had finally been driven from North Africa. (This strategic gain had been crowned by the great Allied victory at Tunis.) The Russians, who had defended Stalingrad with superb heroism, annihilated the German formations besieging it, and began their march to the West which would stop only at Berlin. Still, much hard fighting lay ahead of the Canadians in Italy; and for the First Canadian Army and its formations the hard and bloody struggle from the beaches of Normandy to the Rhine was yet to come.

The 1st Canadian Division's entry into battle had been auspicious. The lightly contested landing was followed by a rapid surge through Sicily, and then a long advance up the Italian peninsula, until German resistance stiffened on the line of the Sangro. Then too the weather turned bad; the troops had to struggle against rain, cold, rushing streams and endless mud.

Although this was a recurrence of the World War I battle conditions in Flanders, there was a great improvement in tactics; in the methods and means for offensive action. During most of World War I, when the infantryman went forward into battle, he was supported by artillery fire only. But in World War II, besides artillery support, which he could call for by radio and which came promptly, he could also call for bombing from aircraft hovering over the battlefront, and within minutes see the bombs fall. His own armament included many more machine guns and mortars; and tanks backed him up or preceded him. When infantry, tankmen, gunners and airmen had got to know one another through training together as a team, and when they were put into battle with the advantages of surprise and a concentration of superior force, victories could be won without paying such a high price in soldiers' blood. Alexander and Montgomery had proved that this could be done in the triumphant advance across Africa from El Alamein to Tunis, and had gained the confidence of subordinate leaders, of the troops and of the nations behind the troops. There were no Sommes or Passchendaeles in World War II.

What I shall try to do in the first part of this book is to set down some of my recollections of World War I, especially of those episodes which seemed to show how troops should *not* be put into battle. The latter part of the book, dealing with my time as Commander of the 1st Canadian Corps in Italy in 1944 may show how these memories of World War I influenced me in the decisions I had to make.

As may be guessed from the title of this book, one of the realities which profoundly affected me was the effect of bad weather on the offensive power of infantry and tanks. I had seen, on the Somme and at Passchendaele, what it meant to attacking infantry when they had to slog through the mud produced by heavy and continuous rain.

It is not easy to cast the mind back fifty years, and recapture the impressions and emotions one felt when first introduced to war. It is hard to remember what one saw and felt in enough detail to form a vivid picture for the reader; to describe convincingly how one felt to find oneself immersed in a war which until then had been something distant, read about in the newspapers, seen through drawings and photographs. Perhaps the years have filtered the mind's record of things perceived, and my recollections focus on what affected thought and behaviour in the second war, twenty-five years later.

Another book of reminiscences by a general may need some justification. The classical excuse is that such works provide material for historians. Admittedly, a general's memoirs may suffer from faulty memory, bias, or untruth. However, the scholar of a later period, winnowing through them, may be able to separate some grains of truth from the chaff. Thus the military biographer may contribute a few footnotes to history.

Ambitious junior officers are advised to study military history and the writings of those who have held high command or staff appointments. This is supposed to provide the student with a stock of vicarious experience on which he can draw when he is faced in war with the necessity to decide. But is the furnishing of such study material any longer sufficient reason for the production of yet another war biography? Many retired generals, since 1945, have become convinced that western civilization could be almost obliterated if there should ever be another great war. If war is obsolete for the settling of international disputes, should the injunction of Micah not be obeyed: "Nation shall not lift up sword against nation, neither shall they learn war any more." If so, no one should teach war any more, or contribute to teaching it.

However, even if the world hopes there will be no more great wars, the United Nations, created "to save succeeding generations from the scourge of war," has not been able to save the generation which came of age after World War II from the whips of many small wars. In some instances, military action taken under the U.N. flag has succeeded in preventing small or incipient wars from growing into great ones. Therefore the military profession, and the need for the study of its practice, is not yet merely a subject of historical curiosity.

Optimists hope that the United Nations may grow in unity and authority—in spite of discouraging trends through two decades. And if this happens, all military actions of any scope should be to repress or prevent breaches of the peace under the U.N. flag. When and if such global policing becomes effective, we shall have reached the epoch when indeed disarmament can be general and complete among the nations. But even then, officers of the police forces operating under the U.N. will need to know something about how to use military force with maximum economy, and consequently will need to study military history.

There is a final reason why I decided to write this book. It is that no Canadian general who has held command in the field has left memoirs. Through the labours of the Historical Section of the Department of National Defence, we now have excellent histories of what Canadian soldiers did in World Wars I and II. I have drawn heavily on these histories in framing the personal account which appears in the following pages. But the Canadian generals of World War I died without leaving books giving their versions of the actions in which they had led the Canadian divisions. I realize that what I may have to say will be of much less value than what could have been put into books by, for example, General Currie, General McNaughton or General Crerar. Canadians who held high command in World War II still live, and may write their stories. But until now, there is this gap in what might be called war Canadiana. I offer this book in the hope it may do something to fill it.

GENERAL MUD

# First days at the front

I was lucky in my employment in World War I. Shortly before it broke out, I had passed into the Royal Military College, and remained there until I had reached my eighteenth birthday—June 1915—when I was commissioned in the Royal Canadian Engineers. After about nine months in Canada, I was able to get overseas with the signal company being formed for the 4th Canadian Division. I went to France as signal officer of the 11th Canadian Infantry Brigade in August 1916, when the division, having completed organization in England, crossed the Channel and a day or so later entered the trenches.

The war was two years old. The autumn of 1914 had seen the drive of the powerful German armies through Belgium, only halted on the Marne, barely forty miles from Paris. This was followed by the "Race to the Sea"—a parallel extension towards the west of the German and Franco-British armies, each trying to outflank the other. By the end of the year a continuous line of trenches from Switzerland to the Channel had been established—a line on which the German and Allied armies wrestled back and forth for the next four years, filling the cemeteries on either side with uncounted thousands of bodies of German, French and British youth. In 1915 there had been the costly and unsuccessful futile Allied attempts to take the offensive and break through the German defences, in the battles of Artois and Loos. In April of 1915, the Canadians had met their first great test in battle, and had proved their steadfastness in defence, in the first gas attack at Ypres. While these inconclusive contests took place on the western front, the Germans had gained great victories over the massive and ill-led Russian armies. German victories in the east continued through 1916. Seven months after the arrival of the 4th Canadian Division in France, we were to hear of the beginning of the revolution, signalling the rapid decline of Russian fighting power.

The Battle of the Somme had begun on the 1st of July. This was one of the bloodiest of the battles in what, unrealized at the time, had become a war of attrition. Into the "mincing machine" the divisions, which Britain and the Dominions had raised since 1914, were fed, and suffered such a toll of their best young manhood that they could never attain the fighting potential they might have had. Generations of military critics have made us familiar with this theme, so that the names of the Somme and Passchendaele evoke all the horrors of the war on the western front. But at the time those of us who were to take part in this battle, fortunately, had little premonition of what it would be like. We thought it was to be the "Big Push," in which the British and French Armies, now superior to the Germans in artillery and munitions, would break through the trench lines and drive the invaders back from the soil of France.

The Somme had been preceded by another horrible grinding battle—Verdun.[1] The German high command had initiated it on the theory that the French army would have to defend to the last the vital territory which Verdun's fortifications covered. Then the power of the German artillery and their supposedly superior offensive tactics would impose such heavy losses on the French that they would be "bled white"—and their military power would collapse. Terrible losses were indeed inflicted on the French armies in the Verdun battle, which raged from February to July 1916, but these losses were almost equalled by those of the attacking Germans.

It was at this stage of the war that the 4th Canadian Division arrived at the front. The 11th Canadian Infantry Brigade took over the sector immediately to the south of the Ypres Salient.[2] It was known as the St. Eloi Sector, and extended about 1,000 yards north and south of the former village of that name. The houses of this village had been destroyed in the fighting of the previous two years, and nothing remained but splintered timbers, bricks and other rubble which could not be distinguished from the shell-tossed earth unless one looked carefully. The last fight in this sector had been a sad history of mud and muddle, not untypical of Allied operations at this stage of the war. On March 27, a chain of seven mines had been blown under the German trenches about 250 yards beyond the village. The German garrison was practically obliterated and a line beyond the craters was occupied by the 3rd British Division. On April 4 the 2nd Canadian Division had relieved the British; they were driven out of the positions gained by a German attack on April 6 and mounted a series of abortive counterattacks in the days following.[3] Canadian casualties were 1,343, German 483.

On June 2, two German divisions had mounted a surprise attack on the Mount-Sorrel–Hill 62 sector, to the north of St. Eloi, then held by two brigades of the 3rd Canadian Division. This flank of the Salient was notorious for the grim battles over a few hundred yards of churned mud, a pudding of remnants of barbed wire, stakes, revetments, stinking of death and chloride of lime. The counterattacks on June 12, by which the 1st Canadian Division retook nearly all the ground lost, were the first operations which were planned and executed entirely under Canadian direction. They may be said to be the first example of the Canadian system of command and staff work which helped to bring success and renown to Canadian arms in World War I, and of which more will be written in the succeeding pages. The British Official History remarked that "the first Canadian deliberately planned attack in any force had resulted in an unqualified success."[4]

In the battles of May-June in the Salient, the Canadians suffered approximately 8,000 casualties, and the Germans 5,765.[5] The depleted ranks of the 1st and 3rd Canadian Divisions were filled by drafts from Canadian battalions in England, including some of those which were about to form the 4th Division. So often I watched the drafts move off from the parade grounds in Bramshott Camp that summer, loaded down with the heavy pack and equipment of those days, with bands cheerfully blaring "Colonel Bogey," "National Emblem" and other popular marches. To this day I cannot hear those tunes without sadness, without recalling how to their strains those thousands of young men marched off to the battlefield–one in five of them marked for death or maiming.

As I have already mentioned, I went to France as the signal officer of the 11th Canadian Infantry Brigade. I remained in that post for about eighteen months. The signal officer lived at brigade headquarters, which was usually a mile or so behind the front line and so nearly always exempt from shellfire; nevertheless close enough for us to have constantly in mind the conditions under which the infantry lived. Brigadiers and their staff officers toured the forward areas day by day, and the record shows that not a few were killed or wounded.

Those who served in other arms felt a certain humility when they compared their lot with that of the infantryman. Infantry casualties, especially in attack, were far greater than those of the artillery, the engineers or other troops. It was they who braved the machine-gun fire, struggled through the mud, got hung up on the wire. In defence, they suffered the concentrations of shell and mortar fire, bore the brunt of the German assault. Even in so-called static periods, they lived permanently at the mercy of the weather, wading through mud and water in undrained trenches, seldom having any adequate shelter from the elements. Soldiers of other arms would speak of "the poor bloody infantry"—abbreviated P.B.I. The bare words may seem to imply a shade of condescension; in fact they were a tribute of respect.

In whatever echelon of the military machine the soldier happened to find himself, he had a profound conviction that the man in the echelon behind him had a pretty easy and safe time of it. The men in battalion headquarters professed scorn for the easy life of the fellows at brigade headquarters, or at the battalion transport lines (usually fairly well back from the trenches); those located at company headquarters had the same feeling about the inhabitants of battalion headquarters. There was a story of a section corporal who spoke bitterly of the "bombproofers" back at platoon headquarters —all of 100 yards behind the front line.

As my men and I approached the front, the first signs of war's destruction we noticed were the wounded trees. It was not until we got within about a thousand yards of the combat area that we saw completely shattered trunks. But for some miles back, here and there we saw a fine tree blasted, usually one of the poplars bordering the long straight granite-block paved *chaussées.* (It was over these roads that the armies in France and Flanders endlessly marched and were carried in buses in the divisional reliefs, concentrations and regroupings necessitated by the strategy, such as it was, in the war of the trenches.) The shell-struck tree might have only a large branch wrenched off, leaving a splintery fragment. But it never failed to arouse the thought, "We're getting near it," and the conjecture that what could happen to the limb of a tree could happen to a human limb. Then, as we came closer to the front line, in areas where there had been intense fighting, as in the St. Eloi Sector, the trees had been whittled down by high explosive and shrapnel to stumps pointing a sheaf of slivers to the sky. What had been blown off was soon collected for firewood, always in short supply.

Then there were the houses with shell damage. We thought of the Bairnsfather[6] cartoon of the inquisitive newcomer to the front asking Old Bill, "Wot made that 'ole?" and the sour reply, "Mice."

As we approached nearer to the front, damage increased, until soon nothing was left but scattered bricks and splintered wood. Some of the farmhouses in the St. Eloi Sector had been used as headquarters of battalions or companies since the Ypres Salient first became a battleground in 1914. Cellars originally provided some protection from shrapnel and air-burst high explosive. They had been strengthened with I-beams and sandbags. Presumably it was hoped that this would enable them to protect the occupants against a direct hit by a shell of 4.2- or 5.9-inch calibre. When I compared these structures with the recommendations in the engineering pamphlets, I hoped that if they should ever be hit, I would be somewhere else.

The 11th brigade headquarters was at the Dickebusch farm. This was the residence of the burgomaster of Dickebusch.[7] At least, we thought he was the burgomaster. The farmhouse and out-buildings were constructed on the standard model for those parts: the farmhouse on one side, the stables and barn on the other two sides, and the whole forming a "U" in plan. They enclosed the midden, on which the animal manure and other refuse was deposited to ripen until it should be required for fertilizing the fields. At first we found the stink formidable but we soon got to know that there were many worse smells in war. Older soldiers informed us that the size of the midden was an index of the farmer's prosperity. It was also suggested that the local people considered the effluvium to be healthy as perhaps conferring some kind of immunity to various diseases.

The farmhouse and buildings were undamaged, although they were within easy range of the medium German artillery. This immunity gave rise to some unkind thoughts; the latrine gossip was that the burgomaster was somehow *persona grata* with the enemy, perhaps even to the extent of supplying them with information. I don't think anyone took this seriously; doubtless the I(b) organization (counterespionage) was effective enough to have detected any improper actions on the part of this locally prominent citizen. But spies and spying were something of an obsession in the early days of the war. Defeats, even minor tactical setbacks, were often attributed to prior German knowledge of our plans, which they discovered by underhanded intelligence methods. But as so many war memoirs and historic reviews have established, the Germans needed no great intelligence apparatus, apart from ordinary ground and air observation, as the preparations for Allied offensives were usually sufficiently obvious. In the last twelve months of the war, however, the Allies relearned the importance of surprise, and concealed their intentions better.

The officers' mess was in one of the rooms of the farmhouse. There was no luxury about it, nor was much time spent over meals. Our Commander, Brigadier-General Victor Odlum, did not touch alcohol himself and this, naturally, did not encourage drinking in others. Relatively little else was talked of but the immediate business of the brigade. A picture of one dinner remains in my memory. A German long-range, high-velocity gun, known locally as "Pushful Percy," opened a strafe of some point in the rear area, and the trajectory of the shells seemed to pass right over our heads. No one mentioned these noises, but as each shell passed (and we only heard them after they had passed) everyone (except the Brigadier) bowed involuntarily over his plate. The effect, in the dark room lit only by candlelight, with its high ceiling and stone walls, gave the impression of monks at their refection, bowing at the mention of holy names.

The immunity of the brigade headquarters did not last for long after we had moved in. Living accommodation and the signal office were in shelters of the cut-and-cover type. That is, a shallow excavation was roofed with semi-circular steel sections, and earth or sandbags were piled on top. They offered less protection than the farm cellars just described. So it was decided they should be strengthened. Our amateurish solution was to pile more layers of sandbags on top of the mounds, which were overgrown with grass and therefore blended in with the tree-bordered little field in which they stood. But the new sandbags were light beige in colour, and showed up like the proverbial banana in a coal-scuttle to German air observation. Anyway, whether or not the Germans knew what it was, they felt that this Canadian industry should not remain without some token of appreciation. So one afternoon they sent over a series of five-nines,[8] very well grouped, in the headquarters area. I happened to be absent at the time, visiting battalion and company headquarters up the line, and returned to find about a dozen shell-craters and a good deal of suppressed excitement. Fortunately, no shelter had been hit, and no casualties incurred—with a minor exception. A shell had landed in the farm midden, and besides spreading some of the manure where it would do no good, one of the shell fragments had wounded the farmer's daughter. This young woman, solidly built on the Flemish rural pattern, had been growing more beautiful day by day—at least in the eyes of the men round the brigade headquarters, deprived of the sight of any other female face and figure. So when the small piece of shell imbedded itself in her ample posterior, numerous solicitous volunteers were there to apply first field dressings.

In my observation, most old soldiers don't "look back in anger." They like to reminisce about funny incidents, the better times, short and inconsequential though they may have been in the whole grim chronicle of the war. All wartime service was not a horrifying sequence of blood and guts, boredom and terror. But to say this is not to minimize the fear, hardship and suffering undergone by nearly every soldier in the infantry, or those in other arms whose duties took them frequently into the zone where the infantry soldier fought and had his existence.

No one *wants* to remember that he was afraid; to remember the death of comrades, the man beside one cut off from life in a second by a rifle or machine-gun bullet, an exploding shell's conversion of the human body from the image of God to offal. It is, I suppose, a merciful dispensation that human beings have a tendency to forget the horrible and to recall mainly the pleasant.

One of the themes I will develop in the succeeding chapters of this book is that a general must keep in mind the limit of his resources in manpower. This may give the impression that a general thinks of the men under his command as mere statistics; so many men fit for duty, so many sick, wounded or killed—statistics, or "bodies" to use the World War II staff officers' slang. In fact, there can have been very few generals indeed who have been so cold-hearted. One reads of the Duke of Wellington, a tough Commander if there ever was one, weeping when he saw the dead at the trenches of Badajoz. But the testimony of many books about World War I, and recollection of personal experiences, cause the chilling conviction that there was a wide gap between some of the top generals and their troops. Not only were their headquarters distant from the front, but they were far from understanding what the soldier had to endure, and what he might be thinking. However, the remote-control general has been made into a stereotype, and that is unjust to many, perhaps a majority, of the generals of that time. In any case, Canadian divisional commanders should be exempted from this criticism. They nearly all had begun the war as battalion commanders, and so had been close to the men in the line.

Field-Marshal Montgomery affirms in his memoirs: "I went through the whole war on the Western Front, except during the period I was in England after being wounded; I never once saw the British Commander-in-Chief, neither French nor Haig, and only twice did I see an Army Commander."[9]

It was plainly a realization of lack of communication, and its unhappy effects, which made Lord Montgomery in World War II adopt the practice of haranguing the troops in relatively small groups, and showing himself to them as often as he could. He wrote, again in his memoirs: "To command such men demanded not only a guiding mind, but also a point of focus . . . It helped, I felt sure, for them to recognize as a person—as an individual—the man who was putting them into battle."[10]

In following this line, he was reverting to the habits of great commanders of the past, when war was simpler and armies were not spread out over such wide spaces. The more hidebound and unreflective of the British officer corps considered his harangues rather ridiculous, an evidence of vanity. Some others who saw his point tried to follow his example, but, lacking his personality and skill in public speaking, did not make much impression. Being a poor speaker, and thus averse to talking to larger groups than could fill a medium-sized room, I never tried the Montgomery technique. Looking back, I regret that I never had any instruction in public speaking—or thought that I needed it, until with seniority in rank I appreciated its importance. It is an art which any young officer aspiring to rise in the military profession should learn and practise. General Maxwell Taylor, in his book *The Uncertain Trumpet*, remarks that the skill he found most useful when he was Chairman of the U.S. Chiefs of Staff Committee was what he had learned as a member of his high school debating society.

Every commander knows that whatever order he may give depends for its execution on the soldiers at the base of the military pyramid, not only those who are facing the enemy at close quarters, but also those carrying out some supporting operation under fire or hardship which tries their courage and endurance. He will not see them with his own eyes while the operations are at their critical point: this is impossible for the most part on the modern battlefield with its wide dispersion of men and weapons. So as he tries to estimate what is happening, how the battle is going, he will consciously or unconsciously fill in the gaps in the exiguous information that comes back to him from subordinate commanders, and from air and ground observers, with an imagined background supplied from his own firsthand experience.

It will, I think, be obvious to the reader that the commander of a higher formation who has worked up through the command of lower formations and units, where he has been close to where the fighting is, has a great advantage, and, ideally, no higher commander should be without such experience. He will know what men can do, the probable limits of their endurance and what can be expected from them in the attack. It will not be a precise knowledge, on which exact calculations can be based, but war is not an exact science; generalship is not a matter of applying computer readouts.

It is not by coincidence that the most distinguished and able British commanders of higher formations in World War II—Alexander, Montgomery, Slim—were graduates from the cruel school of the infantry in World War I. I unfortunately lacked this hard-won knowledge as a qualification for high command. The limits of the experience which I did have will become clear in the following pages. As already mentioned, I commanded an infantry brigade signal section. What had such a unit to do, and what kind of men comprised it?

In 1914 the commander of a brigade or higher formation could no longer direct a battle, as Napoleon did, by watching events from some vantage point, sending off messages, oral or scribbled, by mounted aides-de-camp, or even going himself to points where the battle was critical, and giving orders directly to the officers on the spot. This being ruled out by modern battlefield conditions, the commander's best substitute for face-to-face talk is to use the telephone. In World War II, portable two-way radios usually provided a reliable telephone link, but in 1916, when my war experience began, the best available form of communication was the line telephone. It was the task of the brigade signal section to lay and maintain the telephone lines, and if these were broken by shellfire, or otherwise disrupted, the signallers had to get the messages through by some other means; for example, by visual Morse signalling, or, in the last resort, by runner.

There are, of course, exceptions to the general rule that a commander does not nowadays exercise his function in battle through direct contact with his subordinates. Sometimes situations, critical to success or failure, occur in some limited sector where a higher commander can and should intervene by going to the spot himself. Of course, he should frequently visit and confer with his immediate subordinates, and less frequently with the commanders one level below; that is, the divisional commander will regularly see his brigade commanders, and should quite often see the battalion commanders. He should try to see as much as possible for himself, but seeing for oneself is not easy on the modern battlefield.

The personnel of the brigade signal section was divided between linesmen and office staff. The linesmen had the duty of laying the telephone lines, and repairing them when they were broken—consequently theirs was the most dangerous task, as they were exposed to shellfire and sometimes small-arms fire when carrying it out.

Sergeant Cartwright was the sergeant in charge of the linesmen. He was a stocky young man of medium height, who before the war had been a drugstore clerk in Montreal. Red-haired, with a longish nose usually bright pink in the cold weather, and by no means interested in spit and polish, he was an excellent leader, and always had the respect and willing obedience of the somewhat tough and unmilitary characters under his charge. He won the M.M. on the Somme, and was evacuated, suffering from the effects of mustard gas, during the Passchendaele operation.

The man whose face and voice first comes to my mind when I happen to think of my signal section in World War I is 2nd Corporal Wilde. He had been a power linesman in civil life, and was a tall, loose-jointed fellow, with brown eyes and hair, and a face tanned by his outdoor occupation. He constantly wore a cheerful smile, the effect of which was somewhat marred by a missing front tooth. During the days of training at Bramshott he had been a sore trial to me, as he seemed incapable of going through three consecutive movements in foot drill without making some mistake. (I was trying, with slight success, to bring the section's standard of drill nearer to that of the Royal Military College.) However, when we got into the field I soon found he was about the most valuable man I had; skilled at his job, and fearless. I became very fond of him. I have forgotten what his first name was. Anyway, he was generally called "Oscar," after his celebrated namesake, and it was a stock article of section humour that he shared the notable aberration of that unhappy aesthete. But Wilde always grinned patiently at this hard-worked joke.

Another important element in the section was the telegraph operators, a class of tradesmen which I imagine is now extinct. These men were professionals, who had either worked on wire services for commercial telegraph companies, or for railroads. They translated the clicking of the Morse instrument into letters written down by hand on the army forms, and vice versa. I was lucky in having several very skilled operators. Their task was to take and receive messages coming from the division, to which it was generally possible to maintain a line good enough to allow the telegraph instrument to be used. They all had a very clear cursive handwriting—a necessity in their trade, and a rarity today.

The signal office, which had to be systematically run in order to ensure that all messages and despatches had been properly delivered and registered and reached their proper destination, was under the charge of Sergeant Ayris. He was English by birth, and had been a bank accountant before joining up. A methodical careful man, in character with his former occupation, he managed the office efficiently. After the war he returned to banking, and when I last heard from him he was a branch manager.

As I have said, most communication was by line telephone, and the brigade office had a switchboard of twenty lines or so. The operation of this exchange was naturally important in providing the staff with the service they needed. I was fortunate in having another group of intelligent—and what was more, patient—young men to perform this thankless task. Summers, Huston, Whitmore and the Marritt brothers were aspirants to the Methodist ministry, who had been students at Victoria College of the University of Toronto, and had enlisted in a group. Sometimes staff officers grew rather testy if communication was not instant and trouble-free, and would blame the operators in vigorous military terms. The Christian humility of my ministers-to-be was a distinct asset in these circumstances. Once, however, I happened to be standing behind the switchboard, unknown to the operator, when he was on the receiving end of one of these tirades. Presently he pulled the jack from the switchboard, so that what he said could not be heard by the irate staff officer who was abusing him, and pronounced loudly and very distinctly, "B . . . s!"

Summers, Whitmore and Huston all entered the ministry after the war; I like to think that their wartime experiences made them the better pastors.

Last, but not least important, were the "runners." They were men attached from the battalions of the brigade, and their task was to carry written orders, administrative instructions and general "bumf" on foot to the battalions and other units. When the lines were cut and there was no alternative means of communication, they had to carry the messages by hand, usually through shellfire. In action forward of battalion, the battalion and company runners were usually the only dependable way of getting messages through. The literature of World War I contains many stories of the bravery of the infantry runners. Of course, the runs from brigade to battalions were seldom dangerous, nevertheless the men were taking greater risks than the regular members of the section. Some of them also helped as linesmen, while others worked as registry clerks in the office.

One, whom I remember best, had a rather peculiar form of expertise. The section had an establishment of six bicycles, which the runners used when the roads were suitable. One day I discovered that we had only two or three bicycles—the rest, I was informed, had been purloined by miscreants from other units. While it was possible to get replacements for missing equipment by "indenting" (explaining that the missing articles had been "destroyed by shellfire") it usually took a long time for the item to come forward, and sometimes it did not come at all. In the case of the bicycles, it seemed to me, speedier methods were required. I thereupon let it be known that anyone who succeeded in "finding" one of the missing bicycles would be given two days' leave. In a very short while we had nearly a dozen bicycles. The most successful of the runners in this restoration of our bicycle establishment was Private Denis, of the 87th Battalion. I have often seen him since the war in Ottawa, and we usually discuss this rather unorthodox proceeding. To make sure that false claims to possession would not be entered by any other unit which might be missing a bicycle or two, Sapper Smith, our instrument artificer, painted them with our identifying symbols, and, as a further precaution, changed the serial numbers stamped on them.

At the time I took over command of this signal section, I had not reached my nineteenth birthday. In World War I very many subalterns were no older. Civilians perhaps may think that it was not very sensible for a youth of eighteen to be made responsible for the performance and well-being of a group of twenty or thirty men, many of whom would be older than he was.

The relationship of age to command responsibility was rather amusingly expounded to me three years later, after the war was over, when I was travelling by train to Montreal. I was in uniform, sitting in the smoking compartment, and the negro porter engaged me in conversation. He said he had served in the U.S. Tenth Cavalry, a regiment which I believe had a high proportion of negroes in its ranks. The ex-cavalryman asked me what my rank was, and when I told him I was a Captain, he said: "My goodness, I don't know how I'd be able to *obey* a young captain like you." I laughed, and told him I'd never had any difficulty about being obeyed.

Why was this? I suppose it was because I had absorbed the concept of discipline in the R.M.C.; one obeyed orders, and acknowledged the right of officers to give orders. So when one became an officer oneself, with the King's commission, one never thought that one's orders (if lawful) would not be obeyed. To disobey a lawful command was an offence under the Army Act! One fitted into the institutional framework of the army; one obeyed the orders given by those senior in rank, and in turn one was responsible for giving orders to one's subordinates, and seeing that they were obeyed.

These were the men I commanded. In this, and succeeding chapters, I shall try to set out the view I had at the time of my superior officers, and, primarily, of Brigadier-General Odlum, Commander of the 11th Canadian Infantry Brigade. I suppose that in seeing them and watching their way of doing things, I formed my picture of how a general functioned in war—an impression which probably was more lasting and important than anything one could acquire from reading military history.

Brigadier-General Odlum took command of the 11th Canadian Infantry Brigade when it was formed, in the summer of 1916, and continued to command it until demobilization. Before that he had distinguished himself as Commander of the 7th (B.C.) Infantry Battalion, in the Second Battle of Ypres, and in organizing and carrying through successfully the first operationally-planned trench raid. This was in the winter of 1915-16, and from that time on the raid became a feature of trench warfare. He was also a veteran of the South African war. Wounded three times, twice while commanding the 11th Brigade, he earned the C.B., the C.M.G. and the D.S.O. with two bars. This should tell enough of his personal courage, and the concentration and energy he devoted to the duties of his command. He was constantly in the forward areas, observing the condition of his troops, the state of the trenches and the lie of the land.

In the months when I served as his signal officer, there was little scope for any tactical originality at any echelon of command, from corps down. Offensives were carried out with the artillery as the major partner. The organization for a big attack was more like laying out railway schedules, or for a large civil engineering project, than for planning and preparing a battle in either the classical or World War II manner.

At one point during the winter of 1916-17, General Odlum decided to cancel the rum issue in the brigade. Instead, the troops in the forward area were to be served hot cocoa. Now it is a fact that the rum ration sometimes led to abuse; some soldiers got less than their share, while others managed to scrounge more and became drunk. A favourite soldier's song included the line, "Where's the Sergeant-Major? I know where he is; boozing up the privates' rum." But as can be imagined, General Odlum's innovation got minus zero in the front-line opinion polls. After a time he was overruled by the divisional commander, and the rum ration was restored.

In spite of this and other somewhat puritanical attitudes, General Odlum was a true leader, and held the respect and confidence of all who worked under him. And he, in turn, gave his confidence to anyone who did his job properly. Perhaps his loyalty was sometimes excessive. Junior officers on the brigade staff thought that he retained certain battalion commanders when they might better have been replaced. He certainly was not a ruthless man, although his manner sometimes made people think he was.

The Divisional Commander, Major-General David Watson, had been a militia officer and a newspaperman in Quebec. He had taken the 2nd Infantry Battalion to France in 1915 and had commanded the 5th Infantry Brigade before his appointment to command the 4th Canadian Division. At brigade headquarters, we frequently saw him about. But his personality was rather put in the shade by that of his General Staff Officer Grade I—Lieutenant-Colonel E. Ironside. The general opinion was that Ironside was the real commander of the division. It is not surprising that this view was current—whether it was true or not—when one recalls Ironside's subsequent career, towards the end of which he became Chief of the Imperial General Staff—the top appointment in the British Army.

At that time, many of the senior general staff officers and brigade majors in the C.E.F. were British. Up to 1914, few Canadians had passed through the Staff College at Camberley, and so the British supplied the men for the most important staff jobs. To some extent this resembled the Prussian system, under which a senior but somewhat obsolescent general would nominally command a formation, but the real control would reside in a younger member of the Great General Staff. The British officers selected to serve in the higher staff positions in the Canadian formations were professionals of high quality. They included many whose subsequent careers were very distinguished: Alan Brooke, Ironside, Charles Harington, for example. There was also Charles Portal, the World War II Chief of the Air Staff, who had commanded No. 16 Observation Squadron, R.F.C., which for a long period co-operated with the Canadian Corps.

These were the men who served under me, and the exalted ones whom I viewed from a distance. The 4th Division's breaking-in spell in the quiet Kemmel-St. Eloi Sector soon came to an end, and we were plunged into the Battle of the Somme as October began.

# The Somme

When people of the British Commonwealth learned the truth about the conditions under which the Battle of the Somme had been fought, it did more to create the horrified reaction against war than anything else that had happened between 1914 and 1918—except perhaps the Third Battle of Ypres, generally known as Passchendaele. After fifty years, what can be said that has not been said before? Not much, perhaps. However, most of the writing has been about the earlier days of the four-and-a-half month long struggle. The fighting then was fiercest, the casualties heaviest. No one thinks of the Somme without remembering the frightful losses of the first day of battle—the 1st of July, 1916—when 60,000 of the British attacking divisions were killed, wounded and missing; greater losses than in any day in the long history of the British Army. But I shall concentrate mainly on conditions towards the end of the battle, after September, when the weather got bad, and the troops were fighting and enduring in endless mud.

The Somme has been held up in many books as a prime example of the bankruptcy of the strategic thinking of World War I generals. They have been denounced for pursuing victory through attrition, for feeding men into this battle and others as butchers feed meat into a grinder. And, as already mentioned, they have been blamed for not knowing the conditions in the front lines, where the infantrymen pigged it until it was time for him to "go over the top with the best of luck."

However, it should not be accepted as a fact that the generals who ordered these attacks from the safety of their headquarters were inspired by the motives Siegfried Sassoon pins on them, in the following passage from *Memoirs of an Infantry Officer.*

> . . . the military caste who were making the most of their Great Opportunity for obtaining medal-ribbons, and reputations for leadership; and if I am being caustic and captious about them I can only plead the need for a few minutes' post-war retaliation. Let the Staff write their own books about the Great War, say I. The Infantry were biased against them, and their authentic story will be read with interest.[1]

Nearly every general who attained high command had proved his courage in former wars, former battles. They were probably *too* brave; too brave to realize the fear that might oppress and eventually freeze lesser men. They would doubtlessly have gallantly led their men, if chance had somehow put them in the van of the battle, but most of them did not seem to be able to imagine the exhausting will-sapping effect of struggling through mud, living in mud, for days on end.

It was not only the British who suffered terrible casualties, and the privations of the trenches and the shell-holes—for little gain. It was not only British generals who for years failed to find the right tactics to overcome the initial enormous advantage given to the defence by the machine gun, barbed-wire obstacles, trench systems and covered machine-gun emplacements. The Germans in their attempt to bleed the French army white at Verdun had attacked in the same desperate way, and the French resisted them; both sides pouring out blood in the mud. The French learnt their lessons, perhaps the most severe of any of the combatants, when they slaughtered off the prime of their youth in the early battles, hurling waves of men against machine guns and rapid firing artillery. In 1917 Canadians stared with open mouths at the cemeteries behind the Vimy Ridge where thousands upon thousands of wooden crosses showed where the valiant French soldiers lay.

Sir Basil Liddell Hart, in Volume I of his memoirs, tells of his experiences in the Somme battle. He was one of four officers who led seventy men of his battalion, the 9th KOYLI's,[2] out of the battle after the attack on July 1 into which they had gone 800 strong. A fortnight later he was badly gassed with phosgene, and was evacuated. During his convalescence he wrote a short book on the Somme Offensive, the "Impressions" of "a Company Commander." He remarks that on rereading it, he was amazed at the enthusiastic praise he gave to the British high command, and to Haig above all. That Liddell Hart should ever have held such an opinion, especially after his own recent experience of the Somme battle, will probably astonish anyone who has studied his subsequent writings. But it is not inexplicable; the British (including the Canadian) soldiers and junior officers really knew very little about the higher command; they were Olympians whose pictures were seen in the paper, with respectfully phrased commentary. The operations of the British Army were always victorious; and the undeniable setbacks only temporary. The British had always won, even if it was by muddling through. Wellington and Marlborough were among the greatest of generals of history; this greatest of wars would surely bring forth worthy British successors. So during most of the war the British soldier and subaltern trusted their superiors. Disillusionment came after the war, when the military historians and critics examined the record, and Lloyd George and Churchill employed their devastating rhetoric against the generals and admirals whose errors they had not had the prescience or political courage to prevent.

Our division was relieved in the St. Eloi Sector about September 21, and we went into reserve in the St. Omer area, about twenty-five miles west of Ypres. Lee-Enfield rifles were issued in place of the unsatisfactory Ross; we received the new box-type gas respirators to replace the PH helmets, and the troops were trained in the tactical methods which were being employed in the Somme battle, which we were soon to enter.

These tactics were based on the idea that, "The artillery conquers, the infantry occupies." The enemy was protected by trenches, in machine gun emplacements and behind barbed wire entanglements, which had first to be destroyed by prolonged artillery bombardment to enable the infantry to advance. Then, just before the assault, there would usually be an intense period of shelling all along the enemy forward positions, to keep the heads of his riflemen and machine-gunners down. After this a "rolling barrage"—which really progressed in lifts, or jumps of fifty or a hundred yards—would be laid down by the field pieces, while the shells of 4.5- and 6-inch howitzers detonated in a zone in front of this line of bursting shrapnel, with the 60-pounders ranging farther to the rear. At the same time the defensive fire of the enemy artillery would be silenced by counter-battery fire of a proportion of the heavier calibres of the Corps Artillery.

The infantry were supposed to advance behind the barrage, following it as closely as they safely could, so as to fall on the enemy defenders, dazed and shaken by the bombardment, before they could bring effective machine-gun and rifle fire to bear. The infantry attacked in "waves"—long straight lines, following each other at intervals of fifty or a hundred yards. The bayonet and the hand grenade were relied on to finish off the defenders who were left, and who did not surrender. Rifles and Lewis guns would come into play against counterattacks, after capture of the objective. This was the offensive system—it can hardly deserve the name of tactics. Only later in the war was it realized that the infantry platoon was a tactical unit that could employ fire and manoeuvre in the attack, still with the support of artillery, and sometimes in co-operation with tanks. But for infantry tactics of this sort to be possible at all, to give the infantryman half a chance to really fight the enemy with skill and craft, he had to be able to move—and move very fast. And, obviously, he could never move fast through ankle- or knee-deep sticky mud, weighed down by the impedimenta of trench warfare, loaded upon him by a military hierarchy which had gone sadly astray in its thinking.

> The men . . . who attacked . . . at Beaumont Hamel were weighted down with 120 rounds of ammunition, two sandbags, two grenades, helmet, smoke helmet (pre-gas-respirator), rations, water bottle, a groundsheet, and a first-field dressing. Forty percent of them carried shovels and ten percent picks. . . . A steady walk was the most they could manage, and the width of No Man's Land in this sector meant that as many as four attacking waves were exposed to the enemy fire at one time.[3]

The system of long preliminary bombardments had two effects which prevented the subsequent attack from being decisive—from piercing the enemy's organized defences, and achieving the breakthrough which the generals dreamed of from 1915 to 1917. As a first effect the terrain of the battle was broken up into a crater-field, which only needed a few hours' rain to become sticky, foot-clogging mud. This massive ploughing of the ground by high explosive made it impossible for the field artillery to move up rapidly. So when the infantry had struggled forward a thousand or so yards to their objectives in the first phase, the field artillery were at the limit of their range, and were no longer able to support a further infantry advance with barrage fire. The guns could not be moved forward until the engineers had laboriously reconstructed roads for them.

As I now see it, the most lasting impression which I carried forward from the First World War to the Second was the difference between what soldiers could achieve on the offensive when the weather was fair, the season was right and the ground reasonably firm under foot, compared to the heartbreaking struggle to advance a few hundred yards through the mud in the later battles on the Somme and in Passchendaele.

"Russia has two generals in whom she can confide—Generals Janvier and Février," said the Emperor Nicholas, after other Russian generals had failed to halt the Allied advance in the Crimea. Officers learning their trade at the staff colleges are taught that the weather is one of the important factors that must be taken into account in planning operations. But when one reads recent military history—or takes part in the actions which become military history—one sadly perceives that in practising the art of generalship, or the staff officer's trade, the effect of weather on operations is often left out of account. "General Mud" has to be added to the two cited by Emperor Nicholas. German soldiers got to know this unrelenting enemy only too well, and gave him his name when he brought their drive for the capture of Moscow to a halt in the late autumn of 1941.

Meteorological science at present does not allow one to predict the weather in Europe—except for the very short term. However, those who plan operations for the better seasons of the year may leave the weather factor out of their calculations, knowing that in all probability a few days of rain will be followed by a fine period. Moltke wrote in 1864: "An operation cannot be based on the weather, but it can be based on the season." But during several campaigns in both world wars in Europe, the planners and directors seemed to ignore the lesson which the kings and generals who had led mercenary armies in the seventeenth and eighteenth centuries had learned: it is advisable to go into quarters in the winter, and save manpower and other military assets to be used when the weather does not add to the difficulties of the offensive.

Military writers have tended to depreciate this and other practices of the great leaders of that epoch as no longer applicable in the days of universal conscription. Higher commanders and the military profession generally have seemed to think that they had an unlimited draft on the nation's manhood, that they did not need to think too much about how they should economize manpower. It did not occur to them to apply the famous military principle of economy of force to the expenditure of their capital in able-bodied soldiery. This expenditure is not counted only in the number of dead, the most poignant loss, but in all casualties: the wounded, who may not again be fit for service in the forward echelons of the infantry; and the missing, which usually means those taken prisoner, a loss which tends to increase as the war goes on. To sum it up, if a general uses up his capital in able-bodied soldiery before he has defeated his enemy, then he is defeated himself. This principle remains valid in the twentieth century, when the highest military staff organ of a nation, and not an individual general, is responsible for overall national war strategy.

Napoleon wrote, *"Il n'est aucun qui n'eut fait plusieurs campagnes, qui ne sache que la qualité la plus essentielle d'un soldat est de savoir supporter les privations avec constance."*[4] One might add, that if the general makes too many drafts on this quality, even the most doughty and enduring troops will come to an end of their endurance. To attack successfully, the assaulting troops need all their vigour, all their vital force. If they are exhausted by struggling through mud, the drive to break through the enemy's resistance, and more important, to exploit the gains, will not be there. I do not think it is too arbitrary to assert that in all the history of war, cold and snow have inflicted less misery and hardship on the soldier than has mud. Marshal Foch is quoted by Churchill as saying. "*Boche* is bad, and *boue* is bad, but Boche and *boue* together. . . . Ah. . . ."[5]

So much for the effect of the long preliminary bombardment in producing mud. The second effect was to destroy the possibility of surprise. The enemy knew where the attack was coming, and although his forward defences might be obliterated, he could still organize and strengthen more defensive lines to the rear, and have reserves in readiness for counterattack. As a result, the attacker could attain no decisive results either by breaking up enemy units and formations, or by the occupation of vital terrain. The battles became essentially like the combat of bulls, a head-on shock. In the battles of attrition, each general staff grimly counted its own casualties in dead, wounded and missing, and justified its losses by imagining that those of the enemy had been even greater.

In spite of all this, morale was certainly not low among the Canadian troops. We in the 4th Canadian Division were confident, perhaps due to the valour of ignorance. We had read in the newspapers that the Battle of the Somme was the long-anticipated "Big Push," in which the British and French armies would break into and through the German defensive system of fortifications. Then the shattered German armies would be driven out of France and Belgium. Lack of success of the British armies in previous battles was generally put down to shortages of guns and shells. As the Somme battle opened, it was understood that these shortages had been remedied. The British and Dominion troops that had suffered for two years from the pounding of the more powerful German heavy artillery would no longer have to fight with this disadvantage. German 5.9- and 8-inch howitzers would be matched by a greater number of 6-, 8- and 9.2-inch British pieces. Further back there were even batteries of 12 and 15 inches to counter the 420 mm. siege howitzers of which we had heard so much in the first days of the war, when Liège and other Belgian forts were captured quickly after their main works had been destroyed by these monster weapons.

It may be obscure to the non-military reader why the soldiers fighting in the front line, manning their own trenches, or attacking the enemy's, should be greatly concerned about whether there were guns of large calibre behind them or not. They would hardly ever see where the shells from these giants exploded. But since 1914 it had become clear to every front-line soldier that the trench war was for the most part an artillery war. In the trenches he was safe from rifle and machine-gun fire, except when defective communication trenches or fire positions gave concealed enemy snipers a chance. But hardly anywhere was he safe from the shells of the German howitzers, and later the numerous *minenwerfer* (mine-throwers).

An infantryman's sardonic definition of an "artillery duel" consisted of the artillery of each side pounding the opposing side's infantry trenches. There was truth in this, especially in the earlier stages of the war, before counter-battery methods had been fully developed. But whatever the targets were, the men at the very front had a lively sense that it was very important that if the enemy began shelling, he should get back as good or better than he gave; and, of course, on the offensive it was vital that the advancing infantry should be supported by overpowering fire. The symbol of artillery supremacy was the size of the greatest guns, although many gunners felt that the money and manufacturing effort put into the largest calibres would have been more economically and effectively spent by increasing the number of medium batteries—6-inch, 60 pounders.

Entraining at a station near St. Omer, we journeyed slowly to Doullens. A young staff learner and I had under our charge an unfortunate elderly officer who had seen fit to prepare himself for the rigours of the Somme by getting very drunk, and had been deposited by some Samaritan in General Odlum's compartment to sleep it off. Naturally he had been placed under arrest when the General arrived. We passed a train full of French soldiers going the opposite way at a junction and gave them cigarettes, while they invited us to sample their "*pinard*." Then we marched up to Albert, saw the famous hanging statue of the Virgin, and heard the legend that if it fell the Allies would lose the war. After bivouacking in a muddy brickyard in the rain, we moved up to a temporary headquarters in Sausage Valley, to the south of Pozières,[6] with heavy batteries thick all round us. The blast of the 60-pounders compressed the air in our headquarters dugout, the first well-constructed timber-lined German deep dugout we had seen. Why were their dugouts—deep shelters—so much better than ours?

Nearby was the village of Pozières, captured weeks before by a gallant assault by the Australians, who had moved out of the battle on relief by the Canadian Corps. Only brick and stone rubble and fragments of wood now remained where Pozières had once stood.

One day on the Albert-Bapaume road a little forward of the village, I happened to see Sir Douglas Haig with one or two of his staff. A trooper rode behind him with a lance, and from it a red and white pennant fluttered. Sir Douglas made a fine figure on a horse, and I admired him from a distance. He gazed for a while in the direction of Bapaume, and then departed. Of what was he thinking? Since 1952 his diaries have been available to the public.[7]

About this time he wrote in his despatch to the Chief of the

Imperial General Staff that the enemy might be close enough to the breaking-point for the Allies to achieve a success which would afford "full compensation for all that had been done to attain it." If the winter were normal, Haig went on, Allied operations could continue with profit as long as sufficient reinforcements and greater supplies of ammunition were forthcoming. If the winter were normal? Normal rain implied abnormal mud. And "continue with profit"? We shall look at the profit and loss account of these operations at the end of this chapter.

Perhaps I should say I was lucky to have seen the C.-in-C.; not many junior officers and men had. Officers from General Headquarters may have visited the forward areas periodically, but if so, few of the front-line troops knew of it.

It was October 10 when our division arrived on the Somme. By October 17th we had relieved the 1st and 3rd Canadian Divisions, taking over 2,000 yards of front roughly north of Courcelette (under command of the 2nd British Corps). Canadian Corps Headquarters and the 1st, 2nd and 3rd Divisions departed for the Vimy area, leaving their divisional artilleries to support the further Canadian attacks. About this time the weather really began to break. *C.E.F. 1914-1919* records that, "After a few days of fine weather, rain began falling steadily, and conditions steadily became worse in the front line trenches. In many places these had been reduced by the rain and the enemy shelling to mere ditches knee-deep with water."[8]

The constant rain permeated the ground to form the infamous Somme mud. No one who struggled through it will ever forget it. The overlying clay soil, saturated with the downpour, was puddled with the chalk turned up by shellfire and trench digging, and became a viscous mass, sticking to our boots in great heavy lumps, covering our clothing, rendering every step a burden, treacherously slippery, causing many falls.

During the few days of fine weather mentioned, the 11th Brigade prepared to take over its sector of the line. Reconnaissances went forward, and for me this meant going up to the place selected for battle headquarters, in the North Practice Trenches, about 100 yards northeast of Courcelette.[9] The road foward led past the sugar factory, south of the village, where there had been heavy fighting in the battle of September 15. A broken-down tank remained to mark the area where tanks had first been used in war. I remember another grim monument to the battle—the first dead man I had seen. He had been an artilleryman, a big strong-looking fellow. His body was leaning against a shattered tree, his limbs stiffened and swollen, almost bursting out of his uniform, his face entirely blackened with the changes of death. "Battlefield clearing"—which in particular means the burial of the dead—had somehow passed him by.

As we passed through Courcelette, along the road which ran along the southern side of the village, there was a burst of shellfire, and my little party paused, huddled together. On moving to the Somme, the 4th Division had been issued with steel helmets, which had come into general use in the British Army about that time. It was fortunate for me that we had them, for while we were standing there a fairly large lump of shell came down on top of my helmet with a resounding thump. It did no more harm than to make a big dent in the helmet, and a considerable bump on the top of my head. I retrieved the piece of shell and carried it round with me for some time. I recall also some of the men in the section arguing about the value of the "tin hat," as it was usually called. One of the telegraph operators clinched his argument by saying, "Look at Burns! He'd of been S.O.L. if he hadn't had one on."

Another time I was passing along the same route with some men when shelling began we decided to make our way along what passed for a communication trench near the Courcelette cemetery. In many places the trench was over knee-deep in liquid mud. At one point I stepped on something which yielded, and there rose up before me the rear end of a dead German. His clothes had been torn off, and his flesh, visible in places through the mud, was green. By that time we had been living for many days in the stink and visible presence of dead men, and so this very horrid sight excited no more than a moment's shock and disgust. But the memory has remained.

Brigade headquarters was in a deep German dugout, driven into the side of the valley in the North Practice Trenches (presumably so-called because they were not a component of the German defensive trench system, but seemed to have been dug for training purposes). The South Practice Trenches were on the other side of Death Valley—a shallow draw that had acquired its name because of heavy casualties suffered there in previous attacks. It was open to observation from the northeast, the infamous Quadrilateral and Le Sars.

German artillery observers were ready to bring down fire on groups of even two or three men moving in this dismal hollow.

The trouble with most of the German dugouts we took over was that their entrance faced the wrong way. The one which our headquarters occupied, however, faced the west, and was consequently away from our front. There were two tunnels which ran into the side of the valley, well and continuously revetted with solid timber; and our sappers had connected them together by a transverse tunnel. In one gallery General Odlum and his staff lived and worked, while the other was occupied by the signallers and runners, with whom I lived. Communication from the rear was by telephone and Morse buzzer. Forward, that is to battalion headquarters, communication was by telephone, with the wires laid in the trenches when possible, and otherwise overland. Every now and then they were broken by shellfire, or by someone putting a pick through them. Then the linesmen had to go out and repair them.

I recall that one evening in the signal section's part of the dugout, some of the men had begun to heat up the Maconochie "M. and V."[10] or pork and beans which we shared together. The cooking, such as it was, was done on a Primus stove. This generally-dependable article was designed to use kerosene as fuel. However, gasoline was often substituted, as it was more readily available, and this was rather dangerous. On this occasion the man using the Primus pumped too hard, and suddenly the burning gasoline spurted out of it in a great flame. Someone yelled "The Bombs!"—for the dugout was filled with boxes of trench mortar bombs—and in an instant there was a rush towards the steeply-sloping muddy dugout stairs, towards which, I blush to say, I also jumped. But Wilde kept his head, seized a blanket and began to smother the flames. His example showed us what should be done, and with more blankets we quickly put out the fire. I quote this incident because it taught me how panic can arise like a flash—and how the example of a brave man can halt it.

The objective of the 4th Canadian Division in its first operation during the declining days of the Somme battle was the notorious Regina Trench.[11] This position had previously been attacked three times by the three senior divisions of the corps, on a front of about 3,500 yards. They had suffered from 2,500 to 3,000 casualties. The

Regina Trench lay on a reverse slope; that is to say, it was situated on the other side from us of a rise in the ground, and this meant that it was difficult or impossible for the artillery officers to observe fire on it. Consequently in all these attacks the barbed wire entanglements had not been properly gapped. Nor had the bombardment by heavier pieces succeeded in destroying the fire positions in the trench itself. At this period of the war, shrapnel, fired by the 18-pounders, was depended upon to make gaps through the wire, through which the infantry could rush to overpower the remaining defenders, whose power of resistance would have been reduced by long, heavy bombardment. The barrage of the attack, preceding the infantry waves, was supposed to force the defenders to keep their heads down until the last minute, when the attackers could be on them.

It is to be remembered that before the 1st, 2nd and 3rd Divisions began their attacks on Regina Trench, they had been in the battle since August 30, and had been attacking almost continuously since the 15th of September. Although they had gained successes, considerable in the scale of the Somme fighting, they had suffered very heavy casualties. Even when the ranks of the battalions were filled up with replacements, their fighting power was not the same, for few of the replacements were fully trained even in the basic infantry skills, and none were battle-wise.

A temporary clearing of the skies afforded the artillery a chance for continuous observation, and it became possible to cut the wire properly in front of Regina Trench. On October 21 our division attacked, together with three British divisions on our left, under command of the 2nd Corps. The attack went in at noon—a variation from the usual dawn zero hour. The 87th and 102nd battalions of the 11th Brigade took their objectives, and 160 prisoners, at a cost of 200 casualties, most of which were from shellfire after the objective had been taken.

On October 25 another operation to extend our holding of Regina Trench by the 44th battalion of 10th Brigade was held up, with 200 casualties, owing to insufficient artillery support and heavy flanking machine-gun fire from the Quadrilateral.

There was a pause for a fortnight, necessitated by the rainy weather. Since the 4th Canadian Division had entered the line there had been rain on sixteen out of twenty-one days, and the state of the front trenches was indescribable. But on the night of November 10/

11, an attack by two battalions of the 10th Brigade and one of the 11th was successful in capturing the remainder of Regina Trench. "Repeated bombardments had reduced it to a mere depression in the chalk, in many places blown twenty feet wide, and for long stretches almost filled with debris and dead bodies."[12]

On November 18 the 4th Division attacked and captured Desire Trench, some five to eight hundred yards north of the Regina Trench position. The main effort was by three battalions of the 11th Brigade (54th, 75th and 87th) with the 38th Battalion of the 12th Brigade under command, on the left. Snow fell during the night, changing as the attack went in at six a.m. to sleet, and later to rain. The infantry, cold and wet, advanced in four waves, at intervals of fifty yards, struggling forward through mud, and found their objectives with difficulty. By eight a.m. the troops had established themselves in Desire Trench and were digging in. The 38th and 87th battalions had even pushed patrols out a further 500 yards or so to Grandcourt Trench, but these were later withdrawn under orders, since they had advanced far beyond the formations on both flanks, and would have been very vulnerable to a counterattack. The division had taken about 625 prisoners, for a loss in casualties of 1,250, and must have inflicted further heavy loss in dead and wounded on the enemy.

During the 11th Brigade attacks my brigade signal section had been fortunate in being able to maintain telephone communication from the headquarters in the North Practice Trenches to all battalions almost continuously. As I remember it, there were only a few short intervals when any of the lines were "out." This was partly due to luck; for the most part the shells did not fall where the lines lay. However, when the shelling was heavy and the lines were broken, disregarding all danger the linesmen went out and repaired the breaks, working day and night. Sergeant Cartwright, Corporal Wilde, and Sapper Schindler took a leading part in this and won Military Medals. My section was fortunate in this battle and suffered no serious casualty.

The capture of Desire Trench on November 18 was the last operation of the 11th Brigade. During November, as might be expected, the weather had grown steadily worse, there was more rain, which made more mud, which made everything the soldiers had to do more difficult. It was strenuous for the linesmen, hauling rolls of cable through the mud, though of course this was nothing to the dangers, hardships and drudgery of the infantry.

I remember one night a particularly hard struggle in the mud, getting the line across to the 38th Battalion on the left flank, in preparation for the attack on Desire Trench. I was astonished when one of the linesmen, a big burly fellow who had always seemed to be the real tough guy of the section, dropped his end of the reel of cable and burst into tears. After a little encouragement he pulled himself together and we went on.

On the whole, the 4th Canadian Division had succeeded in these two relatively small operations, nearly the last in the Somme battle. "Much has been made of Ypres, much of Courcelette, to say nothing of later victories. But, for sheer guts and endurance of the men who took them, the names of Regina and Desire trenches should be emblazoned on Canadian history in letters just as tall."[13]

It is difficult for me now to understand just why the attacks of the 4th Division happened to be successful. Perhaps they hit an enemy exhausted by previous and prolonged battering. Probably in the division's first entry into offensive battle the 4th Division infantry had an *élan* which had not been eroded by trench war and the attrition battles. Before leaving Bramshott we had been reviewed by Lloyd George, then Secretary of State for War. After the march-past, the officers were called up, and he spoke to us. The little man perfectly resembled the cartoons of him in the newspapers. His flowing statesman's mane was lightly ruffled by the breeze. Altogether he did not impress—until he began to speak. I recall nothing of what he said, except that if the Empire could put new formations into the war of such high quality as we displayed after two years of hard fighting, it was certain we should be victorious. He didn't speak long, but the orator's magic was there; somehow he made us feel that we were members of a great army, about to march forth to conquer.

Our division remained in position on the Ancre Heights until November 28, when we were relieved and returned to the Canadian Corps, in the Vimy Sector. We had been nearly seven weeks continuously in the line.

Canadian battle casualties at the Somme had totalled 24,029. Looking at the battle as a whole, what had been gained? The British official historian sets the British losses at 419,654. He puts the losses of the French at 204,253; a total for the Allies of 623,907. Against these he estimates the German losses at between 660,000 and 680,000. There has been much controversy over the real number of German losses, as their method of reporting casualties has never been exactly established. Consequently it has been impossible to strike a generally accepted balance in the attrition battle.

What seems to be more certain, from the examination of German unit and formation histories, as well as the various generals and other senior officers, is that the old German Army suffered such losses in the Somme battle that it never recovered its skill and high morale. Many regiments record losses of half to three-quarters of their strength. And in the infantry those most likely to be wounded or killed are the leaders of all grades, the machine-gunners and other key members of the fighting machine. "The bloodbath of the Somme" was what the German soldiers called it. In weight of material, in guns and ammunition, for the first time they found themselves the underdogs; before they had always had the advantage. The battle, or series of battles, had, as the Canadian historical record[14] notes, destroyed the illusion of German invincibility on the western front. But it goes on to say that "after all has been said in vindication . . . we cannot close our eyes to the horror of the mass butchery to which the C-in-C's tactics had condemned the troops under his command. The proof of successful attrition is to be found in convincing casualty figures—and the . . . casualty figures from the Somme are not convincing."

But in condemning the deficiencies of the British strategy and tactics, we might remember that at that time neither the Germans nor the French high commands had better records. It was not until a year after the close of the Battle of the Somme, and immediately after the worst experiences of the 1917 Flanders battle—usually known as Passchendaele—that the Battle of Cambrai saw the introduction of the tactics which would bring final victory in the autumn of 1918. But that victory would be won over a German army depleted by the attrition battles, brought to a halt after its initially successful offensives in the spring and early summer, and finally deprived of any hope of victory by the massive entry of the American armies on the western front.

# Vimy Ridge

Canadians who fought in World War I took more pride in the conquest of Vimy Ridge than in any other of their battles in the four long and bloody years. In the Second Battle of Ypres, April 1915, the 1st Canadian Division held on in the face of the first gas attack and proved themselves to be gallant and great-hearted soldiers—but it was a defensive battle, hardly a victory. The greatest Canadian success on the Somme, the battle on the 15th of September during which Courcelette was taken, tends to be slightly diminished by all the grisly struggles which preceded and followed it, and at no time during the Somme battles did all Canadian divisions attack together. Of the battles which followed Vimy, Hill 70 was intended as a diversion to help the more important operations in Flanders, in the autumn of 1917; and Passchendaele was an experience even more dismal than the Somme. The continuous series of victorious advances beginning with the Battle of Amiens on August 8, 1918 and ending at Mons on November 11 were in their sum a greater success than Vimy. In that autumn of triumph we felt that the Canadian Corps was the spearhead of the British armies, and that the final defeat of the great German military machine which had defied all assaults for so long was near at hand. But it seems to me, looking back through fifty years, that no other battle stands out so eminently as a Canadian victory as does Vimy Ridge.

The capture of the Ridge took place in the framework of the far wider Battle of Arras, the first British offensive of 1917. The Canadian Corps under command of the British First Army was on the left flank, and we attacked together with seven other corps in the Third, Fifth and Fourth Armies on our right. A few words about the general situation at the beginning of 1917, and the Allied strategy developed at that time, may be useful as orientation.

In December 1916, General Joffre had been replaced as Commander-in-Chief of the French armies by General Robert Nivelle. Nivelle's recent successes in limited offensives in the Verdun Sector had persuaded French politicians that he had discovered the tactics which would lead to the victory which had so long eluded their arms. Lloyd George also was impressed by Nivelle and assented to the British armies participating in his grand plan for the western front in 1917. First there would be offensives by French and British armies to the south and north respectively of the Somme battlefields. But these would be only preliminary operations intended to pin down as many German formations as possible. The French would then launch the main attack, which was hoped to achieve surprise, between Reims and Soissons, employing the same shock tactics which Nivelle had used to recapture Fort Douamont at Verdun. Lloyd George visualized a decisive battle, which would be exploited to final victory.

However, this plan was thrown out of gear somewhat by the German withdrawal to what we called the Hindenburg Line—a defensive position some twenty miles to the German rear, which shortened their line by about twenty-five miles and enabled them to bring thirteen divisions into their strategic reserve. These could be employed in offensives on the Russian or Italian fronts where great strategic successes might be—and in fact were—obtained. So there were no Germans to attack in the sector south of the Somme for which the French preliminary operation had been planned. The northern attack became an all-British operation, its thrust line directed towards Cambrai, outflanking the defences of the Hindenburg Line. It would open on April 9; and would be followed, as planned, by the main Nivelle offensive on the Champagne front a week later.[1]

That was the general picture. A few more paragraphs on the plan of operations of the Canadian Corps, and the tactical importance of the Vimy Ridge feature may be useful, before I pass to the main part of the narrative in this chapter, relating to the fortunes, or misfortunes, of the 11th Canadian Infantry Brigade, and my personal experiences in the battle.

The Ridge did not look to be a very formidable obstacle from the west; for a distance of several miles the terrain sloped gently up to the crest. The highest points were Hill 135 to the south, and Hill 145 towards the northern end. But these high points were not isolated and distinct features, only terminal elevations of the generally high ground, which through nearly all its length afforded excellent observation for the German artillery over the whole of the area to the west. It was only when we had taken the Ridge, and looked back over the trenches in which we had spent the winter of 1916-17 and which the French and British had held before us, that we realized what an advantage the Germans had gained when they seized this feature in the so-called "Race to the Sea," in the autumn of 1914. Furthermore, the Ridge, dropping sharply to the Douai plain on its eastern side, gave observation over the lower land, to the banks of the Scarpe, to the east of Arras and beyond. Its capture was thus vital for the success of the Battle of Arras. If it had remained in German hands, the British corps, in attempting to advance, would have suffered greatly from artillery fire directed from the commanding ground.

In the great Battle of Artois, of 1915, the French armies had unavailingly tried to capture the Ridge. The British Army had supported this offensive in the Battle of Loos,[2] further to the north. This battle, on a smaller scale than the French Artois offensive, was in its way as great a failure. Harold Macmillan, in his book *The Winds of Change,* describes his experiences at Loos as a Lieutenant in the Grenadier Guards. He had been thrust into a battle without clear orders and no artillery support; a battle which resulted in the sacrifice of hundreds of the finest of Britain's young soldiers. Robert Graves, in *Goodbye to All That* gives a more extensive and even more harrowing account of the slaughter of the fine British soldiery in this terribly mismanaged battle.[3]

The Canadian success at Vimy Ridge was due to excellent planning and careful preparation, without which the bravery of individual Canadian soldiers and the fighting spirit of the veteran Canadian battalions would have gone for nothing. The Canadian commanders and staffs, by and large, had now grasped what was needed for success in the offensive, under the tactical systems of the day. It is true that the infantry still were advancing in linear formation, in waves up to six or eight in number, relying mainly on the power of the artillery to overcome the enemy resistance. But the Canadian command had learned, through hard experience, how to work the system to best advantage.

The divisions were now all together within the Canadian Corps, commanded by Sir Julian Byng, who went on later to command the Third Army, and after the war to become Governor-General of Canada. He stood in the first rank of the higher British commanders. It was a great advantage to the Canadians, at Vimy and in later battles, that they always operated together, under a corps commander and staff whom they could trust, and whose methods and abilities they knew and understood. In contrast, British divisions moved about from one corps to another, and sometimes suffered from misunderstandings arising from different operational and administrative practices in the different corps, and personality clashes between officers on the divisional and corps staffs. From 1916 on, people began to speak of "battles of *matériel*"; in these the artillery played the predominant part, and, for the best effect, had to be controlled at corps level, so that the fire of field, medium and heavy guns should all be co-ordinated to give maximum support to the infantry. For proper co-ordination, corps headquarters had to control the immense amount of engineering work needed in preparation for an assault, carried out by divisional, corps and army engineer units. Good administration—the supply of munitions, food, medical service, shelter and the evacuation of the wounded—also depended on co-operation between corps and division. Given the role of the corps staff in these areas, the importance of good understanding between corps and division is obvious.

During the advance of the last "100 days" in 1918, I remember being asked by a young British flying officer from an attached RAF observer squadron who had come to our brigade mess: "You Canadians always get your objectives. How do you do it?" The question was somehow embarrassing, and I forget what I answered. Certainly we Canadians at the time had "a guid conceit oursels," and we felt we were the spearhead of the British Army. Of course there were British divisions as good or better than any of the Canadian divisions, and the British soldiers were just as brave as the Canadians. Nevertheless, there was some point in the flying officer's question, and the answer to it lay in the factors I have just mentioned; the homogeneity of the Canadian Corps and its unchanging composition. Another answer, of course, was that the battalions in the British formations were on the average much lower in strength than were the Canadian battalions. The drain on the British manpower fit for war service had been far more severe than on the Canadian. The adoption of conscription in 1917 had enabled us to keep our ranks fairly well filled. When the strength of a fighting formation falls below a certain critical point its efficiency, particularly in the attack, falls off very rapidly.[4]

It was in the third week of January 1917, that Sir Julian Byng was told to prepare for a spring offensive, in which the objective of the Canadian Corps would be the whole of the Vimy Ridge, a front of about 7,000 yards, or four miles, with a mile to a division. Immediately the planning and construction and accumulation of supplies was taken in hand, and went on at increasing tempo until the days just before the assault.

As the many books and articles about the battle published in 1967, its semi-centenary year, impress on us, a most notable feature of the preparations for the offensive was the driving of many tunnels, which served to allow the attacking troops to move up to the front in full security, instead of having to struggle through encumbered communication trenches, subject to enemy shellfire. These tunnels also provided shelter for the attackers until they had to go out into the jumping-off trenches,[5] just before zero hour. Enlarged bays, or caves, in these underground lines of communication held battalion and brigade headquarters, forward dressing stations, munitions dumps and water supply. They also provided a secure route for the telephone lines connecting the various headquarters.

The tunnelling which served these purposes in the battle had originated as mine warfare which had been underway for a year or more. The purpose of mining was to get under the enemy's important strong points and then blow them into the air. The chalk which underlay the clayish soil of the Ridge, and indeed most of Artois, made tunnelling relatively easy. Several offensive mines were driven and laid, to be exploded when the battle opened: more than one of them on the front of the 4th Canadian Division, which included Hill 145 where the great Vimy monument now stands.

My task in these preparatory weeks—in addition to my regular work as brigade signals officer—was the simple one of supervising night-time working parties digging deep trenches to protect the telephone and telegraph cables from the divisional H.Q. up to the tunnel entrances. These cable trenches protected the communications through the zone behind the infantry positions where the enemy shellfire found secondary targets. (The bulk of the shells always fell on the forward positions.)

Cable-trench working parties consisted of a hundred or so infantrymen under command of one or two lieutenants or sergeants. This task was regarded by the weary foot-soldiers as onerous and disagreeable, and one to be avoided as much as possible. Digging cable trenches in the relatively safe rearward areas, where the soil had not been much disturbed by shellfire, was far easier than digging infantry defences in the front and support lines. Nevertheless this job was only a shade less disliked. However, once allotted their six feet of trench to dig, most of the men worked with a will, knowing exactly what their task was, and that when they finished it they could return to their billets. Those men who were more used to pick and shovel, after completing their own part, would often help out their softer-handed fellows, so that the task would be accomplished sooner. When the whole length of trench was excavated to the correct six feet in depth, and checked by the officer in charge, the strands of armoured cable would be laid in the bottom by the signalmen, and then the trench would be filled in. The cable so installed would be safe against any shelling, except a direct hit on the trench by a 15 cm. shell.

I recall a brief episode on one of these working parties, when the sergeant in charge of the infantry asked me, "How long have we got to dig to-night, sir?" I replied facetiously, "About half-an-hour," and was immediately reproved by a war-shaken boy's melancholy voice coming out of the darkness: "Don't kid the troops, you mustn't never kid the troops!"

The outline plan for the attack required the four divisions to attack in line. The deepest advance was to be made by the 1st Division on the right flank, about two and a quarter miles, while on the left flank the 4th Division would have only 1,000 yards to advance to its final objective. The tactics were generally to be the same as those with which the Somme battles had ended, an advance in waves, following and timed by the field artillery barrage.

An important training innovation was the practising of the troops over a full scale layout of the corps objectives, such as destroyed villages and hamlets, woods and roads—all of these indicated by tapes and signs. This, with the aid of a relief model of the ground to be captured, and a plentiful supply of maps, were the means chosen to ensure that the attackers would know where they were, where they were to go, what trenches and other defended points they were to overrun, and where the final objectives lay. The same methods had been used for some time by the Canadians, but on a smaller scale, in preparation for trench raids.

The sector which the 11th Brigade was to attack included Hill 145. Excepting this sector and part of that of the 12th Brigade to the north, success was won practically on schedule on all of the Canadian front. How was it that the 11th Brigade, whose attacks had been so successful on the Somme, failed to take its objectives on the 9th of April? The story has taken its place in the official history, and in the several books and articles about the Vimy battle which have recently appeared. But as one who was actually on the ground that day, having gone "over the top" with one of the later waves, and who knew also what went on in the brigade before the battle, I may have a footnote or two to add to the history.

The main reason for the failure was the very heavy casualties suffered by two of the battalions in the brigade in the disastrous gas raid which was carried out on the night of February 28/March 1. In *C.E.F. 1914-1919* this event is given only a paragraph and is not related to the lack of success of the 11th Brigade in its attack on Hill 145 on the 9th of April.

I do not remember to what extent the battalions of the 11th Brigade carried out the training for the offensive, over the taped representation of the area to be captured. If they did it before the gas raid, those trained, and in particular the key officers and N.C.O.'s, were probably killed and wounded in the raid; if it was done after the raid, the reinforcements which had brought the battalions up to strength would be completely new to the battlefield, and to their officers and comrades. Consequently the unit would not be organized and in condition to receive and retain the information and instructions it needed to play its part in the attack.

During the defensive period between arrival in the Vimy Sector and the deployment for the attack, the 11th Brigade had in use a system of reliefs, or rotation of units in front-line, support and reserve roles which was not a good one from the standpoint of providing proper training of the infantry for the offensive. The system was that each of the four battalions had a permanent sector, and had always a company in the front line, while the others were in support or reserve positions.

The defect of this was that only one company of each battalion at a time was in the reserve position, which might be several thousand yards back, or even farther. At this distance from the enemy it was possible to carry out training in company and platoon tactics and weapon training. Such out-of-the-line training ought to have been done under the eyes of the battalion commander—like every other activity of his unit. But if he was responsible for a sector of the front, his eyes would generally be turned in that direction, and the training would be left more or less to the company commander, whose standards might not be as high.

I had my first leave to England about the middle of February, and returned to find brigade headquarters in a state of tension. The preparations for the gas raid had been completed for a week or more, but the attack had been postponed because the wind was not in the right direction to carry the gas into the enemy trenches. It was to be released in a cloud, the same method used by the Germans in the first gas attack against the Canadians at Ypres in April 1915. The cylinders, containing chlorine and tear gas, were installed in our front trenches by sappers of the Special Companies, Royal Engineers.

According to the plan, the gas would take the Germans by surprise, and either knock out those defending the forward trenches, force them to put on their gas masks, or take refuge in gas-proof dugouts, and so enable the Canadian raiders to enter their positions with little or no opposition.

This night-by-night postponement, waiting for a wind in the right direction and of the right strength to take the gas effectively to the enemy positions, extended for more than a week and must have allowed the Germans to learn what was intended. The officers of the raiding battalions and brigade headquarters concluded that there would be no surprise and that therefore the whole operation ought to be abandoned. These views were pressed on division and corps headquarters, but the higher command decided that the operation should nevertheless take place. I well recall overhearing General Odlum arguing with division for the cancellation of the raid, using very stiff, almost insubordinate language. Nevertheless, against the opposition of the officers who would have to carry it out, the raid took place early in the morning of the 1st of March.[6]

Some witnesses report that a German bombardment of our front lines had broken a few of the gas cylinders, and the escaping gas caused the first trouble. When the gas was released in bulk, the wind drifted it to the south, almost parallel with our lines, instead of across into the German positions. It caused some casualties to the 75th Battalion on the right flank and even to the infantry in the next brigade sector. Seemingly, little or no gas was blown to the German trenches on the front of attack. So when the 54th and 75th Battalions went forward at five-thirty a.m. they found the Germans on the alert waiting for them. Under a murderous fire, and faced with substantially intact barbed wire obstacles, the unfortunate attackers were mown down. The gallant commanding officers of the 54th and 75th Battalions, Lieutenant-Colonels Kemball and Beckett, went out with their men and were both killed. No man's land was full of dead and wounded Canadians.

After a few hours, the Germans offered a truce, to enable the casualties to be collected and brought back to our lines, which must be put down as a credit to German military chivalry. They may have been moved to pity by the hopeless mess of the attack, by the bloodless victory they had won—or been presented with. A German staff officer came out to no man's land and met with Major Ferrers-Guy, our brigade Major, while German soldiers helped in the task of collecting wounded and dead.[7]

The shattering effect of these losses on the 54th and 75th Battalions, just a month before they were to take part in the great battle for the Ridge, hardly needs explaining. The disappearance of experienced leaders was the most serious result. In the battalion there were four company commanders, sixteen platoon commanders and the same number of sergeants, sixty-four section leaders—about 100 leaders of all grades. It is the leaders who suffer the most casualties in any attack. It may be assumed that probably over half of the leaders in each battalion were killed or wounded. There must also have been a great lowering of morale—and not only in the battalions which had been involved in the attack. The other battalions knew about it, of course. How could their confidence in the higher command not be enormously shaken when the two battalions had been ordered into a misconceived operation, against the violent objections of the brigade and battalion commanders, and the results had been so disastrous? How could these battalions be rebuilt into effective assaulting troops in the one month that remained?

Nevertheless, the final preparations for the attack went on. Among the matters which most affected me was the planning of signal communications within the brigade attack sector. One of the great difficulties in the offensives so far carried on by the British armies was to know exactly the situation of the forward troops, after they had kicked off behind the barrage on the way to their objectives—quite often only defined by a line on a map. Communications by telephone could usually be maintained pretty well as far forward as battalion headquarters. In the Vimy battle there was no difficulty about this, as they were in the tunnels. But it was almost impossible for the battalion signallers to establish links to the companies; enemy artillery and small-arms fire usually prevented carrying telephone lines forward, even if the company commander and his headquarters had survived the assault and his location was known. So runners were the only means of sending messages. These men took great risks in their journeys back and forth from the front to headquarters, as the many decorations won by them prove. Carrier pigeons were tried, and indeed an extensive organization was built up for the purpose. Unfortunately it produced more jokes than useful results.

Between the battles of the Somme and Arras someone in the higher signals organization produced a plan for more reliable communications to the zone between the most forward elements—on the farthest objectives reached by the attacking infantry—and battalion and brigade headquarters. Roughly, the idea was that there should be a main artery of communication forward, running up the middle of each brigade attack sector. This would be established by the brigade signal section, and the battalion signallers would only have to tap in their phone lines from the companies, or bring their messages to the report centre to be established at the end of this signal artery. At the report centre would be concentrated all the alternative means of communication—power buzzer,[8] pigeons, runners and visual signalling lamps. This seemed to be a very sensible way to organize and concentrate efforts to get messages back and forth between companies and battalions.

In the 11th Brigade sector there was another special reason for wanting to get reliable communication to the top of Hill 145. This height was expected to give very favourable observation to the artillery, whose forward observing officers could make use of the "artery" if their own lines back to artillery batteries and brigades were not working. In theory it seemed good, and after getting the agreement of the Commander and brigade Major, I planned to organize accordingly.

The brigade forward signal party would start out from the jumping off trenches with one of the latest waves of the attack, some ten minutes after zero. The telephone lines would run forward from one of the tunnels on the brigade front, at the head of which I established a relay post under Corporal Wilde. He would be listening in on the telephone line, and if it was broken would send linesmen out to try to repair it. It did not turn out that he had to.

I decided to take command of this forward party myself. It would be the key to the success or failure of the whole brigade communications plan, and therefore I should be with the group. They were to go over the top a little behind the infantry; consequently into considerable danger, and I did not like to send one of my sergeants or corporals to take charge while I remained safe in the tunnel at brigade headquarters.

Although I had a bunk at brigade headquarters, I did not sleep much the night before the attack. Like nearly every other man who is to go into action, I was mainly thinking of whether I might be killed or wounded. A deeply religious person, I suppose, can get comfort by resigning his fate to God's will; nevertheless the various glands and organs in the complex human anatomy don't often respond to reason, will or faith in a high and just ruler of all things. However, before zero hour I was in the proper place in the jumping-off position, with my little groups of signallers, runners and carriers.[9]

Zero—five-thirty a.m., and still dark—was marked by the explosion of several large mines on the 11th and 12th Brigade front. Huge inverted cones of flame and flying sparks shot up to the sky, like monstrously large fireworks, flinging clods and debris all round. This happened almost simultaneously with the opening of the barrage, which drowned out the possibility of speech, and almost of thought.

As I recollect, when we started to plough across no man's land in the growing light of the dawn, my principal emotions were curiosity and a not unpleasant excitement. The noise of the barrage dominated all other impressions: imagine the loudest clap of thunder you ever heard, multiplied by two, and prolonged indefinitely. The sky was a cupola of lead, and the appalling uproar, reflected down from it, pressed on one like deep water. The shells burst only thirty rods ahead, but they were invisible, except for brief flames and showers of sparks. Our supporting machine guns poured forth their 800 shots a minute in insane stammering rhythm, just audible against the deep note of the artillery. No doubt all this noise had a stimulating psychological effect, and built up a sense of power in the attackers. I could identify no enemy reply; the barrage, on our immediate front at least, seemed fully effective.

We reached the German front line, which at this point was relatively unbattered. I telephoned back to General Odlum, reporting that the attack seemed to be going very well. We also had a prisoner —a small and terror-stricken Bavarian, who hopped up and down precisely like a small boy who had wet his trousers, until he decided we were not about to slaughter him, and obediently wandered off in the direction of our lines.

Then we moved off again, towards the high ground to the front. By this time a few other oddments of personnel—ammunition carriers and the like—had attached themselves to my party. Up to this point the action had been "according to plan"; now there was a sudden change. The barrage had moved some distance ahead, and the surviving enemy now crawled out of their shelters and turned upon us. A machine gun fired a burst directly in front of us, less than 100 yards distant.

There is no more vicious noise than that of a machine gun trained directly at one: in the half-light long streaks of flame reached out like adders' tongues. Fortunately, shell-holes were everywhere, rim to rim, and Hadow, the man who carried my telephone, and I took cover with one jump. As we did so I heard a faint clang from my tin hat and, when well down in the hole, I removed it to find a neat longitudinal crease. The machine-gunners had nearly scored. I did not reflect long on this narrow shave, for just then a man came up from behind, one of the ammunition carriers I have mentioned. He was a middle-aged fellow, with a foolish, fat face, and stood grinning in a diffident manner, as if to apologize for intruding on our privacy.

"Get down, you damned fool!" I yelled at him, and down he came —knees sagging first, and then gently collapsing until he rested on his back, his feet doubled under him. The grin had faded before he fell, and as he slumped down his eyes rolled upward with a mechanical finality, till only the whites were showing. There was no sign to show where he had been hit. Once he was dead and a corpse, he took his place in the general category of corpses on the battlefield, to which sadly, one had become accustomed.

After ten minutes or so, I decided to go back and see what had happened to the remainder of my followers. This was achieved by a rapid scuttle from one shell-hole to another. Hadow, the telephonist who was following me, got a neat blighty, through the *gluteus maximus*, just as we arrived among the rest of the men. It turned out that several of them had been wounded in the first burst of fire. We were now all immobilized by the rifles of a group of the enemy who occupied a mine crater to our left front. These were bold fellows, and were standing exposed from the waist upward, apparently as unconcerned as if they were shooting at bottles in a pond. I was in a shell-hole with an infantryman—a straggler from one of the last waves, I suppose.

"Have a shot at those Fritzes," I suggested. He gaped at me as if I had ordered him to capture the Kaiser single-handed. He didn't seem scared, but he told me he hadn't fired his rifle since he had come to France—that that was the business of the sniping specialists. After some persuasion he cautiously loosed off a few rounds, but I don't think he hit anything. This episode remained firmly in my memory. It showed with such force how useless, indeed how wicked, it is to send men into battle who have not been properly trained in the use of their arms. They are merely moving targets to be shot down by a better trained enemy. Perhaps my infantryman knew how to throw a Mills grenade—esteemed in 1917 the most important offensive weapon of the infantry, but he certainly had not been taught how to use his rifle, and so he thought he was helpless against the

Germans on the crater lip, who probably were no braver than he was but who knew how to shoot.[10]

I had the telephone hooked up to the line which had been brought as far as our shell-hole, and got through to Wilde; then to brigade headquarters, where I spoke to General Odlum. I reported what had happened, and told him that it seemed the later waves of the infantry had somehow diverged to either flank, leaving enemy riflemen and machine-gunners who had stopped the signal party's advance, and who were dominating the area. I could hear General Odlum saying something, but the line was too weak for me to understand him. I asked Wilde what he was saying. "He says it's all poppycock," Wilde reported, somewhat disconcerted. That terminated that conversation.

About this time I observed an officer and a couple of men making their way up what had been a communication trench (now practically obliterated by shellfire) some twenty or thirty yards to the left. I saw they would walk right into the enemy if they kept on, and as the noise of the barrage would have made it impossible to hear a shout, I ran over, from shell-hole to shell-hole, and intercepted them. These people were a scouting party sent up from the headquarters of one of the battalions to ascertain the situation. I told the officer what was going on immediately around us, and suggested that he might get forward by going towards the right flank, where I had seen some men of the next brigade moving. I had seen nothing of the infantry of our own brigade since reaching the German front line, but judged that in their first rush after the barrage they must have passed over the enemy detachments who were now troubling us. The scout officer thanked me, and went off in the direction suggested. I heard afterwards that he got through, and back to his battalion to report. Making a second trip, he was wounded.

From the ruined communication trench I got back to the old German front line, which I had left about an hour before. I found eight or ten men—some of my party and some infantrymen—sitting on their backsides with no idea of what the immediate future was to bring forth, but quite cheerful, on the whole, in this comparative safety. Two or three of them had rifles. A Lewis gunner, a lance corporal, arrived just then, his gun covered with mud and out of action. I told him to clean it, set some of the men to collecting

German bombs and posted a sentry. It appeared to me that a supplementary attack would soon be made by our reserves, and that in the meantime the best thing to do was to hold on where we were.

This done, curiosity (or it may have been a subconscious desire for safety) led me to enter a deep dugout, in which some of the men were ferreting about, and I spent a quarter of an hour or so prying into the affairs of the late occupants.

Suddenly someone shouted down the entrance: "Mr. Burns, Mr. Burns, quick! Fritz is counterattacking." I climbed the stairs, telling myself that I must try to appear less frightened than the men. On arrival in the trench I soon found the counterattack to be nothing more than a dozen or so *kamerads,* nearly 300 yards away, making for our lines under escort. As we watched, one of their own five-nine shells dropped in their midst, and sent two or three flying through the air.

One of the men warned me not to expose myself in a certain direction, saying in an awed voice that there were snipers further down the trench we were in. I peered over the parapet cautiously, and saw two or three Germans standing waist high in the trench (just as the others in the mine-crater had stood), and not more than 150 yards away. As I looked at the Germans, behaving as if they were at a rabbit shoot, and the men around me, who seemed to be about as warlike as rabbits, I grew rather angry and asked one gaping buck private what he thought he had a rifle for. Taking it from him, I fired several shots. Whether I hit the Germans at whom I was aiming, I don't know, but all of them disappeared from view. I was feeling rather pleased with my skill with the rifle when a shot struck the parapet a foot away, sending a shower of tiny stone splinters into my face, and making a most demoralizing crack. I was considerably shaken by this, and squatting down, asked the man next to me anxiously if I had been hit. He inspected my face solemnly and reported only a few scratches.

I was given no time to be dismayed by thoughts of death barely escaped, for one of the other men, a smallish, red-haired intelligence observer, began staggering and making strange whistly noises. I held him up and saw he had been shot through the jugular vein, probably by the bullet which had just missed me. An inch and a quarter long split, purplish at the edges, sucked inwards at each pulsation of his heart and produced the queer whistle. I had a notion that if this gap could be closed he might live, and tried to do this with my fingers, but as I held him his face became scarlet, and then purple. Finally he ceased breathing. Possibly the bullet had gone on through the spine. He made no articulate sound in dying. I laid him down at the side of the trench, and wiped my fingers on his jacket.

The rest of my personal history on that day may be told briefly. A short time later, I endeavoured to work around by the right flank, to look into the situation there. This attempt was terminated by a bullet through my gas respirator—a third warning which it seemed should be heeded. After seeing that the little post in the old German front line was all right (by this time the Lewis gun was ready for action), I went back across no man's land and reported to brigade headquarters.

That ended my own involvement with the battle on the 9th of April. By the time I returned to brigade headquarters General Odlum had decided to put in an attack with two companies of the 85th Battalion—Nova Scotia Highlanders—who had just come to France, and were to replace the 73rd Battalion of the 12th Brigade. It was their first time in action, and they had to advance without a barrage. They went forward gallantly, helped somewhat by the setting sun at their backs which tended to blind the remaining German defenders. They succeeded in advancing about to the crest, and joined up with the surviving elements of the 87th and 102nd battalions.[11]

> The 11th Brigade's attack was initially successful on its right, the 102nd Battalion seizing its half of the forward slope and the 54th passing through to consolidate on the summit. Farther north, however, things did not go so well. A portion of German trench had been left undestroyed by the heavy artillery at the request of the left assaulting battalion (the 87th) who hoped to put it to good use when captured. From this position machine-gun fire cut down half the 87th's leading wave and pinned the right of the supporting 75th Battalion to their assembly trenches. Those who could pressed on, though harassed in flank and rear by machine-gun fire from the uncaptured sector, and from Germans who emerged from mine shafts and dugouts after the attacking wave had passed. Then came murderous fire from the second trench, whose garrison had been given ample time to man their positions. The entire left wing of the 11th Brigade's attack broke down, and the 54th Battalion, its open flank under counter-attack, was forced to withdraw. Thus for a time the

> Brigade was left with only the 102nd Battalion on its objective, the south-western slope of the hill. The presence of this unit prevented any artillery bombardment of the German-occupied trench; but at one o'clock bombing parties of the 87th Battalion supported by Stokes mortars and machine-guns, successfully attacked the troublesome position. Before dark, two companies of the 85th Battalion overran the two remaining trenches on the west side of the summit, silencing the harrying enemy fire from the hill.

In the afternoon of April 10, two battalions of the 10th Brigade, the divisional reserve, made a further attack with a barrage, and their left flank protected by a smoke screen. They carried the final objective on this sector, the Brown Line, located on the forward slope, looking down on the Douai plain.

On the 13th of April, it was discovered that the Germans had retired from their positions on the lower part of the eastern slope of the Ridge. They had gone back to the 4th Division sector to a prepared position on the Line Avion-Lens, a little over two miles from the foot of the Ridge. General Odlum was on the front looking over the situation and I accompanied him with a few signallers. We went cautiously forward with patrols of the 85th Battalion across the practically undisturbed green plain leading towards the far mining villages. Walking above ground on fresh grass, instead of struggling through muddy trenches and shell craters, was exhilarating. Not a shot was fired at us, and I remember Colonel Borden of the 85th hurrying along the parapet above a deep communication trench, pausing at each deep dugout entrance, and inviting the non-existent Germans to come out, emphasizing his remarks with a revolver shot or two into each. General Odlum sent me to investigate a group of buildings a few hundred yards away on the right flank, where my runner and I came on an abandoned gun—an old Austrian piece, 80 mm or thereabouts. I tried to claim this afterwards for the signal section as a captured trophy, but the claim was disallowed!

In the Vimy Ridge battle, as on the Somme, my section had been fortunate in suffering few casualties. The only man killed was Sapper Jardine. His regular job was driving the section's wagon, but he had volunteered to go with the forward party to help carry the reels of telephone cable. He was a farmer and lumberman from Eastern Ontario, considered rather a simple soul by the rest of the boys.

They used to like to get him to tell of his post-war plans. He was saving up his pay ($1.10 a day, at that time) and was going to buy a "steam-enjine" tractor, with which capital equipment he could make good money in the woods. The poor fellow was hit through the chest when we went forward from the first German trench, and lay silent in the shell-hole with the other men around him, his face paler and paler, a first-aid dressing on his wound, his life slowly ebbing away.

What had been gained by the capture of Vimy Ridge, and in the Battle of Arras, of which it was a part? As explained above, it had been, in the larger strategic picture of the western front, a preliminary operation, a diversion intended to prepare the way for the decisive French attack on the Aisne, between Reims and Soissons. This main offensive opened on April 16, and, partly due to the German advance information of Nivelle's plan, it resulted in a costly failure, with a total French loss of 134,000 in ten days. Considerable ground was gained, it was true, but the excessive losses, and disappointment from the glowing expectation of total victory produced a profound discouragement, which by May had reduced many French formations almost to mutiny. Pétain replaced Nivelle, and his estimate was that the French Army would be in no state to undertake offensive operations on any large scale for the rest of the summer. This resulted in the British Armies having to carry on the offensives in Flanders for the rest of 1917. These had, as their main strategic objectives, the freeing of the Belgian coast, which included submarine bases. They were also intended to keep the Germans on the defensive so that they could not attack the weakened and discouraged French armies, and perhaps finally have broken their resistance. In these circumstances, the chief effect of the Arras battles lay in the attrition to which they subjected the Germans. The importance of the winning of the Ridge in relation to the larger Arras battle is indicated in the following passage.

> While the task of the Canadian Corps was primarily to form a strong defensive flank for the Third Army's effort, the Vimy operation was significant in its own right. The high ground between the Scarpe and the smaller Souchez River, of which the

> Ridge was the dominant feature, formed a nine-mile barrier across the western edge of the Douai plain. Overlooking Lens to the north, Douai to the east, and Arras to the south, Vimy Ridge was tactically one of the most important features on the entire Western Front. . . . The Ridge was the keystone of the defences linking the new Hindenburg system to the main German lines leading north from Hill 70 to the Belgian coast.[12]

In the six days from April 9 to 15, the Canadian Corps had advanced some 4,500 yards, and captured fifty-four guns and more than 4,000 prisoners. Canadian casualties were 10,602; 3,598 of them fatal. The capture of the Ridge and the advance of the British in front of Arras and to the south had resulted in the capture of more ground, more prisoners and more guns than any previous British offensive on the western front.

> For Canada, the battle had great national significance. It demonstrated how powerful and efficient a weapon the Canadian Corps had become. For the first time, the four Canadian divisions had attacked together. Their battalions were manned by soldiers from every part of Canada fighting shoulder to shoulder.[13]

In 1967 the Canadian Government organized a special ceremony in honour of the fiftieth anniversary of the battle. It took place in front of the great and beautiful Vimy memorial situated on the summit of Hill 145. Through the Department of Veterans' Affairs a representative was sent over from each unit that had taken part in the battle. I had the honour of acting as the leader and spokesman of these veteran survivors, as they were reviewed by the Duke of Edinburgh (who represented the Queen). There were guards of honour of Canadian and British regiments, and a band, of course. But what touched us most was the immense crowd of the French people from surrounding villages and towns, who thus showed that they did not forget the Canadians who had come over the sea and had fought and died by the side of the sons of France.

# Vimy to Passchendaele

After the capture of Vimy Ridge, the 1st and 2nd Canadian Divisions were engaged in further attacks, extending the northern flank of the Third Army offensive which had been resumed on the 23rd of April. The 1st Division captured Arleux[1] on April 28, and from May 3rd to 8th both the senior divisions were fighting hard in and around the village of Fresnoy, immediately east of Arleux. It was taken at last, though subsequently lost to counterattack after the Canadians had handed it over to a British formation. The 3rd and 4th Divisions carried out only minor operations after advancing across the Douai plain to regain contact with the Germans in the positions to which they had withdrawn.

By early May the strategy to be followed by the British armies on the western front during the 1917 campaign had been determined, and Field-Marshal Haig briefed the army commanders on it at a conference at Doullens on the 7th of May. The object of the Allies would be to "wear down and exhaust the enemy by systematically attacking him by surprise."[2] The main blow was to be delivered on the Ypres front, with the eventual purpose of driving the Germans back from the Belgian coast and occupying this territory, which would reduce the enemy's ability to destroy British shipping by submarine attacks.

It was planned that operations would also take place in the Arras-Lens Sector. These would be a diversion, to mislead the enemy as to the direction of the main offensive, and also to distract his attention from the French front. The plan called for the attacks to be made about the end of June, in a direction which would threaten Lens and Lille. Weather and other factors caused considerable delay in setting up this diversionary offensive. It was not until August 15 that the battle took place in which the Canadian Corps captured Hill 70, east of Loos, where in 1915 the British had fought.

In the minor operations during April and May on the left flank of the Canadian Corps, the 4th Division was given as objectives various fortified positions between the Souchez River and Avion.[3] Several attacks were carried out, each by one or two battalions. These followed the same pattern. With an initial success, the objective would be occupied and some prisoners captured. But then, after prolonged heavy shelling by the German artillery, the survivors of the attacking units would be driven out by counterattack. As we did not have enough artillery to ensure protection of the attacking troops against the German counteraction over a prolonged period, General Currie suggested a change of tactics.

> Short of supporting guns, the Canadians could not keep the enemy from concentrating overwhelming fire on the newly won trenches. The Army Commander therefore, at Currie's suggestion, decided against trying to hold captured ground at great cost, and ordered that operations take the form of large-scale raids in which the assaulting troops would attack in sufficient strength to ensure breaking into the German trenches, but having disposed of the enemy garrison and inflicted the maximum damage on his position, would withdraw under cover of a rearguard.[4]

One of these raids, as described in *C.E.F.*[5] involved "strong groups" of the 11th and 7th Brigades employed on a two-mile front. Owing to careful rehearsal over tapes and strong artillery support, the operation was very successful. As I recall it, "box barrages" were laid down. This term meant that the area within which our troops were operating was sealed off from enemy counterattack by our field guns firing barrages not only on a line drawn just beyond the objective, but also on the two flanks, roughly perpendicular to the front. The two brigades took 136 prisoners, and claimed to have inflicted over 700 casualties on the enemy. Canadian casualties were 709; 100 of them fatal.

I mention this operation, which was followed by raids by other Canadian formations prepared in a similarly elaborate manner, because it came to my mind when we began to hear the sad news of the outcome of the Dieppe raid, in August 1942. Of this, more in Chapter VII.

After the Arleux-Fresnoy operations the Canadian Corps' next serious engagement was the attack on and capture of Hill 70, which lay about two miles north of Lens. The objective was limited, and the operation was carried out with the increased skill which the Canadian Corps had been acquiring over the past two years. While all objectives were taken, it is clear that the principal purpose for which it had been devised was not achieved; that is, it failed to create uncertainty in the minds of the German General Staff as to the strategic intentions of the British.

In this battle, the 11th Brigade had only a small part to play: to hold the line on the southern flank and to push forward fighting patrols towards Lens to test the enemy defence there, (which, it turned out, was solid).

About this time I was slightly wounded in the hand by a shell splinter travelling in a parabola from a burst more than 100 yards away. This earned me a shot of anti-tetanus serum, pumped into my chest by what looked like a horse-syringe; which was the system in those days. It also earned me (pretty cheaply) the right to wear the little gold braid wound-stripe, and another leave to England.

The next scene is the swamps and ridges before Passchendaele,[6] a theretofore obscure Flemish village which lent its name afterwards to the three-and-a-half months' battle. For the British and Commonwealth troops that fought there it became a symbol of all that was most horrible and desperate of the war on the western front. Many pages have been written in an attempt to describe the hopeless morass in which the soldiers of the British armies struggled forward yard by yard against a stubborn enemy.[7] The Germans held the limited areas of high ground where the water table was below the surface, and were protected within the concrete pillboxes which became a feature of their defensive arrangements for the first time in this battle.

The general strategy of attrition and surprise on which the 1917 campaigns of the British Army was based has already been mentioned. In its initial aspect, Haig's strategy doesn't seem faulty, given the condition of the French Army at the time. But it has been the subject of a controversy which continued acrimoniously between the world wars, and perhaps will never be settled.[8] The fundamental question remains: if the British Army had relaxed their attacks in this particular sector of the western front, would the Germans have been able to launch a shattering offensive against the French Army, said to be demoralized and mutinous after the failure of Nivelle's offensives in May? Could the Germans have finally broken the French capacity to resist, and won the war before the American armies could intervene?

A second question: if indeed the overall Allied situation in the West demanded that the British armies should pin down the Germans by taking the offensive, should the Flanders attack have been continued, when the rainfall and the state of the ground was found to be such a terrible obstacle? Vimy, and the British successes at Messines before the Flanders offensive, and at Cambrai after it, showed that with adequate planning, an element of surprise and reasonably *dry ground,* victories could be won without a terrible price being paid in soldiers' lives. By "victories" I mean here battles in which the enemy is made to suffer the greater loss.

The Flanders offensive had opened on July 31, and after some initial success on the first day was checked short of its later objectives by German artillery fire and counterattacks. Then heavy rain began falling, and continued for four days. It brought operations to a halt. The nine attacking divisions had lost from thirty to sixty percent of their strength, and were in no condition to continue the advance. The offensive resumed on August 16th, but little ground was gained and the weather grew worse. That August was the wettest in four years. The only credit item was that the enemy was being worn down; the heavy losses caused Ludendorff to worry. But the first four weeks of the offensive had cost 68,000 British casualties, and the strain of fighting in the mud and the lack of real success in the attacks had begun to tell on morale. No post-war witness was in a better position to know of conditions on the battlefield than Sir Hubert Gough, the Commander of the Fifth Army, which held the principal role in the battle when it opened. At the time, his reputation and that of his army staff were very bad among the troops, or perhaps it would be more correct to say among commanders and staff officers in lower formations. The stigma stuck, and in March 1918 when the German offensive broke through the over-extended Fifth Army, it resulted in General Gough's removal from command. The belief that he was a reckless and rather incompetent commander, careless of his troops' lives and well-being, persisted until some time after the war. There was considerable satisfaction when it was found the Canadian Corps was to operate in the Flanders battle under Plumer's Second Army, and not under Gough's Fifth. The front between the two armies had been adjusted.) I recall General Odlum remarking, "Gough—that's the man who kept us plugging in the mud in November last year on the Somme."

Looking back, and having read General Gough's books *The Fifth Army* and *Soldiering On*, it seems to me that he became the scapegoat for failures and inadequacies which were not his alone, but were shared to a degree by all the British higher command and staff. But let us see what he says about the desperate handicaps under which the Flanders battle was fought. The following extract describes the situation after the attack on August 16, 1917.

> The state of the ground was by this time frightful. The labour of bringing up supplies and ammunition, of moving or firing the guns, which had often sunk to their axles, was a fearful strain on the officers and men, even during the daily task of maintaining the battle front. When it came to the advance of infantry for an attack, across the water-logged shellholes, movement was so slow and fatiguing that only the shortest advances could be contemplated. In consequence I informed the Commander-in-Chief that tactical success was not possible, or would be too costly, under such conditions, and advised that the attack should now be abandoned.
>
> I had many talks with Haig during these days, and repeated

> this opinion frequently, but he told me that the attack must be continued. His reasons were valid. He was looking at the broad picture of the whole Allied cause.[9]

One wishes that Gough's advice had been taken. The lives of thousands of good soldiers would have been saved, and the reputation of British generals in World War I would have been higher.

Haig changed his general plan, and directed the main thrust to be carried out by Plumer's Second Army on the southern flank. This entailed extensive preparations, and the next important attack was not launched by Australian and British formations until the 20th of September. It was followed by others, each with limited advances and very heavy artillery support. These tactics were successful in producing an advance of 4,000 yards in two weeks, but objectives that were to have been taken on the opening day of July 31 were still in enemy hands. The forward troops of Plumer's Army were still a mile from Passchendaele. Continuous rain began to fall on October 4 and continued off and on for the next three days turning the shell-torn shallow valleys into almost impassible bogs. Plumer and Gough told Haig on the 7th that they favoured stopping the offensive, because of the ground conditions, but Haig decided that as a minimum the high ground of the Passchendaele-Westroosebeke Sector had to be gained, as a suitable line to be held throughout the winter. It had at last become clear even to GHQ that General Mud had defeated all hopes of attaining the ambitious strategic object—the Belgian coast. The over-optimistic intelligence reports that persuaded Haig that he was winning the battle of attrition became irrelevant, because he had hardly any reserves left to add to his stake in this grisly game.

At this point Haig decided to bring in the Canadian Corps. A GHQ directive of October 13 called for General Currie to submit plans for the capture of Passchendaele. It was a task which he accepted with reluctance, because it was clear that no strategic success could be gained, and what ground could be won would be only at the cost of great hardship and many casualties. However, all but nine of the sixty British and Dominion divisions on the western front were drawn into the Flanders battle; the Canadians could hardly refuse to do their share. On October 18 the corps took over, from the Second Anzac Corps, a front in the valley of the Stroombeck between Gravenstafel Ridge and the heights about Passchendaele. It was almost the same front as the 1st Canadian Division had held prior to the April 1915 gas attack. A period of preparation followed, mainly occupied with roadbuilding and getting the field and heavy artillery into position to support the Corps' operations. All this was accomplished under great difficulties.

In successive attacks on the 26th and 30th October, and the 6th and 10th of November, the Canadians captured the high ground up to the village of Passchendaele and beyond. Many deeds of great gallantry in which numerous Victoria Crosses were won marked this struggle through the mud. What was achieved in terms of ground won, and what was the price paid for it in casualties? The Canadian Corps had advanced starting from a front of 3,000 yards to a depth of 3,000 yards, narrowing down to a blunted salient in front of Passchendaele. The cost of conquering this piece of ground, little more than two square miles in extent, was 8,134 casualties, 2,623 of them fatal.[10]

My own memories of Passchendaele are limited, though still vivid. There were the endless duckboard tracks, winding erratically towards the front. To leave them was to sink into a slough. As far as the eye could see, through rain or generally misty autumn air, there were shell craters, great and small, in patterns which so many have compared to the moonscape. But these craters were full to the brim with water. Originally a swamp, this low-lying part of Flanders had been made cultivable by elaborate ditching and drainage—all of which the month-long bombardments of unprecedentedly heavy concentrations of artillery had destroyed. The land had reverted to the primeval bog, except that all trees, bushes and other vegetation had disappeared under the storm of high explosive, and there remained only mud and muddy water.

There were areas of high ground, for example the Gravenstafel Ridge, conquered at high cost by the Australians. And there was the Passchendaele Ridge which had become the final objective.

On these ridges there were the remains of a few farmhouses, bearing such homely names as "Lilac Cottage." But they existed only because the Germans had reinforced them with concrete from within, so that the outer brick walls became a kind of camouflage for the essential structure. There were a few shattered stumps of trees, but the desolation was hardly less than on the lower lands. The vista of shell-holes and mud presented in every quarter was accented by the pillboxes. These were reinforced concrete structures, generally not much larger than needed to hold a pair of machine guns and their crews. These emplacements were raised slightly from the mud, and, when captured, usually served as headquarters for companies, battalions and brigades.

Marking the stages along the roads or tracks on which guns, munitions and heavy supplies were carried forward were the bloated carcasses of horses and mules. These were to be met on any of the battlefields of World War I; but in Passchendaele, owing to the swamp, clearing the battlefield of dead men and beasts had fallen far behind. Many bodies of dead soldiers, unburied for weeks, were to be seen. I remember well the site of an assault by the Irish Division on one German stronghold, where the bodies of the brave Irish soldiers lay in rows, seeming to keep their alignment in death.

The 11th Brigade carried out no attack in this battle. Our task was to hold the line between assaults of the 10th and 12th Brigades. But to hold the line in such conditions was a bitter trial, though less costly in casualties than an attack. The enemy harassing fire was heavy and unremitting, and there was no shelter nor continuous trenches—because digging in the sodden earth, even in the high ground, was almost impossible. Our short spell in the battle, however, cost my brigade signal section heavily. Nearly all the linesmen and many of the office staff were evacuated suffering from the effects of mustard gas. This new means of chemical warfare had been introduced by the Germans about the time the Flanders battle began. Mustard gas lingered in several of the pillboxes and reinforced farmhouses which served for headquarters. In small concentration its effects were not noticeable until the damage to the eyes and respiratory passages had been done. It was usually not severe enough to leave lasting effects, but a few days after exposure its victims could not carry on, and had to be sent out to hospitals in the rear or in England for treatment.

Our brigade headquarters was located in one of the concrete-reinforced wrecks of farmsteads. The battalions were on the Passchendaele Ridge, several thousand yards ahead. Ground conditions being what they were, there was of course no possibility of burying cable; and there were no trenches which could afford telephone lines any protection. It was impossible for the linesmen to keep overland lines intact. The shelling was constant and frequently heavy. To struggle through the mud, lifting the clogging masses that attached themselves to the feet soon exhausted even the strongest men.

There was a pillbox on the western slope of the Passchendaele Ridge that faced towards the brigade headquarters, and this was our forward "report centre." The system of communications we took over from the brigade we relieved was to pass messages by lamp signal between this station and headquarters. From the report centre we tried to keep telephone lines working to the battalion headquarters. The state of the ground being somewhat better on the ridge, it was possible for the linesmen to patrol, but the continuous heavy shelling broke the wires almost as soon as they were mended.

Corporal Wilde was the head linesman stationed at this report centre, and Ben Summers (one of my theological students) was the lamp signaller. The pillbox was one of those contaminated by mustard gas, but we found this out too late. The new agent, in low but still effective concentration, did not have the warning smell of the chlorine or phosgene. In spite of increasing irritation of eyes, nose and throat, both my signallers carried on. Wilde insisted on working until he could no longer see, and hardly walk, and then the stretcher-bearers took him out. Of the many men of my section who were gassed he was the only one who died from the effects. Summers, also evacuated suffering from the gas, was awarded the Military Medal.

Wilde was given a bar to the Military Medal he had won on the Somme. Some time after we heard of his death there arrived for him the little silver rosette, the symbol of a bar to a decoration. This contained, I suppose, about a third of the amount of silver in the then current Canadian five-cent piece. I remember holding it in my hand, and thinking it did not seem a great recompense for those who like Wilde risked their lives and set a brave example to others in fighting the nation's battles. Wilde had risked his life many times, and in the end he lost it. He was one of the bravest men I have known, and always cheerful.

While the Flanders battle was floundering to its end, GHQ initiated another operation which was to stand in brilliant contrast to it. It was carried out under the Third Army, commanded by Sir Julian Byng, who had commanded the Canadian Corps. The plan which had been maturing over several months was a bold one: it was hoped to break into the German front—the Hindenburg Line—from St. Quentin to the Sensee Canal—a front of twenty-two miles. But the initial penetration, to be expanded with success, would be effected on a smaller front centred on Cambrai in the northern part of the sector.

The battle, launched on November 20, 1917, began with a surprising success, and caused great jubilation in the British armies in France and Flanders. The deep penetration of the strong German defences on the first day, and the launching of the cavalry into action was in such contrast to the muddy and bloody struggle in the Flanders swamp that it made the quick success seem all the more wonderful; the troops and the people at home could say to themselves, "At last we've found a way to win!" But the celebrations which included the ringing of church bells for the first time since the war began were premature. Most of the ground gained was lost to German counterattacks, and the battle came to an end on the 5th of December. The ensuing disappointment seemed almost to exceed the early euphoria. Nevertheless, in spite of the discouragement that followed the effective German riposte, the tactics that were to win the battles in the last months of the war had been learned.

What were the elements of these tactics? First and most striking, was the massed use of tanks on firm ground which had not been turned into a waste of craters by prolonged bombardment. Second was that surprise had been attained. To take the enemy by surprise in attack or by some strategic move had always been the test of generalship, but this principle of war had been almost entirely neglected in the offensives of the Allies on the western front.

Before Cambrai, artillery bombardment had to be relied on to make gaps in the enemy's barbed wire entanglements—obstacles which if not destroyed held up the attacking infantry long enough for the enemy machine guns and rifles to do their deadly work. But at Cambrai, it was the massed tanks that broke down the wire in wide avenues, through which the infantry could rush. And so wire cutting was no longer a reason for the guns to begin firing before the zero hour came. Furthermore, a remarkable advance in artillery technique had done away with the necessity to "register" the guns, that is, to establish where their shells would fall by trial shots. This procedure in earlier offensives had been enough to give away the presence of a concentrated mass of artillery, which was a definite indication of a forthcoming attack. Now, procedures had been developed to locate the position of each battery of guns accurately by survey. So located, they were tied in to the large-scale map on which the enemy defences had been plotted, mainly by using air photographs. The gunners were thus able to determine the range and bearing (direction) of their targets, and could open fire on them without preliminary ranging, and with the necessary accuracy. So at zero hour, the intense field artillery barrage, the longer-range destructive concentrations by the heavies, and neutralizing fire on the enemy's batteries could come down with crushing weight and stunning surprise on the unsuspecting defenders.

The tanks were employed *en masse*—as many of them as could be assembled, so that the enemy field guns could not pick them off one by one. Even though in one or two places a few brave and skilful German gunners inflicted heavy losses, the tank attack was successful in breaking through the wire of successive strongly-fortified trench positions, and leading the infantry through to crush the last resistance of the demoralized defenders. The commanders and higher staff of the new Tank Corps, the best-known of whom was the then Colonel J.F.C. Fuller, had long been urging that the tanks should be used in this way; not in the "penny packet" manner of allotting a few tanks to each infantry unit, under which their effect was too dispersed to be decisive in making a breakthrough. The lesson that tanks should generally be used in heavy concentrations was one which was taught at the staff colleges between the wars. It was a principle which I tried to apply in the 1944 battles in Italy. There was always a temptation and pressure to split up tank units into too small elements. Every infantry unit wanted tanks working with it in defence as well as attack. But there were not enough tanks to satisfy all demands, and hard choices sometimes had to be made.

It was intended that the cavalry should exploit success by disrupting the enemy's communications, and by breaking up the troops he might be trying to move forward as reinforcements. However, the cavalry action did not succeed, in spite of much bravery by individuals and units—and notably the units of the Canadian Cavalry Brigade. The horse was too vulnerable to machine-gun fire, and obstacles such as the canals in front of and to the flanks of Cambrai held up the troops during critical hours. Although Haig and other high-ranking ex-cavalrymen kept on hoping from 1914 until 1918 that one day there would come the great breakthrough when the cavalry would come into their own and take up the pursuit of the shattered and fleeing German armies, that day never arrived. The Germans managed to keep up a substantially unbroken front until their final capitulation on November 11, 1918. This is not to say that there was not some gallant and successful cavalry fighting—and not the least of it was when the Germans made their breakthrough on the Fifth Army front in March. But the experience of World War I finally brought it home to the most die-hard equestrian enthusiasts that the horse no longer belonged on the battlefield. The cavalrymen turned to the mechanical equivalent of the charger—the tank, and fought just as bravely in them.

Taken all together, the tactics first practised at Cambrai were those which brought victory in the Battle of Amiens on August 8, 1918—the Black Day of the German Army, as Ludendorff called it. They were also successful at the Battle of Arras, on the 26th of August, and the following actions in which the Canadian Corps drove through to Mons and final victory.

Early in the new year, 1918, when the Canadian Corps was again in the Vimy Sector, I was appointed a staff learner. The system of recruiting junior staff officers in those days was for captains or lieutenants who were judged to have some aptitude for staff work to be attached to brigade or divisional staffs. As a rule, they would be given any odd job that might come up. Their capacity for staff work would be assessed by staff and commander, and if they displayed the necessary qualities, in due course they could be recommended for an appointment as staff captain. I had observed the staff learners who had been attached to the 11th Brigade, and had concluded (perhaps conceitedly) that I could do as well as some of them. I was only twenty years old at the time. But it was a "young man's war." (Is there any other kind?) and some of the officers on staffs and even commanding officers or seconds-in-command of battalions were not much older than I. After the Vimy battle I had screwed up my courage and asked General Odlum if he would recommend me to go on the staff learner list. He kindly did so.

It must be admitted that while commanding officers were urged to put forward the names of competent officers who had done well in their regimental duty for staff training (such as it was), not infrequently they would recommend an officer who was a misfit in their unit, or whom for some reason they wanted to get rid of. These regimental rejects, as they might be called, quite often managed to get a staff appointment through the operation of a somewhat inefficient selection system, and this did not help the reputation of the staff. Of course every veteran of World War I, and indeed everyone who has any acquaintance with World War I literature, knows that the troops spent a good deal of time commenting, with much flavouring of four-letter words, on the deficiencies and inefficiencies of the staff, who were blamed for everything that went wrong. It was fair enough; the staff were supposed to be there as assistants to the commanders with special responsibility for elaborating the plans and writing the orders for the operations into which the fighting troops were to be thrust. It was also their duty to see that all possible arrangements for the comfort of the troops when they were not in combat were made; and when they were fighting that they were supplied with all the munitions, food and other items they needed.

It seems rather extraordinary that it was always the staff who were blamed for what went wrong in battle or in billet—and never the commander! In theory, it was the commander who was responsible for everything, however he was usually a remote and glamorous figure, while the staff officers were to be seen close at hand, very distinctive in their red tabs and red hatbands. As war is full of miseries and frustrations, the fighting soldiers—and the non-combatant troops who support them—need some person or persons on whom to blame their troubles and misfortunes. The advice in the song "Pack Up Your Troubles in Your Old Kit Bag and Smile, Smile, Smile" was, to say the least, not universally adopted. "Dump out your troubles on the dugout floor, and grouse, grouse, grouse" would, I think, be a better description statistically of what the soldiers usually did. In fact, some experienced officers would tell you that it was a sure sign of bad morale if the soldiers were not grousing. Of course, good officers paid attention to what the men were grousing about, and if there were reasonable grounds for it the officer tried to put it right. The men did not usually expect more than this; they knew that in war everything could be expected to go wrong, and often did.

# 1918 and victory

Early in 1918 I left the 11th Brigade and was attached as a "staff learner" to the 9th Brigade of the 3rd Canadian Division. The commander was Brigadier-General F.W. Hill, C.M.G., D.S.O., who had previously commanded the 1st Battalion in the 1st Division. Not long after I joined the brigade, General Hill was succeeded by Brigadier-General D.M. Ormond, C.M.G., D.S.O. He had distinguished himself as Second-in-Command and then Commanding Officer of the 10th Battalion, when in France with the 1st Division in February 1915. He was only thirty-two years old in 1918 and was, I think, the youngest brigade commander in the Canadian Expeditionary Force.

It will be seen that the brigadiers I served under had all qualified for their appointments by having been successful battalion commanders. And they all had the mental grasp enabling them to master their increased responsibilities. This was the pattern for most of the infantry brigadiers of the corps, although, of course, there were a few appointed who did not measure up, and who were quietly transferred to other duties in England or Canada.

A rough calculation shows that of the forty-four officers who held the command of infantry brigades between 1915 and 1919, the average tenure was seventeen months. Seven of these brigade commands ended on promotion to command a division. This average period in command contrasts with the rapid turnover in the Canadian Army during World War II; and the same contrast between the two wars is to be seen in the length of time officers commanded battalions.

The 9th Brigade throughout my time with the formation had a remarkably able group of battalion commanders. Lieutenant-Colonel Urquhart, D.S.O., M.C., of the 43rd Battalion (Cameron Highlanders of Canada), raised in Winnipeg; Lieutenant-Colonel W.W. Foster, D.S.O. (with two bars) of the 52nd Battalion (New Ontario), raised in Port Arthur; Lieutenant-Colonel R.A. Macfarlane, D.S.O. (with two bars) of the 58th Battalion; Lieutenant-Colonel George Pearkes, V.C., D.S.O., M.C.—the only Canadian Army officer to win the triple decoration—who commanded the 116th (Ontario County) Battalion.[1] As these decorations attest, these men had all led their troops with outstanding bravery. They were confident, and held the confidence of the battalions they commanded. I noticed this particularly, as there had been periods in the 11th Brigade when certain commanding officers had been less than satisfactory.

The influence of the commander of an infantry battalion, and of commands in the other arms comparable in size, can scarcely be exaggerated. His character is of the first importance in determining the training, the discipline and the morale of his unit; in short its efficiency as a fighting machine. The lieutenant-colonel's command is the highest in which an officer has direct and constant contact with all ranks under him. The battalion or equivalent is the largest *unit*; above that, the units are grouped into formations, and the commander of a formation cannot exercise the *direct* influence over all the officers and men under him as can the commander of a battalion. The higher commander's will and influence has to be exerted through his subordinate officers. To be successful he has to be able to choose them with discretion, promote the right men, get rid of those who don't measure up to their responsibilities, arrange for commanders and staff officers from outside his own formation to do the jobs when there is no one ripe to take them on within his own command. Thus, judgment of men, the ability to inspire them with confidence, and to generate in them the *will* to execute his will are essential requirements for a higher commander of a formation.

For the commander of a battalion or tank regiment (who exercises direct command over all ranks) to be fully successful requires visible evidence of character, personality, courage and, ideally, a series of virtues too long to enumerate. Not very many officers are to be found who possess these qualities to a superior degree; those who do generally rise to higher command in wartime, if they survive. There are some commanding officers, however, who reach their ceiling in the command of a battalion or equivalent unit: they may lack the mental ability or versatility needed to supplement the more physical qualities which have brought them success as a unit commander.

Although I have no statistics to prove it, I believe that in World War I battalion commanders held their commands for considerably longer periods than did the battalion commanders in World War II. Some officers in World War I commanded battalions for several years. I suppose there are various reasons for this: in World War I the Canadian Corps was built up gradually, with selection of commanders who had been tested in fighting from April 1915 on until the end. In World War II, promotion went more quickly; many able officers were drawn away from units to provide the very numerous staff officers required for Army Headquarters, two corps and five divisions. This left a smaller pool of above-average officers to draw upon for unit commands. Once the fighting started in World War II, it went on with little pause; there were not the long static periods of holding the line in trenches (a great mercy on the whole) which allowed more stability in battalion arrangements. I was surprised, during my time with the 1st Canadian Corps in Italy, how often changes in command were proposed on the grounds that the incumbent was "very tired" or worn down, when perhaps he had only held his appointment for six months or less. I suppose it was easier to say that he was "very tired" than that he was incompetent, or unsuited to his job. I feel that there was too much tendency to simply dismiss the commander of a battalion if its performance was not satisfactory, rather than to try to train him in his job. But once it had started for the Canadians the war went on at a rapid pace, and there was not much disposition to give doubtful commanders a second chance.

The spring of 1918 was a period of sore trial for the British Armies, when Ludendorff launched the great offensive of March 21 against the sector defended by the Fifth and Third Armies. The Germans broke through on a wide stretch of the Fifth Army front, and drove towards the west, creating a great salient with the apex close to Amiens, a penetration of nearly forty miles. This was followed by a subsidiary drive in the direction of Arras, to widen the front of advance; there the Third Army managed to slow down and eventually to halt the German push; the flanks of the great salient were held, and the impetus of the offensive was reduced and finally stopped, as Ludendorff decided to switch to the second of the vast offensives against the British armies which he had prepared.

The Germans did not attack on the front held by the Canadian Corps, in front of the Vimy Ridge and north to Lens. However, the Canadian Cavalry Brigade, which was in the 3rd (British) Cavalry Division, fought first dismounted, and later mounted, in a series of actions in the Fifth Army area, to help cover the retirement of the divisions falling back before the powerful German offensive. The Canadian Motor Machine-gun Brigade also came into action in the Fifth Army sector, where its mobility and firepower enabled it to play a valuable role in slowing up the German advance.

General Headquarters, urgently needing divisions to stem the breakthrough on the Fifth Army front, ordered the 2nd Canadian Division into G.H.Q. reserve, and the 1st Canadian Division into First Army reserve. A few days later, the 3rd Canadian Division was placed under the command of the 13th Corps, while the 4th Canadian Division was withdrawn from the line to G.H.Q. reserve. The Canadian Corps Headquarters, with only corps troops under its command, was also placed in reserve. General Currie protested the orders which had removed all four divisions from his command, but in the event, within twenty-four hours, the 3rd and 4th Divisions came back to him. By April 8, the 1st Division had also returned, and thus reconstituted the Canadian Corps which held a ten-mile front between the Scarpe River and Lens. The 2nd Division, however, remained under command of a British corps until July.

I have previously decribed at some length the advantage, in fighting efficiency, which the Canadians enjoyed by being integrated in a homogeneous corps. The rapid series of shifts in command just outlined illustrates the point that in World War I—as in the subsequent world war—it was the division that was the unit of manoeuvre for the higher commanders. They distributed their forces for offensive and defensive situations by shifting the position and concentration of divisions. The division, of course, is the lowest formation which comprises units of all arms, and is capable, in theory, of operating independently, although this did not happen very often in either world war. In the later years of World War I the staffs became very skilled in arranging divisional moves in which the horses and mechanical vehicles usually went by march routes, while the soldiers who normally marched were carried by train or bus column. For longer moves the whole division—men, horses, guns and wagons—travelled by train.

The higher commanders could move divisions about almost like chessmen; but it was much more difficult to move a whole corps as a body. Nevertheless, as we have seen, in 1916 and 1917 the Canadian Corps had moved from the Ypres front to the Somme, to Vimy, to the Hill 70-Lens area, then to Passchendaele and back to Vimy again. But in the emergency of March 1918, when divisions were needed quickly to plug gaps in the deepening salient created by the German advance, or to stand in reserve behind threatened sectors, the move of a whole corps could not have been accomplished with sufficient speed. There was thus a conflict between the desire of the British higher commanders to dispose of divisions freely, in accordance with the need to move formations to meet the sudden emergencies of the defence, and the desire of the Canadians and their commanders that the Canadian Corps should fight as a unit.

This conflict resulted in protests, or at least firm requests, that the Canadian Corps should not be broken up by detaching its divisions. These requests were made not only to Field-Marshal Haig by General Currie, but also to the British Government by the Canadian Government representative in London. Field Marshal Haig did not take very kindly to these complaints and the consequent necessity to keep the Canadian Corps intact, thus lessening the flexibility of manoeuvre of his command. His diary entry of April 18 shows his irritation:

> He [Currie] wishes to fight only as a 'Canadian Corps' and got his Canadian representative in London to write and urge me to arrange it! As a result, the Canadians are together holding a wide front near Arras, but *they have not yet been in the battle*! The Australians have on the other hand been used by Divisions and are now spread out from Albert to Amiens and one is in front of Hazebrouck.

The opinion of this scattering held by Sir John Monash and the Australians he commanded is not recorded.

The irritation of some British generals was increased by certain rather tactless remarks by General Currie and other Canadians to the effect that some of the British formations did not fight very tenaciously. It is quite possible that the facts justified such an observation. It would indeed be surprising if there had not been loss of morale in some of the understrength British divisions that had been through the blood-and-mud baths of the Somme and Passchendaele. Their losses in the 1917 battles were probably made up only by the reinforcements which could be scraped up from Britain's dwindling manpower. A good many of these 1918 reinforcements were either eighteen-year-olds or older men in lower physical categories. The payment for the reckless expenditure of the lives of young and strong men in the offensives of 1915 to 1917 had come due.

As previously mentioned, there had not been such heavy drafts on Canadian manhood. Canadian formations were finally being reinforced by the men called up under the Military Service Act of 1917. Our ranks were practically full, and we had not been obliged, for lack of manpower, to reduce the number of battalions in our divisions from twelve to nine, as the British had. We were not very sympathetic to the difficulties under which British formations laboured.

After the German offensive between Armentières and the La Bassée Canal, in April, which drove a deep wedge into Allied-held territory in Flanders and adjoining France, a joke was current among the Canadians who continued to hold the only part of the British line that had not been attacked and pierced by the Germans. The tale went that the real German strategy was to isolate us by the offensives to the north and south of our sector, and then make a separate peace with Canada. However, a certain self-satisfaction and truculence, unpleasant in ordinary life, is not a bad attitude in fighting soldiers.

At the brigade headquarters level, we knew little or nothing of the controversies about the splitting off of divisions from the corps —the separation and return took place too quickly for it to percolate down to the lower levels. We knew that the 1st and 2nd Divisions had been hustled off to the Third Army front, but, as mentioned above, the corps was soon reconstituted with the 3rd and 4th divisions in line, shortly afterwards rejoined by the 1st Division.

I have touched on the subject of the temporary breaking up of the Canadian Corps at this time[2] because of a somewhat similar problem I faced in Italy in June-July 1944. This was the desire by the British higher command, for operational convenience, to employ Canadian divisions separately from the 1st Canadian Corps. Of course there were many dissimilar factors in the two situations; all of which will be discussed in later chapters.

From the early part of May 1918 until about the middle of July, the Canadian Corps, with the exception of the 2nd Division, still detached, were out of the line in reserve. This period was used for some reorganization of the Engineers and Machine-gun Corps; and also for some very valuable tactical training. It was at this time, as I recall, that the conception of how the infantry should fight was changed. Instead of advancing in straight lines of a series of waves following a field-gun shrapnel barrage, the foot soldiers within a platoon were now to fight their own battle using their own weapons —rifle, hand and rifle grenades, smoke bombs, and light (Lewis) machine guns. The infantry would practise fire-and-movement tactics autonomously, so to speak. Of course, every advantage was to be taken of the supporting artillery fire, but the idea that the infantry only "occupied" after the artillery "conquered" was superseded. The training carried out in this period when the corps was in reserve had a great deal to do with the success of the almost continuous offensive operations which took the Canadian Corps from in front of Amiens on August 8 to Mons on the 11th of November.

The German offensive against the British armies in Northern France and Flanders came to an end on the 29th of April. After a month's pause, Ludendorff launched a series of attacks on the French front, which continued until mid-July. These attacks penetrated deeply, even to a crossing of the Marne, from which the invading armies had been thrown back in 1914. But then, on July 18, the Allies seized the initiative under the direction of General Foch, who had been appointed Supreme Commander of the Allied Forces in the Western Theatre in the very critical days at the end of March.

The first counteroffensive was carried out by twenty French and four American divisions, and forced the Germans to withdraw from the Marne. This was the turning point of the 1918 campaign. The Allies were now on the offensive, which they continued in a series of blows until the completely defeated enemy was forced to sue for an armistice.

The French-American counteroffensive of July 18 saw the recession of the enemy's offensive tide, but the eighth of August was, in Ludendorff's well-known phrase, the "Black Day of the German Army." British, Australian, Canadian and French formations penetrated deep into the German positions on the first day, destroyed completely several of their divisions and threw back many more in confusion. This powerful blow made Ludendorff realize that the German Army, weakened by the heavy casualties of his spring offensives, could no longer be relied upon to repulse the attacks the Allies would be capable of mounting, much less be able to take the offensive again. So, while the war might be prolonged, for the German Army and for its directing genius, Ludendorff, at the supreme headquarters, it was lost.

The Canadian Corps moved rapidly and secretly from the Vimy-Arras area, deployed in front of Amiens, and in the ensuing battle won a great tactical success at relatively low cost in casualties.[3] The attack on the Canadian front was supported by a total of 646 field and heavy guns; a concentration of one gun for each twelve yards of front, which was heavy indeed. The effect of this powerful artillery was all the greater, as the unfortunate German divisions caught in the blast were completely surprised. They had no warning from preliminary registration or bombardments, because the Allied artillery was able accurately to bring down its barrage with harrassing and counter-battery fire without previous registration, employing the new survey techniques already mentioned.

A battalion of forty-two tanks was allotted to each of the assaulting Canadian divisions, and these tanks were distributed to the infantry battalions, each of which was supported by a section of three tanks. This was the "penny-packet" method of employing tanks, which had begun to receive strong criticism from Tank Corps officers. Of the forty-two tanks that started out with the 3rd Canadian Division on August 8, only eight remained in action when the intermediate objective had been gained, some three miles from the start-line.

But tank tactics and the best way for them to co-operate in the assault carried out by large formations were in the early stages of development. There were not very many tanks, proportionate to the infantry. It would have been a difficult decision to mount a concentrated tank assault on a relatively narrow front, leaving most of the infantry formations without tank support. It was considered then—quite rightly—that accompanying tanks were a great morale-booster for the attacking infantry, apart from their effective destruction of wire obstacles and enemy machine-gun nests.

The results of the first day's fighting in the Amiens battle are summed up in *C.E.F.*[4] as the greatest defeat the enemy had suffered since the beginning of the war. The front attacked by the French, Canadians, Australians and British extended some twelve and a half miles; in the Canadian sector the Germans had been thrown back eight miles, and in the Australian sector, seven. The German Second Army, according to official German figures, suffered about 27,000 casualties, including many officers, with nearly two-thirds of the loss accounted for by those who had surrendered as prisoners. The Fourth Army's casualties, British, Australian and Canadian, excluding those of the air force and tank corps, were approximately 8,800. To balance these against the German losses, we should have to add the losses for the French attacking divisions (which are not given in *C.E.F.*). The Canadians (whose casualties were included in the above Fourth Army total) lost 3,868, and captured 5,033 prisoners and 161 guns.

The Canadian formations continued to be engaged in the Amiens battle until the 17th of August. Good gains were made on the second day, although they remained far short of the first day's great success. After that the momentum slowed down, as the enemy reinforced his broken front.

My own experience in the Amiens battle was very limited. I had been allowed leave shortly before it began, and did not return until the later stages. The main impression I retain is that of riding over the part of the battlefield where the 9th Brigade had advanced to its farther objectives, and finding with surprise how little the terrain had been disturbed by shellfire. Also, as a result of continued fine weather, there was no mud. There was a great contrast between the conditions of the Amiens battle, and the preceding ones of the Somme and Passchendaele. Victory was in the air, and I suppose that a connection was established in my mind between good weather, firm ground and victory.

Yet it would be wrong to suggest that these favourable factors alone accounted for the extent of the Fourth Army's victorious advance. There was the fact that the enemy was no longer fighting with that dogged courage with which he had opposed us in the battles of 1916 and 1917. The same factors which I have mentioned as accounting for the less determined defence of some British formations during the German offensives of March and April applied also to the Germans during and after the Amiens battle. Units were understrength, and were reinforced—when they were reinforced at all—by drafts of underage youths and less fit older men. Disappointment at the failure of the great German offensives earlier in the year to bring the promised victory, and the long toll of casualties and hardships also made hearts sink. And the Germans suffered too from the food blockade imposed by the British Navy; they were not as well fed as our soldiers were. It is hard to keep morale high on an empty stomach.

Was the "war of attrition" really necessary to wear the enemy down before final victory could be won? It seems improbable that against such a courageous, skilful and determined enemy as the Germans any magic formula of generalship, or any innovations in strategy or tactics could have brought quick victory, victory unaccompanied by horrifying losses on both sides. But when all is said, recognizing that victory over such opponents as the Germans could only come through offensive action and wearing down their capacity to resist, the object was not likely to be attained through prolonged offensive operations in bad weather, where mud is the ally of the defenders and the enemy of the attackers.

When the hardening of the enemy's defence, and the increasingly difficult obstacle imposed by the old trenches and wire of the 1916 lines showed that further pressure on the Germans in the Fourth

Army sector would produce diminishing returns, consultations between the higher echelons of command—in descending order, Foch-Haig-Rawlinson-Currie—resulted in a decision to open another offensive front. This brought about the move of the Canadian Corps from the Amiens battleground to the Arras front. As a measure of deception, before the corps had moved to Amiens, plans had been drawn up and conferences had been held purporting to be in preparation for an attack on Orange Hill and Monchy-le-Preux, five miles to the east of Arras. Now these "cover" plans became reality. The 2nd and 3rd Divisions were disengaged from the Fourth Army front, and, moving north, came under the command of the First Army. The 3rd Division was moved by bus and train to the area in rear of Arras on the night of August 20/21. At dawn on August 26 it was launched into the attack on the left of the Arras-Cambrai road, together with the 2nd Division on the right, and on the left the famous 51st (Highland) Division which was under Canadian Corps command for the opening phase of the offensive. This was a rapid switch in the main line of thrust. The war was indeed opening up.

At this time I was transferred from my job as "learner," assisting the staff captain A. and Q.[5] in the 9th Brigade, to the general staff (Operations, Training and Intelligence) of the 3rd Divisional staff. My particular employment was to be reconnaissance during operations; the task for which "liaison officers" were provided in World War II. As previously explained, the great difficulty in tactical command of the offensive battle during World War I was to know how far the attacking troops had advanced, whether and when they had taken their assigned objectives, or whether and where they were held up. Lacking such information, it was impossible for commanders to employ their reserves and supporting artillery effectively to reinforce success, or to remedy the situation when objectives had not been taken. In World War I there were very few portable radio sets for operation forward of divisions. So in battle, messages reporting the situation had to go by runner from front line companies, back as far as battalion H.Q. It usually took hours for the reports of what was happening on the front line to get back through battalion and brigade headquarters to divisional ones.

To get a picture of the situation at the front, the reconnaissance officer would go forward, visit brigade and battalion headquarters, learn what they knew about what was happening, and then have a look at the battlefield himself, to the extent that the features of the terrain would permit observation. To carry out his task he was not required to go up to the foremost companies, as he had naturally to avoid being caught in the actual fighting. Having gained the best picture he could of the progress of the operation, he was supposed to get his report back to divisional headquarters as quickly as he could; by telephone if he could find one working back from any forward headquarters; otherwise, by returning to his division and reporting personally.

A few words on the organization and functioning of a divisional staff, as it was at this time, may be useful for the non-military reader. The General Staff Officer, Grade 1 (G.S.O. 1) was the kingpin; and was responsible for directing the "general" staff side of the work. This included planning and executing operations, writing the orders for them, as well as intelligence and training. The chief staff officer on the administrative side, the A.A. and Q.M.G. (Assistant Adjutant and Quartermaster-General), was equal in rank to the G.S.O. I, but as between these two (to adapt George Orwell) the G.S.O. was more equal than his colleague. In brief, the G.S.O. 1 had the co-ordinating responsibility to see that the commander's plan was translated into action through the necessary staff, to write orders, to ensure they reached those who had to take action on them in time and to check that they were carried out. In the conditions of World War I, when divisions operated on a narrow front, with other divisions on both flanks, there was not a great deal of scope for the exercise of tactical genius by a divisional commander. The orders came down from above and they framed the action of the division pretty tightly; their execution was more a matter of staff work than of initiative by the commanders.

None of the Canadian officers commanding divisions in World War I had had the benefit of higher training for the direction of operations or staff duties. They were supported by British regular officers as G.S.O. 1's, who had the required training and experience. Generally these British officers were of very high calibre, and in some cases were reputed to be the real commanders of the division. On the other hand, before succeeding to their post the Canadian divisional commanders had all proved themselves in the command of brigades, and sometimes before that, of battalions. Thus they had confidence in themselves and their immediate subordinates could have confidence in them. This was the usual picture, though of course not every subordinate in the echelons of command had full confidence in every superior.

The British establishment of a divisional headquarters included one General Staff Officer Grade 2, and one General Staff Officer Grade 3, who handled operations and intelligence duties, under the G.S.O. 1. Canadian divisions had two of each. Canadian brigades had two staff captains, one for administrative (A. & Q.) and one for intelligence duties, while there was only one staff captain on the British brigade H.Q. establishment. This doubling of the establishment, I believe, came about in the early days of the C.E.F. when nearly all staff appointments were held by British officers. But Canadian officers in the same grades were put alongside them to learn the business, which in due course they did. When the British staff officers departed, the double establishment was left, and was filled with Canadian officers who had acquired the necessary experience. This arrangement contributed to the efficiency of Canadian staff work. While one experienced and fully-trained staff officer could handle these jobs, when they had to be done by officers whose military training for the most part had begun in 1914, the extra man was useful.

During the period I was attached to 3rd Divisional headquarters, the Canadian Corps advanced from about one mile in front of Arras to Cambrai (captured on October 10)—a distance of about twenty-one miles. In this advance it had broken through the heavily fortified Fresnes-Rouvroy and Drocourt-Quéant Lines, which were extensions of the Hindenburg Line to the north. During the advance the 3rd Canadian Division was in action from the 26th to the 29th of August, driving forward for about six miles from the trench positions where the line had settled down after the spring offensive of the Germans. It was not engaged during the Drocourt-Quéant operation, but was fighting continuously for twelve days from the crossing of the Canal du Nord on September 27, until it entered Cambrai on the 9th of October.

During all these actions I was employed on reconnaissance and liaison jobs. Two minor failures in the operations, due to command and staff errors, impressed me during this period. One happened on the first day of the offensive—the 26th of August. The first objective of the 3rd Division, which was attacking with only the 8th Brigade (Canadian Mounted Rifles) forward, was to the west of Monchy-le-Preux. This had been the scene of much hard fighting in 1917, before its eventual capture by troops of the Third Army. The village had been retaken by the Germans in their drive which began on March 28, 1918. It stood on the highest ground and afforded good observation for the Germans, particularly to the west. The battalions of the 8th Brigade advanced rapidly, meeting less opposition than had been expected.

Zero hour had been at three a.m. I was sent forward, soon after it became light, and rode along to the north of the Arras-Cambrai road as far as seemed practicable, then, leaving my horse with the groom who accompanied me, I went on forward on foot. The battlefield seemed remarkably quiet, with no German shelling or small-arms fire. Presently I came on some machine-gunners, who were in position near what was supposed to be the main objective. This was perhaps 700 or 800 yards west of Monchy. I did not get much information from the machine-gunners, except that everything seemed to have gone "according to plan" and that they were not aware of any enemy to their front. At this point I noticed some men in khaki riding into Monchy (a gunner observation party probably). The machine-gunners then told me that they thought our troops had been in Monchy for some time.

This news was very important; it had not been expected that this tough village position would be captured easily, but might require an attack by one of the reserve brigades, which, according to the divisional plan, would be used to exploit success after capture of the main objective. I therefore turned back and was able to telephone the news to divisional headquarters. As I remember it, this was the first information they had that Monchy had been taken. By the time I got back to headquarters the staff were trying to get orders forward to the reserve brigade which, it had been planned, would be the first to be engaged in the exploitation if the main objective were taken. But here a delay developed—the brigade commander and his brigade major could not be reached at their H.Q. They had gone off on a personal reconnaissance of the battlefield, which lasted several hours. While they were away it was impossible for the division to convey orders to get the brigade moving, and thus take advantage of the apparent gap in the enemy's defences.

The official history states that shortly after the capture of Monchy two battalions of this reserve brigade pushed through to attack enemy-held woods east of Monchy. My recollection was that this move forward did not take place until well on in the afternoon, and that a good chance for exploitation was thus lost.

The lesson I derived from this was not at all a new one. It was that, as a rule, during the critical phases of a battle, a commander should remain at his headquarters from which he can communicate to the formations or units under him, gain information from all sources, and receive orders from the next higher echelon of command. This lesson, as I have said, was a commonplace. The conditions of battle, as they were from 1914 to 1918, made it practically impossible for a general to gain a comprehensive view of what was happening on the front he was attacking or defending. So the accepted view was that if he did go forward he would probably give undue importance to the limited action he had actually seen, and so get a distorted picture of the battle.

Conditions of command in World War II were different. Better means of transport for generals and staff officers—jeeps, armoured cars and tanks—with efficient radio communication, allowed a commander more freedom to move out from his headquarters, as he could still communicate with it to receive information and issue orders.

Another lesson occurred a few days later when an attack was ordered, at short notice, to follow up the success of the first day, and exploit the weak and disorganized German defence. To observe the operation I had gone forward with Major "Jonesy" Meredith, one of the G.S.O. 2's of the division, and we had reached a position not far in the rear and a little to the flank of the start-line of the battalion making the attack. When zero hour arrived—about ten a.m. or so—the barrage came down all right, and the line of white puffs from the shrapnel shells, seemingly very accurately placed, continued in short lifts down the little valley towards the east. But no infantry appeared to be following the barrage, until ten or more minutes after zero, when a few khaki figures emerged from an old trench and began to move forward. There was some scattered enemy rifle and machine-gun fire, and the khaki attackers disappeared from sight, doubtless having taken cover in the old trenches which remained from former years. The attack gained nothing.

When reports about what had happened came in, the failure was put down to insufficient time having been allowed for the battalion to get in position for the takeoff, or for officers to have a look at the ground over which they were to attack and to locate their objectives. This little action which I had watched from a front-row seat, gave me a prejudice against "quickie" attacks. There is an adage one used to hear in the staff colleges: "Time spent in reconnaissance is seldom wasted." It might be supplemented by another, which perhaps would qualify as a platitude: "An attack made without enough time for reconnaissance and preparation will usually fail." Of course the problem remains: How much time is enough? If an attack is too long delayed in a fluid situation such as existed at the time of the action I have described, an opportunity to hit the enemy while he is still disorganized may be missed. It is a matter for experienced judgement.

The autumn of 1918 in Picardy was as exceptionally fine as the autumn of 1917 in Flanders had been exceptionally wet. I write from recollection without reference to meteorological statistics. Contrast the photographs of the crossing of the Canal du Nord and the advance towards Cambrai[6] with the photographs of the Somme and Passchendaele. It rained, of course, but it seemed generally to rain during the night, and was never persistent enough to create the morass of mud which had made the battles of 1916 and 1917 so miserable. Allowing even for the deterioration in the enemy's strength and morale, the offensive on the Canadian front could not have been as successful as it was if the weather had not been good and the ground firm. In many of the accounts of the actions given in *C.E.F.* one reads that even without tank or close artillery support the infantry were able to gain ground by platoon and section rushes —infantry fire and movement tactics, inculcated during the training period of the summer. This could not have happened on soggy, muddy ground.

Another element in the operations which stuck in my mind was the way in which the corps as a rule relieved divisions successively after they had been about three days in action. Divisions carrying on a hard driving offensive, and inevitably suffering casualties, required some reorganization and rest for weary infantrymen, on whose leg muscles and lungs the success of the attack depended.

After the capture of Cambrai, the corps side-slipped to the north and began to operate on the axis Douai-Valenciennes-Mons. It was the last month of the war. About this time I returned to the 9th Infantry Brigade, to act as Staff Captain A. and Q. I continued in this job until a month or so after the armistice. Looking back, it was rather a large responsibility for an officer only twenty-one years old. However, I got through it without any serious troubles, perhaps due to the indulgence of Brigadier-General Ormond, and the fact that the brigade was not in any serious engagement during this period.

The 3rd Division was advancing towards Mons, the little Belgian city which had seen the first action of the British Army in the war, and from which the famous retreat of the "Old Contemptibles" had started. But now, instead of retreat and the possibility of disaster, it was an advance to final victory, and it was the Canadians who were leading the way. The German armies were in retreat across the whole western front. Their resistance was reduced to a series of rear-guard actions. The leading troops of the 3rd Division and the 2nd Division on our right probed this resistance cautiously.

Negotiations were under way for an armistice, but these were shrouded in secrecy and uncertainty, and little news of what was happening reached the forward troops. The newspapers told us of many events presaging the end of the war, but those who had been through years of it had listened to so many promises that this or that offensive would bring the final victory that they found it hard to accept the evidence that this time the war would really end. Would there really be an armistice or was it just another rumour? Every soldier far forward enough to be within range of the enemy artillery, which continued to fire sporadically until almost the last hour, must have wondered whether he was going to survive, or whether some shell "with his number on it" would wipe him off the rolls in the last hours of the long war.

Early in the morning of November 11 the 7th Infantry Brigade entered Mons and cleared out the few remaining Germans. After the war, General Currie was unjustly attacked because he had ordered operations to continue during the last twenty-four hours, when presumably he knew that the armistice was to take place. He was accused of unnecessarily sacrificing men's lives for the sake of prestige. But in a libel suit his action was completely vindicated.[7]

In fact, it was not until five a.m. on November 11 that the German plenipotentiaries signed the armistice agreement. This news, and orders for the ceasefire at eleven a.m. only reached corps headquarters at six-thirty a.m. Until then, the directive had been to continue the advance. But the occupation of Mons, effected by strong fighting patrols, had been finished before dawn. Of the sixteen Canadian casualties on November 11, only one was fatal.

The victory parade through the square at Mons was a memorable event; troops of the 3rd Division marching past General Currie and the burgomaster of the city. Somehow the battalions had brushed off the grime of combat, and with the guns and teams of the artillery, almost at horse-show standard, they made a brave appearance. The pipes and drums of the Scottish regiments played the marchers through.

John Brophy has the following to say about the mood of the men at this time:

> On the Western Front the advancing troops were too tired for junketing and too sceptical: there had been false alarms of peace before. The Allies halted: the Germans withdrew out of sight and out of range of rifle, machine gun and artillery fire. This agreed "disengagement" brought about a sudden relief from mental and nervous tension, after four and a half years.[8]

I think this probably describes the general mood. As for myself, I certainly recall the feeling of relief. There was no introspective analyzing of personal feelings, or pondering over my uncertain future. I had survived, and that was enough for the moment. Besides, I was kept pretty busy; while the armistice had brought operations to an end, administrative staff work continued.

The 9th Brigade took over the line in front of Mons from the 7th Brigade. After the victory parade there was still immediate business to attend to, settling the units in new positions, as well as the usual administrative routine. I remember that as the junior on the staff, I was left to hold down the brigade headquarters while the brigadier and the more senior officers went off to be entertained by the joyful citizens of Mons, most of whom had managed to conceal a few bottles of wine from the German perquisitions. Shortly before I went to bed, a staff officer from division called up and told me he was going out (presumably to celebrate), and that my line was switched through to corps headquarters, but there was considerable vagueness as to who was in charge there. I went to sleep with the pleasing fantasy that there I was, as a Lieutenant, acting staff captain, responsible for the whole corps front. That in about twenty-five years' time I should in fact be commanding a Canadian corps in another war would have seemed even more fantastic! Early the next morning I was awakened by the sound of exploding shells, and what sounded like rifle fire. My first thought was that the Germans had played a trick on us, and reopened hostilities—a possibility on which some gloomy souls had speculated. But it turned out only to be shells and small arms ammunition exploding in a German munitions train in Nimy, on the other side of the canal, that some idiot had managed to set on fire. And so ended the war.

I had one more lesson before leaving the 9th Brigade. General Ormond with some other senior officers had arranged to visit the 1st and 2nd Divisions which had marched to the Rhine, and were part of the occupation force there. He was to leave early in the morning, and was to travel in the recent and gratefully received addition to the brigade transport—a model T Ford touring car. It was not a really comfortable vehicle for a long drive. The divisional staff, thinking of this rather late, sent the brigade a telegram offering one of the divisional Vauxhalls for the trip. This telegram came in the middle of the night and was brought in, waking me from what must have been a very sound sleep. I signed for it and told the runner, it seems, that there was no further action. In the morning when I woke up and looked again at the telegram I was horrified to realize that the General and his fellow-travellers had gone off in the Ford! I perspired over this slip considerably until telling the General on his return. Rather to my surprise he treated it as a bit of a joke. I did not understand how I had managed to read and initial the telegram, but remember nothing at all about it until I woke the next morning and found the sheet of paper by the side of my bed. It was probably due to a prolonged poker game the night before, during which I had drunk quite a few glasses of port. Going to bed, I felt quite normal, but perhaps the port had a delayed effect.

Above: Author, late summer of 1917 / P.A.C.

Below: Passchendaele, November 1917 / P.A.C.

Opposite, above: Tank in action, Wailly, October 1917

Opposite, below: Crossing of Canal du Nord, September 1918 / P.A.C.

Left: Releasing the odd dove / P.A.C.

Below: "Dinner up" for the 87th / P.A.C.

Left: A street in Liévin / P.A.C.

Below: A big crater, Vimy Ridge /

Lieutenant-Generals Crerar and Burns,
Italy, March 1944 / P.A.C.

Above: King George VI inspecting Canadian troops, Italy, July 1944 / P.A.C

Below: The Hon. J.L. Ralston talking to men of the 22nd Regiment / P.A.C.

Left: A roadside conference between the Metauro River and the Gothic Line / P.A.C.

Below: Men of the Carleton and York Regiment, Liri Valley, May 1944 / P.A.C.

Above: On the road to Pontecorvo, May 1944/P.A.C.
Left, below: Pontecorvo, Italy, May 1944/P.A.C.
Right, below: Major-General Chris Vokes and author/P.A.

In World War II, remembering this incident, I did not drink any alcohol (with the exception of an occasional pre-dinner glass of sherry) while I was in command of troops in the field.

I returned to England with the 9th Brigade headquarters in the early spring of 1919, still a Lieutenant in the routine of repatriation and demobilization. But I then received a regular staff appointment carrying promotion to the rank of Captain. This was to the 12th Infantry Brigade which was still in Belgium. The 4th was the last division to be returned to Canada. Nothing remarkable occurred during this period of my service, except that I got to know Colonel J.L. Ralston, D.S.O., who had commanded the 85th Battalion (Nova Scotia Highlanders) with great distinction, and who acted in command of the 12th Brigade during the last few weeks before it broke up in England. This acquaintance stood me in good stead in World War II, when, as the Hon. J. L. Ralston, he served Canada very ably and honourably as Minister of Defence.

# Between the wars

It is a well-worn gibe that soldiers always prepare for the last war. I suppose that, on the whole, this cannot be denied. Soldiers are limited in methods of fitting themselves for the task for which the country pays them; that is, to be ready to defend it by force of arms if the politicians don't succeed in keeping it out of war. As there is no science of war, based on firmly established data and laws which will allow the solution of military problems by logical deduction, soldiers must, as their principal means of intellectual preparation, study military history, and try to derive lessons from it. It is natural that they should pay most attention to the more recent military history, especially that of wars in which their own nation participated. There is also likely to be a difference in the line of thought and consequent military practice and preparation between the military of a nation which has met defeat and of one which has emerged victorious. If a nation has been defeated, its soldiers are likely to take a more critical view of the doctrines and procedures which they have traditionally followed than the soldiers of victorious nations would do. There are many examples of this, the most recent of which is the German preparation for the 1939-45 war, as contrasted with the lack of, or wrongly directed, preparation by the British and French armies.

In the years following the 1918 armistice there was a great deal of vigorous military criticism and controversy in Great Britain, in spite of having "won" the war. It was inspired, in large measure, by the post-war shocked realization of the tremendous losses in men and wealth which had been incurred. As I have already mentioned, Major-General J.F.C. Fuller and Sir Basil (then Captain) Liddell Hart were the most noted among the British military theorists who advocated new methods of warfare, based mainly on the power of the protected mobility of the tank. Of course, there were also the airmen who saw air power directed against enemy industry and civilian population as the magic means by which future wars could be won. The airmen were unquestionably right about the increasing importance of air power in warfare, but, as I have argued elsewhere,[1] they were sadly astray in thinking that the use of airpower against civilian populations would make for the greater future security of the people of the British Isles, or any other people for that matter.

The controversies in Britain concerning the future of military tactics and strategy had echoes in the Commonwealth, and excited the interest of the professionally alert members of the Canadian Permanent Active Militia—as the regular Canadian Army was then called. But interest, activity and investment in the Canadian military forces was at a very low ebb in the 1920's and early 1930's. We had just won a war to end all wars, so why spend money and thought to prepare for another? James Eayrs has presented the history of those years—melancholy from the point of view of the Canadian professional soldier, sailor or airman—in his book *The Defence of Canada.*

Nevertheless, a good deal was done in the education—the higher military education, one might call it—of Canadian regular officers. When the Canadian Expeditionary Force had been organized in 1914, there were only two or three Canadian regular officers who had been through the Staff College at Camberley.

When the war was over, in 1919, Camberley reopened for its full two-year course. There were two vacancies each year for Canadian officers. Some years later there was added an additional vacancy at the Indian Army Staff College, at Quetta. So that when World War II broke out, there were nearly fifty Canadian officers who had received the regular staff college training. Consequently, all the staff appointments in the first contingents of what was called in 1939 the "Canadian Active Service Force" were filled by trained Canadians.

An Imperial Defence College was established in London in the twenties, and each year two Canadians, any of Army, Navy or Air Force officers, and occasionally a civil servant, attended the year-long course. There were six officers each from the Royal Navy, British Army and Royal Air Force, officers from the other Dominions, and officials of the British civil service. The purpose of the instruction was to inform the students on the problems of higher command and strategy facing the British Commonwealth. Politics, economics, foreign relations and all matters affecting the defence of the Commonwealth were included in the curriculum, with lectures from eminent authorities in many of the fields. For those fortunate enough to be selected to attend the course, it gave a broad view of military and defence problems, enabling the students to understand the problems of the politicians directing the war effort.

The officers of the Non-permanent Active Militia in Canada—part-time soldiers—who were professionally keen and were interested in more than just regimental soldiering and the amenities of the officers' mess, were offered yearly militia staff courses. These included a winter of lectures and paper exercises, followed in the summer by two week's exercises on the ground in one of the militia camps. Later an advanced militia staff course was set up for those non-regular officers who wanted to carry their professional training a stage farther.

When mobilization was ordered in 1939, there was therefore a respectable cadre of theoretically trained staff officers, of whom the more senior had had experience that would fit them for command of brigades and divisions.

The Canadian militia, permanent and non-permanent, had qualified a fair number of Chiefs, although the Indians—non-commissioned officers and privates—had been low in numbers in the drill halls and camps. This was due to lack of money to pay the men for their time, and to buy equipment which would make training interesting enough to attract recruits. There were exceptional units however, that, by a combination of hard work, enthusiasm and social help for members of the unit who were having a hard time in the depression years, managed to turn out respectable numbers on parade. All honour to them.

This book, however, is not intended to cover the history of the trials and endurance of the Canadian military forces between the wars. A certain amount of connective narrative seems necessary to explain how I worked up the military ladder, between the demobilization of the C.E.F. in 1918-19, when I had attained the rank of

Captain, and 1939, by which time I had become a brevet Lieutenant-Colonel, with the training supposed to fit me to assume a responsible post on the General Staff.

My first job in peacetime was as an engineer officer in the Saint John Military District—Military District No. 7 as it was then called. The work consisted mainly in travelling round to various parts of New Brunswick, overseeing the restoration of drill halls (this was necessary because most of them had been used for the accommodation and training of the C.E.F. units). After about a year of this, I was sent to the School of Military Engineering at Chatham, England, where, with about thirty officers of the Royal Engineers of my age and seniority, I was given training in the subjects which a Royal Engineer was expected to know something about. These included building construction, military bridging, mechanical and electrical engineering, and topographical survey. As can be imagined, in the eighteen months allotted to instruction in these very extensive branches of the engineering profession, only the elements could be taught. Having been through several years of war, it was assumed the members of the class should need no instruction in tactics, nor in military engineering as practised in the field—field fortifications, road maintenance and so on. However, quite a number of the R.E. officers had served in the signal units, as I had myself (the Royal Corps of Signals and its Canadian counterpart were only established after World War I). This gap in my training as a military engineer didn't worry me particularly, until some years later I was suddenly posted to be instructor in Military Engineering at the Royal Military College. This was by orders of General McNaughton, then Director of Military Training. I told him that I really knew hardly anything about field military engineering, but he brushed this objection aside, saying I would learn the subject in teaching it. I suppose I did, in the course of a year or so, but my "learning on them" seemed a little hard on the cadets I was supposed to instruct. Some of the victims of my early attempts rose to high rank in World War II, notably Guy Simonds, Chris Vokes and "Johnny" Plow.

The subject taught at Chatham which I liked best was topographical surveying. I received a good report in this subject, which resulted in my being attached, for two years or so after I returned to Canada, to what was then called the Geographical Section General Staff. Actually it was the establishment for making military maps, mostly on the scale of one inch to one mile, of some of the areas considered then to be of military importance—generally in the southern parts of Ontario and Quebec. It also involved a few odd jobs covering the areas in which there were training camps, such as Petewawa, Aldershot in Nova Scotia, Sarcee in Alberta, and others. The work was carried out by plane-table using the techniques of the British Ordnance Survey. I spent two summers surveying in the Eastern Townships of Quebec, in charge of small parties of topographers. I enjoyed this healthy existence, and walked up to twelve or fifteen miles a day, carrying plane-table, clinometer and various other surveying implements, filling in the features of the country. Incidentally, there can be no better way of learning to read maps than spending some time making them. The ability to read a map quickly and accurately is a valuable asset to any officer.

It was in the early twenties that I began writing. Only a few Canadian officers felt the urge to communicate their ideas to their fellows (and perhaps the general public) through the written word. In the British Army, to write about military subjects was becoming quite respectable. Had not Haig written a book on cavalry tactics before 1914? Of course it carried a superior cachet to get an article in *Blackwoods* magazine, usually on sport or travel. After various attempts at short stories my real start in writing came about through a letter I wrote to H.L. Mencken. He had published a short piece on the recurrent theme that Canada was bound to be absorbed by the United States one day. My letter contested this prophecy, of course. Greatly to my surprise I got a letter back, continuing the argument briefly, and saying that in his opinion as a professional writer I wrote clearly and well. Why not try writing an article on the subject? This really set me up on a cloud, for like many other young people of that decade, I admired Mencken for his iconoclastic blasts against the stuffy Victorian-Edwardian mores and literature of North America.

Later he suggested I should write on the military art—a department of literature which he said seemed to be non-existent in North America. So I did produce an article, which was published in the *American Mercury*. This article was followed by several others, one of which is reproduced in part in this book, in the chapter on the

Vimy battle. I met Henry Mencken several times and continued to correspond irregularly with him until he was stricken with paralysis. His encouragement, interest and I may say friendship were a great influence in my life, and I have always been grateful to him.

I also published a number of articles in the *Canadian Defence Quarterly*, an inter-war periodical in which Canadian officers were able to exhibit their thoughts about the art and science of war, especially as it might relate to the Canadian armed services. I recall that my first article was an argument, based mainly on experience in World War I, that horses should no longer be used in armies, either to haul wagons or as a means of locomotion for the cavalry. They were too vulnerable to modern small-arms and artillery fire, and also inefficient when compared with motor vehicles. This caused considerable indignation in the regular Canadian Cavalry regiments, and friends told me that the sentries on the gate of the old Stanley Barracks, Toronto (where the Royal Canadian Dragoons had their headquarters) had instructions to bayonet me on sight. However, in the course of World War II, all Canadian Cavalry regiments were "mechanized." I am happy to think that in the expansion of the Canadian Army, which took place in 1940-1, I was able to exert a little influence in getting many cavalry regiments, with their own names, into the armoured divisions and brigades. Riding in tanks or armoured cars rather than astride horses, they played a decisive role in the successful battles of the Canadian Army.

This writing, more than anything else I did during the 1920's and 1930's, brought me to the attention of my superiors, and ensured that in due course I would be considered for senior appointments in the hierarchy.

I attended the Staff College in Quetta, Baluchistan (now in West Pakistan) during 1928 and 1929. These were very pleasant years, during which the military instruction was ingested in a fairly relaxed atmosphere, wherein the students, mostly of the rank of captain with twelve or more years service and war experience, were encouraged to maintain their physical fitness with tennis, golf, polo, riding to hounds (after the jackal) and other exercises suited to ward off myopia and the scholar's stoop. I had married just before leaving for

India, and my wife and I found life in the rather restricted circle of staff college students very agreeable. We were also able to travel during the breaks between terms, and managed to see many of the cities of northern India. It was a very happy time and I suppose that I learned a good deal about the soldier's trade, although as I write this I am at a loss to recall any one thing in particular. Such acquaintance as I scraped up with India's history and physical aspect was perhaps the most valuable gain from these two years. In Quetta society we did not meet Indians. The authorities had just begun the "Indianization" of the Army, that is, the granting to Indians of the "King's Commission," thus making them professional equals of the British officers.

I returned to Canada "East-about"; from Calcutta to Singapore touching at Rangoon and Port Swettenham (for Kuala Lumpur); from Singapore to Hong Kong, where we stayed for about three weeks, waiting for the C.P.R. *Empress*, which brought us back to Vancouver with stops at Shanghai, Kobe and Yokahama.

During the last term of our course at Quetta our class had taken part in a combined exercise, in which we were joined by a number of Royal Air Force and Royal Navy officers—sailors and airmen gathered together from their stations in and about India. The theme of the exercise was the invasion and defence of Singapore. For the practical part of the exercise on the ground we went to Salsette Island, near Bombay, which was roughly similar to Singapore Island in size and shape. Of course the invasion was carried out by landing from the (imagined) south side of the Singapore Island—not the way the Japanese actually came thirteen years later. In 1929 it was considered that it would be impossible for the Japanese to come down in any force through the jungle of the eastern side of the Malay peninsula; although this view had been modified somewhat by the time I studied the question again—in 1939 at the Imperial Defence College.

I found it useful in these later studies to have seen Singapore and Hong Kong, even for a brief period. But at no time in World War II did my duties require me to have anything to do with the military disasters which these names recall, for which I am thankful.

On returning to Canada in January 1930, I was sent back to regimental duty, so to speak, as District Engineer Officer at Quebec, and remained there for a year. The main engineering tasks had to do with the repair of the ancient fortress walls of the city. This enterprise was undertaken less through zeal for the preservation of ancient monuments than to give employment to Quebecers in the building trades who would otherwise have been unemployed. The depression of the thirties was setting in, following the stock market crash of 1929.

After I had spent a year in Quebec, General McNaughton selected me to be in charge of the Geographical Section, General Staff—the map-making organization of the Department of Defence. He had decided that the principal function of the organization should be to carry out experiments in new mapping methods, primarily by making use of air photographs. The actual production of maps would have second priority.

I remained in this appointment for six years, from 1931 to 1936 inclusive. During this time we made very considerable progress, gradually finding more effective ways to use air photographs: to establish the planimetry (designation by conventional signs for roads, railroads, houses, woods, water features), and then the relief (hills and valleys shown by means of contour lines). The methods we developed were mainly derived from the earlier experiments of Captain R. Hotine of the Royal Engineers, a brilliant mathematician and experimenter, who later in his career headed the Ordnance Survey.

From these experimental activities emerged the basis of the methods of map-making employed successfully by the Canadian Survey Company in World War II, and those now in use in the Army Survey Establishment. Today, of course, methods are vastly improved, using optical-mechanical machines for plotting from air photos. In my time these devices existed only in the form of relatively crude forerunners. It is a great satisfaction to have had a share in the pioneering days of Canadian air photo mapping. The year I spent with the Geographical Section were among the most rewarding of all my service. I felt I had produced something of real value to the community when a map was completed, something which would have a thousand uses, from the preliminary planning of great engineering works to the guidance of the week-end hiker across the countryside.

At the end of 1936, I was appointed General Staff Officer 1 in the Montreal Military District. The duties of this job related principally to the training of the Non-Permanent Active Militia of the district, in armouries during the winter and at camps in the summer. There was also the militia staff course to keep an eye on, although most of the instruction was done by other officers on the district staff.

In 1936 the Canadian Militia was slowly beginning to recover from the period of almost complete neglect from which it had suffered during the twenties and early thirties. The rearmament and remilitarization of Germany under the Nazis was becoming more and more menacing. At least the members of Canada's armed forces, both regular and volunteer, could see the menace, although it had not impressed the politicians sufficiently to make them allot the money for training and equipment which was needed to really prepare our services for war. The politicians, of course, with one or two exceptions, merely reflected the Canadian public's lack of concern with things outside the ambit of its own municipality or employment—or lack of employment, for the depression still lay heavily on the country.

The two years I spent in the Montreal District under Brigadier R.O. Alexander (later Major-General) were busy and agreeable. Born in Montreal, I found it pleasant to be back in familiar surroundings and renew some school friendships. My office in the Post Office building on the corner of Bishop and St. Catherine Streets was a stone's throw from the small apartment on Bishop Street where my family had lived and which is the scene of my first memories. And across St. Catherine Street was St. James the Apostle Church, where I had attended Sunday School and occasionally been taken to the service. But one special memory was of my father, an officer in the Militia, taking me to the office of the then G.S.O.—Major W.B. ("Grog" or "Wilbo") Anderson. I was about sixteen, and considerably awed at being in the presence of a regular staff officer, who moreover had been through the Camberley Staff College. When about twenty years later I found myself in the same appointment I remembered this interview. While I was very pleased to occupy the post, I had outgrown the notion that the G.S.O. of M.D. 4 must necessarily be a very great man.

As I have said before, during these years it was difficult to make training realistic and interesting, because of the lack of modern arms and equipment. We weren't exactly drilling with broomsticks, in the classical tradition of patriotic volunteers, but we sometimes thought we were not far away from it. I recall the expedients we had to devise in training the Three Rivers Regiment, which had been converted from infantry to a tank regiment in the reorganization of the militia which had recently been carried out. There were no tanks in Canada; the armoured might of the country then consisting of a few machine-gun carriers, mostly located in Winnipeg, where exercises and experiments with them were being carried out under the zealous and vigorous guidance of Capt. F.F. Worthington ("Worthy") (later Major-General) who has been rightly called the father of the Canadian Armoured Corps. What success we did have was in the main due to the drive and eagerness of the Adjutant—Captain Jean Allard. (He was later to command the Royal 22nd Regiment with great distinction in the Italian Campaign, and to end his military career as a full General and Chief of Staff of the Canadian Defence Forces.)

I was selected to attend the Imperial Defence College in 1939. At this time, the course was divided into three terms. During the first we studied the situation which would exist in the Far Eastern Theatre if there were war between Japan and the Commonwealth, and carried out exercises related to it. As I remember it, everyone was confident that Singapore could hold out until a powerful relieving naval force could arrive from British waters. Hong Kong was more of a problem. I think that to the majority of our class the island and territory seemed indefensible, and indeed, some doubted the value of having any larger garrison there than was needed for aid to the civil power, that is, to suppress local disorder if it were more than the police could handle. But the counter-argument, that it would be very damaging to the prestige of Britain if the garrison and fortifications were scaled down, prevailed in the actual event. And this led to tragedy. The hopes for the defence of Hong Kong were tied to the calculation that if there were an attack by Japan against the British strongholds in the Far East, the United States would see this proof of Japanese expansionism so dangerous to their own interest and security. They would therefore enter the war and their powerful naval forces would relieve Hong Kong before it fell. When war did break out in the Far East, of course the U.S.A. did indeed become the ally of the Commonwealth; but the Japanese surprise attack at Pearl Harbour, as well as bringing the United States into the war, inflicted such damage on the American battle fleet that it prevented any aid to the British at Hong Kong and Singapore, and to the Americans in the Philippines.

The second term at the I.D.C. was devoted to the study of what might happen if the Commonwealth should find itself at war with Italy in the Mediterranean. At the time, Mussolini was at the height of his power and full of talk of "Mare Nostrum" and a revived Roman Empire. The Berlin-Rome-Tokyo axis posed a more and more imminent threat, although no one could predict exactly to what extent Germany, Italy and Japan would co-operate in the event of war, nor could it be predicted how or when war would break out. The Germans, of course, were the most immediate menace.

It was intended that in the third term (autumn of 1939) we should study the strategy of a war with Germany. But when September came we were all dispersed to various war appointments, and were engaged in the reality of war instead of its study. I remember that when the Commandant of the I.D.C., Admiral T.H. Binney, bade us good-bye in July at the end of the second term, he said that he hoped we should meet again in September—but if not, well, he wished us the best of luck. Most of us thought he was unduly pessimistic in suggesting the possibility that war could break out so soon.

The plan of study was to deal with war in the three theatres separately. This was necessary, I suppose, in order to study the problems in a manageable framework. But some of us wondered what would happen if it should come about that Great Britain and the Commonwealth should be at war with two or even three of the potential enemies at once. As the British resources on the sea, on land and in the air did not seem really adequate to take on any one of these enemies with much hope of success, the prospects of fighting several at once was not at all encouraging. Of course we thought that we could count on having powerful allies if war should break out, as we had had in World War I. That the Commonwealth would be left alone to face the power of the Third Reich and Fascist Italy from June 1940, to June 1941 (when Hitler attacked Soviet Russia) did not enter into our calculations.

It seems to be a persistent myth among more extreme pacifists that generals, and officers aspiring to be generals, think that their chances of glory and advancement depend on there being a war, and are therefore eager for the test of arms. I can only report that I have never met any such fire-eaters in the military profession. I suppose this may have been because most of the officers who were my friends and acquaintances had been through World War I. I think I have said enough about the circumstances of that war to show that no decent man would want to see it recur, even if advancement in his profession could come in no other way.

In the military profession our duty was to prepare the forces of our countries to fight if war should inevitably come. What did we think about the prospects of another great war? The omens had become more unmistakable year by year since the Nazi party had risen to power in Germany.

As much of the literature concerning the science of photogrammetry was in German, during the years I was heading the Geographical Section I had studied the language. In the course of this study I began to read German periodicals which my teacher, a young immigrant from Swabia, gave me. He was an enthusiastic Nazi—though a mild and pleasant person in other respects—and a leading light in the Ottawa branch of the organization. This was directed from Germany and sought to organize loyalty and support for the *Vaterland* among the *volksgenosse* abroad. There was a good deal in this literature which told of the remilitarizing and rearming of Germany. We also received more specific information on these subjects through military intelligence. It was no great secret. In particular, alarm was caused by the rapid growth of the German Air Force—the *Luftwaffe*—which quickly caught up with and then surpassed the British and French Air Forces in numbers and, by and large, effectiveness of aircraft.

In the course of my studies, I read Hitler's *Mein Kampf* in the original German, a feat of endurance of which I have always been rather proud. He certainly set down very clearly what he thought Germany should do in Europe, and yet many people were very surprised when he went ahead and did it.

Although it began to look more and more probable that Nazi Germany would resort to arms to win her *Lebensraum* and remove the remaining inequities of the Versailles peace treaty, it seems to me that the military people with whom I came into contact hoped in their hearts that there would be no war. Perhaps their minds were fixed on the great unreadiness of the British (and Dominion) armed forces to fight. For so many years their armament and everything else relating to preparedness for war had been neglected. The policy of governments of every political colour was based on the notion that there was no probability of another war, at least not for many years. The British political statement of this thought was the official prediction of "No war for the next ten years," renewed yearly, until suddenly it was realized that war could come very soon.

Those who held responsible positions in the military machine were concerned, above all, with doing what they could to remedy the deficiencies accumulated in the long years in which defence had been disregarded. And there must have been general apprehension that war would come before the defects were made good—as indeed happened. This apprehension was justified by the disasters to British arms from the spring of 1940 until the autumn of 1942.

I can't think of anyone among my military friends and acquaintances who would not have been glad if Mr. Neville Chamberlain had indeed brought back "Peace in our time" from Munich. What had the Commonwealth to gain from another war? Nothing, but very much to lose, as the event proved. The most warlike thought in the military mind, I believe, was that our countries should make strenuous efforts to *prepare* themselves for war; to have sufficient military force to meet aggression or blackmail. The danger we should find ourselves in if war came while we were still militarily unprepared was obvious to all.

# 1939 to 1943

At the end of a motor trip through France, my wife and I were in Paris when the news broke that Hitler had moved his troops into Danzig. It was no longer possible to doubt that there would be a European war, and that England would be caught up in it. With hundreds of other tourists in British-registered cars, we scurried along the *chaussée* to Boulogne, and the next day we crossed to England on the car ferry.

Once back in London, I reported to Canada House and found that all Canadian officers attending courses in Great Britain were being recalled to Canada to take up the appointments scheduled for them in the mobilization tables. I was down in the lists to be General Staff Officer, Grade 1 (G.S.O. 1) of the 1st Canadian Division; a very enviable post. In contrast to the confusion caused by the Hon. Sir Sam Hughes' scrapping of the mobilization plans in 1914, those prepared during the years previous to 1939 were carried out with few modifications. They provided for a corps of two divisions, with corps troops,[1] to be sent to Europe if required. Of course, the mobilization of the Canadian Army and its build-up overseas didn't take place just as the plan provided, but the Government did make its decisions on the basis of a properly worked-out and organizationally sound plan. Most of the mistakes of World War I were avoided, although it cannot be claimed that everything went smoothly.

Earlier in the year (1939) I had been talking to Mr. Lester Pearson (then and still "Mike" to his friends) who held the number two post at

Canada House, under Mr. Vincent Massey, the High Commissioner. I suggested that if war should break out, it would be useful to have a general staff officer at Canada House to deal with or offer advice on the many questions which would be bound to arise if—as we both believed—Canada would decide to send a military force overseas. At that time, the only military officer in Canada House was Colonel G.P. Loggie, of the Royal Canadian Ordnance Corps, whose duties were mainly connected with acquiring the arms and equipment which the Government had belatedly decided to obtain for the Canadian Army.[2]

Mr. Pearson agreed that it would be a good idea to have a general staff officer around, and when I reported on the outbreak of war he sent off a cable asking that I should be allowed to stay in England and serve in this way. This first request was refused, Defence Headquarters maintained that I should come back and take up my designated appointment. So I went down to Southampton with my wife and daughter, with orders to sail back to Canada in the *Empress of Australia.* At this time British troops were pouring through the port to deploy in France in accordance with the pre-war planning. I met several British Army friends on or near the docks, and it was a little uncomfortable telling them I was on my way back home. Canada had not at that time declared herself in the war; Mr. King had determined to submit the issue to Parliament. I felt rather as if I were running out on friends. As it happened, the *Empress of Australia* was requisitioned for troop movement and I went back to London. It was nearly a year before my duties called me back to Canada.

Mr. Pearson repeated his request for my services at Canada House, and this time it was granted. This was partly because it had been decided that a Canadian military headquarters was to be set up in London for liaison with the War Office, and to attend to all the administrative arrangements which would be required following a decision to send a Canadian force to England. Brigadier H.D.G. Crerar was to head this organization, with Colonel P.J. ("Price") Montague as Senior Administrative Staff Officer, and myself as General Staff Officer. Brigadier Crerar arrived in the latter part of October. I had worked under him before, when he was Director of Operations and Intelligence and I was in charge of the Geographical Section. Up to the outbreak of war he had been known chiefly as an exceptionally able staff officer, marked for the top staff posts—which he attained before he was appointed to command the 1st Canadian Corps in England and later, the First Canadian Army. He was a man who liked his subordinates to get things done quickly, with not too much chat about it. Although he did not exude warmth and magnetism, he was a man of determination, of will, and when he had made a judgement on what had to be done, he had the grip and drive to see that it was done. Some who served under him complained that he lacked sympathy. In the seven months that I was his immediate assistant, in the rather cramped offices of C.M.H.Q. set up in the Sun Life, I believe I gained his confidence. Towards me he was understanding, helpful and generous, through various ups and downs.

When Colonel Loggie and I were negotiating with the War Office over the reception and accommodation of the 1st Canadian Division, we were particularly concerned over where our units would be quartered. We were anxious that there should be no repetition of the miserable conditions in which the Canadian troops had passed the winter of 1914/15 in the mud and rain on Salisbury plain, under canvas for much of the time. We were surprised and pleased when the British officers we were dealing with informed us that the Canadians should have the best barrack accommodation available in England—in and around Aldershot. The quarters the Canadians were to take over had been vacated by the regular British Army units which had gone to the Continent. In spite of the generous efforts of the War Office, the troops found enough to complain about during the exceptionally cold winter that was to follow—the coldest since 1894. Grate fires in the barrack rooms, fed by a ration of coal that was economical to say the least, did not come up to Canadian standards of central heated comfort.

During the period of the "phony war" when the German Army was preparing for the lightning blows which it would deliver in the spring of 1940, the work at Canadian Military Headquarters was heavy and without respite. There was so much to be done to bring the armament, equipment and training of the Canadian troops in England up to the standard which would fit them for battle against the Germans. We all thought we would enter the kind of war which had ended in 1918—that there would be a static period of "trench warfare" when the French and British armies would be on the defensive, building up strength to undertake an eventual offensive. It was an anxious time, perhaps particularly for those who had served in World War I. We contrasted the power, organization and experience which the Canadian Corps of 1918 had developed through four years of war, against the largely inexperienced and untrained formation which had landed in England towards the end of 1939. How was this war going to be won? I don't think any of us doubted that we should eventually win it. But almost as bad as the deeply suppressed thought of possible defeat, there was the miserable prospect of a prolonged struggle—as in 1914-18—with long wearing battles and campaigns, blood, mud and more blood.

"For if the trumpet give an uncertain sound, who shall prepare himself to the battle?" Perhaps the lack of a clear and ringing sound from the trumpets of our political leaders was at the root of the unease of the staff officers and commanders at this time. Mr. Chamberlain was essentially a man of peace, and was forced into the war against his will. In his mournfully-toned broadcast announcing that Britain, honouring her pledge to Poland, was at war with Germany, he said nothing to stir the blood or set the adrenalin flowing. And Mr. Mackenzie King, all his life also a man of peace who had sought to isolate Canada from the quarrels of Europe, could hardly be expected to provide the oratory to fan Canadian resolve into a high flame.

As I recollect, the mood of all senior officers of the Canadian forces in England—from General McNaughton[3] and Brigadier Crerar down—during those months was grim, arising from a sense of the urgency of the manifold tasks required to fit the Canadian units and formations to face the Germans in the field. Critics might well say that we were preparing to fight World War I over again. It was only after the lessons of bitter and unprecedented defeats that the armies of the Commonwealth learned how this different kind of war could be fought and won.

On the 9th of April, 1940, Hitler launched without warning his sudden and very successful campaign against Norway and Denmark. This date, some of us reflected glumly, was the anniversary of Vimy Ridge. And from that date on, everything changed—the whole prospect and concept of the war's development was altered for Britain and the Canadian Army in Britain. The 1st Canadian Division prepared to engage, in part or as a whole, in the fighting in Norway, in the Dunkirk area and in France. There were beginnings of movement towards the front, and then countermandings.[4] Looking back, what happened seems to have been of little importance. What it signified for those of us in the Canadian forces in England was a sudden change from preparing for a long and hard war, fought on the lines of 1914-18, to the urgent, almost desperate, preparation to resist the invasion of the British Isles themselves. Invasion seemed fearfully close in those days, although subsequent historical research has since revealed the difficulties and the odds against success, as were estimated by the Great General Staff of the Third Reich.

In early June the 1st Canadian Division was getting ready to go to France as part of General Brooke's 2nd Corps (which was organized from the most battle-ready divisions in England) to join with the remaining French armies in making a desperate attempt to stem the German tide from flowing over all of France. The holding units for Canadian reinforcements, and various odds and ends which were not required to accompany the 1st Division, remained in Aldershot and vicinity. A headquarters had to be set up to command and administer them. Leaving my general staff post at C.M.H.Q., I was given the job of commanding this heterogenous group. By this time I had been promoted to the rank of Colonel.

We came under the British Aldershot Command, and were allotted tasks of defending parts of the area round Aldershot, in case of a lightning invasion of England. In view of the way the Germans had crossed the seas and occupied Norway, and had subdued successively Poland, Denmark, Holland, Belgium and France, this did not seem at all beyond the bounds of possibility. The troops were employed in constructing anti-tank obstacles and other fixed defences—which, I realized later, would have been quite useless for stopping a serious attack by tanks. We kept away the gnawing fear that nothing could prevent the victorious onrush of the *Reichswehr* by working as hard as we could at whatever tasks were laid on us, many of which, as I look back, were of little real value. I recall one item of training which seems funny now, but was solemnly performed at the time. During the few days the British Expeditionary Force had been engaged in Belgium, before the evacuation from Dunkirk, many senior officers had had their motor cars put out of action one way and another, and found themselves immobile, except when they were able to ride on the pillion of despatch-riders' motorcycles. So the order came forth that every senior officer, from lieutenant-colonel up, was to learn to ride a motorcycle. The senior officers of my little extemporized command, myself included, spent an hour or so each week solemnly riding round a barrack square on these rather tricky steeds. I hadn't ridden a motorcycle since World War I, but found that this art, like that of riding a bicycle, was something which once learned was not forgotten. This was a year or more before the production of the jeep, which had become the universal officer's charger by the time Canadian troops got into the war in earnest.

The other memory of that time, something which can never be forgotten, was hearing Churchill's radio speech, made when everything seemed blackest: "We will fight on the beaches, we will fight. . . . We shall never surrender." It inspired us. It filled us with courage and determination. One felt: He has told us what we should do, and that is what we *will* do. There was no doubt about the sound of *that* trumpet.

In July, Major-General Crerar was recalled from C.M.H.Q. to Canada to become Chief of the General Staff.[5] He brought me back from England to be one of his staff, with the cumbrous title of Assistant Deputy C.G.S. Two of my nearest colleagues were old friends: the Deputy Chief of the General Staff, Brigadier Kenneth Stuart, and the Director of Military Operations, Colonel Carl Murchie. Both of these officers subsequently held the appointment of C.G.S.

General Crerar employed me in various special assignments, mostly to do with the organization and build-up of the land forces which we should need if Canada was to take her due part in the struggle which had begun so inauspiciously. With the fall of France, the limits which had been imposed by the previous cautious policy of Mr. Mackenzie King's government were set aside, and the question now was: how much could we do within the limits of Canada's manpower and political situation to build up and train and equip those formations needed for the task?[6] The overall planning was done mainly during the period while I was working under General Crerar, late 1940 and early 1941.

I recall particularly one memorandum[7] in which I proposed that the titles of Canada's land forces, namely Permanent and Non-Permanent Active Militia, and Canadian Active Service Force, should be replaced by the title "Canadian Army," which would have active and reserve components. The active component would comprise those units and personnel mobilized for active service, either overseas or in Canada; and the reserve would be personnel belonging to the former "active militia" units not so mobilized, but undergoing training and ready to come forward into the active category. This memorandum went forward through the C.G.S. and the minister and was approved by the Cabinet.

Canada was fortunate during World War II in the three courageous and able politicians who formed a sort of triumvirate in charge of the country's defence. These were the Hon. J.L. Ralston, the Hon. C.G. Power and the Hon. Angus L. Macdonald. J.L. Ralston had been designated as Minister of Defence, after Mr. Rogers had met his death in an aeroplane accident. He was the senior minister and occupied the office prescribed in the statutes governing the organization of the Department of National Defence. I had become acquainted with him when I acted for a while as his Staff Captain when he succeeded to the command of the 12th Canadian Infantry Brigade in 1919. He had distinguished himself greatly in a long period of command of the 85th Battalion (Nova Scotia Highlanders) and was an extremely conscientious man, possessing also eminent moral courage. Charles G. ("Chubby") Power, who was the Associate Minister of Defence, second in the hierarchy to Ralston, and who acted for him in his absence, had the control of all the affairs of the Royal Canadian Air Force as his primary responsibility. He had also served in the first war, was severely wounded, and won the Military Cross. After being invalided he entered politics. I had become well acquainted with him during my year's service as District Engineering Officer in Quebec, where he was member for Quebec South and a political power in fact as well as in name. He guided me through some of Quebec's politico-military peculiarities, and our friendship continued during the period I was serving in Ottawa, and after. It is sad to think that Ralston and Power, who had done so much in the building up and deployment of Canada's armed forces, resigned from the Government because of the manpower crisis, when victory over the Third Reich was only months away. Their reasons were different. Mr. Ralston left over his recommendation to send overseas non-volunteering soldiers called up under the National Resources Mobilization Act, which was not accepted. Later, when this measure was put in force, Mr. Power resigned because he had promised his electors that he would not consent to the extension of conscription for service in Canada to conscription for service overseas. This meant that in the hour of victory they were far from the centre of the stage, and, to my mind, never have received the credit due them.

I often had to report to these ministers, either when brought along by General Crerar, or sometimes by myself in Crerar's absence when some urgent decision had to be obtained. My previous acquaintance with them was, of course, a great advantage. On a few occasions I also dealt with Mr. Angus Macdonald, the third minister, whose responsibility was chiefly the control of the Royal Canadian Navy; but I did not know him nearly so well. Calm and judicial in manner, he inspired confidence, including that of the sailors over whose destinies he presided.

One of the most interesting of the assignments I had at this time was to sit on the Tank Production Committee, as representative of the General Staff. Another member was Brigadier Worthington, the Commander of the Armoured Corps Training Centre, who is generally regarded as the "Father" of the Royal Canadian Armoured Corps. "Worthy" was a rather legendary figure in the Canadian Army, who up to that time I had known only by reputation, but with whom I was to be closely associated for the next few years.

Canada had already contracted to make a considerable number of the "Valentine" infantry tanks—a vehicle which, however well it compared with other tanks when it was designed, was obsolete by the time it was produced in Canada. When I joined the tank committee, it had been decided to manufacture another type: a "cruiser" tank,[8] which would be built on the chassis, track and engine of a tank being made for the American Army. But this American tank, while it mounted a 75 mm. gun, as well as several machine guns, did not have them in a turret. British tanks had turret-mounted guns which could fire in any direction, no matter which way the tank was heading, and this was tactically of great importance.

We decided that the Canadian tank should embody the British turret principle, and considered mounting a 75 mm. gun, but this proved impossible because of certain mechanical difficulties. If we could have placed the 75 mm. gun into the turret, we should have produced precisely the "Sherman" tank with which eventually American, British and Canadian armoured troops were equipped, and which contributed so much to winning the war on land.

American ordnance officers came up from Washington to have a look at the wooden mock-up we had constructed at the Montreal Locomotive Works, and seemed very impressed. It may be that our Canadian initiative helped to speed up the production of the war-winning Sherman. The Canadian tank was later christened "the Ram" (a ram's head was Worthington's crest) and played a useful role in training the Canadian Armoured Corps, which exchanged it for the Sherman on entering the theatres of war. The "Rams" eventually were modified by the direction of General Simonds, to become armoured personnel carriers, and played an important part in several successful battles in Northwest Europe.

In the spring of 1941 I returned to England, and for some months held the appointment of Brigadier General Staff of the Canadian Corps, under General McNaughton. The Canadian Corps had just been formed, as the 2nd Canadian Division had attained a satisfactory standard of training. Before that, the 1st Canadian Division and Canadian Corps troops had combined with British divisions to form the 7th Corps, whose task was the defence against invasion of a sector of the southern coast of England. The new Canadian Corps was busily engaged in training, and carried out several exercises—which showed up certain deficiencies of organization and staff work in the corps headquarters which I sought to correct. These troubles were due, in large part, to the rapid changes in appointments which were then occurring, as a result of the expansion of the Canadian forces. An officer would hardly have had time to learn his job when he would be posted elsewhere, usually with promotion. This sort of difficulty continued, in fact, up to the time of the 1st Canadian Corps' entry into active service in January 1944.

In order to assess the standard of training and the quality of commanding officers, General McNaughton ordered a series of tactical exercises to be carried out on the battalion level. These revealed a number of weaknesses—and some strengths. I remember listening to an excellent appreciation and plan given out by B.M. ("Bert") Hoffmeister, then a Major commanding a company of the Seaforth

Highlanders of Vancouver (and later to rise to the rank of Major-General, commanding the 5th Canadian Armoured Division).

The weaknesses were often seen in the persons of the commanding officers. Many of them were veterans of World War I, who had loyally served in their militia regiments through the long, dreary days of neglect of the armed forces in Canada. But in 1941, faced with the task of training their unit for a kind of war very different from that which they had known, and with the prospect of commanding in the field, many of them no longer had the necessary physical and mental energy and resilience. A few, sadly enough, tried to buoy up their flagging energies with whisky, which only hastened the end of their command.

About this time the British Army instituted age limits for officers of the several ranks serving with front line units. Lieutenant-Colonels bowed out at the age of fifty, Brigadiers and Major-Generals when they were a few years older. This rule, soon after brought into force in the Canadian Army, enabled General McNaughton to weed out some ineffective commanders without injuring their feelings. The result was that younger and younger officers without World War I experience began to hold commands and senior staff appointments. Many of them seemed to hold the unexpressed idea that to have seen service in World War I necessarily classified any officer as a has-been. By the time the Canadian Army was fully deployed in action in Italy and France, I can think of no other commanders than General Crerar, Brigadiers Penhale, Graham and myself who had entered action with previous war experience.

I remember being present when Field-Marshal Smuts called on the Canadian Corps, and ate lunch with General McNaughton and the senior staff officers. At one point Smuts looked round the table and remarked to General McNaughton, "I don't know how you keep your young men contented here, when they are doubtless wishing to be at the front, fighting along with other Commonwealth forces." General McNaughton replied that the Canadians had been given an important mission in the defence of Great Britain. Besides, in the building up of the corps organization, there had been a good deal of promotion for bright young officers. I think General McNaughton's answer to Smuts' question was the truth, but it was a little embarrassing. It seemed to bear the interpretation that Canadian officers were more interested in quick promotion than in coming to grips with the enemy in the field.

During the period when I was Brigadier General Staff of the Corps, I happened to meet a friend who had been at the Imperial Defence College with me in 1939—Lieutenant-Colonel K.G. MacLean. In the course of conversation he asked if the Canadian authorities had ever considered the possibility of one of our divisions going out to the Western Desert. MacLean was at that time a staff officer in the War Cabinet Secretariat, concerned with long-range planning. This idea struck me as being very good. The 1st Canadian Division had been in England for nearly a year and a half, and it was beginning to seem less and less likely that there would be an invasion of Britain, and a direct British invasion of the Continent appeared even less likely in the near future.[9] Yet Canada had plans for building a large army, that is, large by our standards. Very few of the commanders and senior staff officers of this army would have had war experience, and none of them would have had experience in the current war. If we could send a division to the Western Desert, we should be able to gain that experience, and have war-proved senior officers to lead the expanded forces.

I reported this conversation to General McNaughton, who was very interested, and directed me to follow up the suggestion in an informal way and to find out how serious the thinking actually was about employing Canadians in the North African Theatre. We were both aware of the drawback to the idea: it would involve splitting up the Canadian forces, with some in North Africa, while others remained in England. The principle established in World War I that all Canadian forces should be kept together under Canadian command was still one that no one wished to abandon. Nevertheless, the possible gain in the long run of such a suggested detachment might have warranted a temporary departure from this axiom. There was also the question of morale, both among the troops in England and the Canadian population. In World War I the Canadians had been engaged in France by February 1915—seven months after the outbreak of war. No doubt many of our soldiers and civilians were wondering why our army wasn't fighting after eighteen months.

A while later I was able to speak with the Director of Military Operations in the War Office, Major-General Kennedy. At this time there were plans for sending more troops to reinforce the British army fighting in the Western Desert, which had won notable successes against the Italians and had provided the only bright spot in the generally dispiriting war situation. However, General Kennedy was not too encouraging about sending a Canadian division. "There are a good many formations ahead of you in the queue," he said. That is to say, there were many British divisions in England whose commanders (and presumably troops also) were anxious to get to that theatre of war where they could avenge the defeat in Western Europe which had culminated in Dunkirk. In any case, nothing came of this rather informal and confidential negotiation, and I don't know whether it was followed up further from the Canadian side, as shortly afterwards I was transferred back to Canada.

One of the most important elements in the question of fitness for command was physical fitness. The younger man, other things being equal, would naturally be in better physical shape to support exertion and fatigue and long hours without sleep than would the man in his forties and early fifties. "Fitness" was a fetish with most professional British soldiers, although this was not so much so for the average Canadian professional or amateur soldier. The Canadian officer had probably played games and taken part in athletics in his younger days, but the conditions of service in Canada did not generally make it easy to continue active exercising in his middle years. Golf and perhaps tennis were usually the limit of physical activity. "Fitness" or "fit" were frequent words in the mouth of the British officer, and of course it meant fit for war. As is well known, General Montgomery was one of the most ardent fitness advocates. He was commanding 12 Corps in early 1941. Its area was in Kent, to the east of the Canadian Corps area. The weekly cross-country runs for his headquarters were talked about with a mixture of awe and derision in other formations. Everybody had to turn out, and General Montgomery came along in the rear to note whether any straggled or fell out. The performance was not a competition; the runners could jog along, and even walk part way, provided they kept up a fairly consistent pace, and finished. If they did not finish, their employment with the 12th Corps would.

So ran the legend. On one occasion I had personal evidence of General Montgomery's concern for fitness in all his subordinates. Brigadier M.C. Dempsey ("Bimbo" to his British fellow-officers) had been Brigadier General Staff of the composite 7th Corps, of which the Canadians had formed part, and on its conversion to the Canadian Corps I was appointed to succeed him. Dempsey had served in General Montgomery's 3rd Division in the short campaign preceding Dunkirk, and one day Dempsey took me to see the General. The conversation dealt largely with his efforts to ensure fitness in his command. He had found one battalion commander whose medical history showed that he was suffering from diabetes. Naturally astonished at this, Montgomery had him removed at once to other duties. "Diabetes! Good Heavens!" ran as a sort of refrain through part of the lunch. It sounded rather heartless, but of course Montgomery was right. It was his job to ensure that all his subordinates were fit for their jobs—which included physical fitness.

This meeting took place before the General had achieved celebrity as the victor of El Alamein, a year and a half later. But he was a very well-known personality in the British Army. This was perhaps due to what some of the stuffier officers regarded as his eccentricities, more than for the strength of character which made him a great commander.

At that lunch, his liveliness and good cheer impressed me. He was particularly interested to know what Dempsey would be doing after he left the Canadian Corps, and very clearly wanted to get him under his command again. In this he succeeded, and Dempsey ended up as the Commander of the Second Army in the 1944-5 victory campaign in the West. The episode illustrated General Montgomery's principle in selecting subordinates—"Monty's Boys," as they sometimes referred to themselves. That is, he chose officers whom he knew well and in whose abilities he had confidence. There was a certain amount of grumbling among the discarded or ignored at what they called Montgomery's favouritism. But it has been said that "Favouritism is the secret of efficiency."

In the late summer of 1941 I was transferred back to Canada, and took up the appointment of Officer Administering, Canadian Armoured Corps, at Camp Borden. Borden had been allocated as the centre for specialist training of the Armoured Corps, and also the Army Service Corps. (After entering the service the recruit spent his first two months at a Basic Training Centre. Here he was taught those elements of the soldier's trade which were common to all the arms, such as barrack-square drill and personal protection against gas.) The advanced or specialized training units gave the soldier the further individual training he required in order to be able to take his part as an effective member of a sub-unit in his regiment or corps. In the case of the armoured corps who would fight in tanks or armoured cars, this meant training the following specialists: drivers, gunners, radio operators, and of course the commanders of the tank, officers and sergeants. Once a programme had been established individual training was more or less a mechanical, mass-production process. The tankman had to learn to drive the tank, serve a gun, or operate radio telephone apparatus.

The main difficulty in individual training was to get up-to-date tanks, guns and radios. Obviously the training would be more effective if it were with the equipment with which the men would eventually go into battle. But in 1941 there was a devastating shortage of everything; the tanks and all that would go in them for the war in 1943 were just being manufactured, or had only been designed. And what had been produced had to be sent to the armoured units fighting in North Africa, or to those in the front line of defence in England. So we had to train on whatever was available, and sometimes this material would be very ancient indeed. A prime example was the small Renault tanks; the kind the French Army had put into action in 1918 when the counteroffensive began against the Château-Thierry salient. Brigadier Worthington, after great exertion, managed to have these procured from the United States Army, which had had them in dead storage for years. These "tankettes" could hardly have been more obsolete—but at least they were armoured fighting vehicles. Before the arrival of the Renaults there had been nothing more than the Vickers armoured machine-gun carriers, precursors of the Bren-gun carrier familiar to all Canadian soldiers of World War II.

As I have said, the problem of individual training in the tank corps essentially consisted in training a man to operate a machine. But far more difficult was the problem of tactical and unit training. Astonishing as it may seem to readers, at this time there was no clear and established tactical doctrine for the employment of the armoured troops in the British Army. The pre-war doctrines had been proved shatteringly inadequate by the outcome of the short campaign before Dunkirk. The conceptions which had produced the slow, relatively heavily-armoured Infantry tank and the faster but more lightly-armoured and lightly armed Light tank (which was supposed to exercise the cavalry role) had been shown to be fallacious. All this had resulted from the inability of the British high military organs, heirs of the invention of the tank and its effective exploitation in World War I, to make up their collective mind how the tank arm should be used, and what kind of a tank should be designed to fit that use. This failure had many causes but probably underlying all was the reluctance of the senior officers who had controlled the British Army from 1920-39, brought up in the traditions of one of the older fighting arms—infantry or cavalry—to admit that the infantry was no longer the "Queen of Battles" and would get nowhere without an armoured consort, and that the substitution of the tank or armoured car for the horse in cavalry units required a radical revision of the cavalry's traditional roles.

It was indeed a hard problem that faced Canadian Army commanders: how to train the large army that had been built up (eight divisions, of which five fought overseas) so as to be able to meet on even terms the war-hardened and dismayingly successful *Wehrmacht*. I know this was my main preoccupation from 1941 on, as it probably was that of other Canadian commanders. Practically all the men in the ranks and junior officers had been civilians in 1939. While Canadian senior commanders and staff officers had received training which enabled them to take up appointments in the greatly expanded land forces, there was no trial by battle to winnow the fit from the unfit, as there had been in World War I when the Canadian Expeditionary Force was built up from one division to a corps. On the other hand, the prolonged waiting period while the Canadian divisions "stood on guard" in England against an invasion that never came, offered the opportunity to train the troops, individually and in units and formations, for their tasks when they should finally enter the fighting.

Early in 1942 I was appointed to command the 4th Canadian Armoured Brigade which was composed of the Grenadier Guards, the Governor-General's Foot-Guards and the Sherbrooke Regiment.

The 4th Canadian Division, which was concentrated in Debert Camp near Truro in Nova Scotia, had just been converted from infantry to armour. This was in accordance with decisions taken in 1941 that a large proportion of the Canadian Army should consist of armoured formations. It had been impressed on everyone that the German armoured formations had played a decisive part in their early successes in Western Europe, and against the Russians in 1941. Eventually the Canadian Army overseas comprised two armoured divisions and two extra armoured brigades to three infantry divisions.[10]

Major-General F.F. Worthington who had been in command of the 1st Army Tank Brigade returned from England and took over the 4th Canadian Division in February of 1942. He was noted throughout the Canadian Army as a great trainer, and his enthusiasm and driving power were in large part responsible for the progress the 4th Canadian Armoured Division made. Unfortunately for him (and perhaps for the division too) the age limitation caught up with him in 1944, and he did not have the privilege of commanding in the field the formation he had done so much to train and form.

Worthy was concerned that most of the officers and men of the formation he had taken over did not realize what lay ahead of them when they should meet the Germans on the battlefield. Of course there was a sprinkling of veterans of World War I among the officers, but not all of these had retained the vigour and drive that were needed to keep the training routine going at the desired pitch. It was hardly surprising that a good many of the officers and men in the 4th Canadian division should become somewhat "browned off" after being mobilized for over eighteen months, and still being in Canada with no certain prospect of going overseas.

Worthy constantly thought about inculcating a fighting spirit in the troops, and preparing them to encounter the sights and smells of the battlefield. I recall a conversation at lunch in the mess of the Sherbrooke Regiment, where he and I were being entertained after inspecting their training programme. Worthy had been expatiating on his favourite theme of the necessity of hardening the troops for battle, when he suddenly asked the acting C.O. of the Sherbrookes, "Do you know whether there are any slaughterhouses near here?" The startled Major allowed that with reconnaissance one could probably be located. Worthy then suggested that the men should be taken for a tour of this establishment—to get them accustomed to the sight of blood and guts; this would do them a lot of good. The Sherbrooke Major, his face becoming quite pale, agreed that this sort of excursion would be very nice indeed. (I don't believe that this training exercise was ever carried out.)

In October 1942, the 4th Canadian Armoured Brigade moved to England and continued its training there, together with the rest of the 4th Canadian Division. *Six Years of War* remarks that the division arrived in a somewhat more advanced state of training than earlier armoured formations, mainly because a respectable number of tanks from Canadian production were now available for training in Canada.

This was true; a number of Ram tanks, without armament, had arrived in Debert. Besides giving the tankmen the chance to drive and take their places inside the turret of an actual tank, this was a great stimulus to training generally. The troops felt that they were really going to be in an armoured formation with real tanks—which some had been inclined to doubt before. Nevertheless, after arrival in England there was still a great deal of training to do before the brigade would be "battle-worthy," to use an expression popular at the time. In October, a divisional training instruction laid it down that by February 1943 collective training was to reach the stage where squadrons (some eighteen tanks) could operate as a unit, and that headquarters of formations (brigade and divisional headquarters) were to attain enough efficiency to enable them to handle their units in battle by that date. So we went to work on those lines, and, I think, advanced fairly well. But there was still the uncertainty about what the role of an armoured division would be in the operations that could be expected to follow the establishment of a beachhead for the invasion which was to liberate Western Europe.

In April 1943 it was decided to send the 1st Canadian Division and the 1st Canadian Armoured Brigade to take part in the invasion of Sicily. The final battles in North Africa were being fought, as the 1st British Army and the American Army closed on Tunis from the west, and the 8th British Army from the east. It was clear that the Germans and Italians could not hold out much longer, and active planning had for some time been under way for the next step; the landing on Sicily. The North African campaign was brought to an end by the brilliant victory of the Tunis battles, directed by General Alexander, in which some 250,000 Germans and Italians were taken prisoner. The knowledge that at last Canadian formations were to take part in the fighting raised morale greatly, both in those units which were to go to the Mediterranean and those which were left in England. I think it is fair to say that the long period of "standing on guard" had in many officers blunted the keenness essential to make training for war effective. And the Dieppe raid, once the real extent of the casualties and failure to achieve planned objectives had become known, did not greatly add to confidence. But it should also be said that the first feelings general among the troops, in spite of the casualties and limited achievement, were of relief and pride that the Canadians had fought at last. It was felt an honour to have been selected for this operation which was supposed to be preparatory to the invasion of the Continent.

Major-General Harry Salmon had been in command of the 1st Canadian Division since September 1942, and was to lead it in the forthcoming operations, but to the sorrow of his many friends he was killed in a flying accident while *en route* to North Africa. Guy Simonds had recently been promoted to command the 2nd Canadian Division, but Salmon's death occurred before he had taken over. It was then decided that he should take command of the 1st Canadian Division, which he led with such striking success in its entry into battle in Sicily, and through the subsequent operations in Southern and Eastern Italy.

On the 6th of May, 1943, I was appointed to command the 2nd Canadian Division. This division had supplied the bulk of the troops in the Dieppe operation. The two infantry brigades which had fought at Dieppe, the 4th and 6th, had lost so many men that they had to return to individual and platoon training.[11] This was late in 1942. However, by the time I took over command much leeway had been made up, and these formations were ready to take their part in the programme of more advanced training which occupied most of the summer and autumn of 1943.

I have already mentioned the large raids which had been carried out by formations of the Canadian Corps in the spring and summer of 1917, in the interval between the Vimy operations and those which resulted in the capture of Hill 70. When the real facts of what had happened at Dieppe began to be known, there was a certain amount of discussion among officers who were veterans of World War I about the soundness of the tactics which had been adopted.

There were some who contrasted the way in which those raids of the summer of 1917 had been mounted with the conditions under which the 2nd Canadian Division had attacked. Consider some of the differences.

1917—the attack was over a relatively flat plain, which afforded little advantage to the enemy; in 1942, the attack was over beaches commanded by enemy-held cliffs or high ground.

1917—there was precise information about enemy defences, because of preceding close contact; in 1942, knowledge of defences was limited to what could be learned from air photography.

1917—there was strong artillery support by barrages fired by field artillery established in position and registered; in 1942, fire support was given only by air strikes and naval gunfire.

1917—raiding battalions had previously fought in several major battles; in 1942, troops went into action for the first time.

1917—attacks were launched from behind firmly held positions on land, behind which troops could form up in the exact way required by the operational plan; in 1942, attacking troops came on shore from landing craft, under fire from some distance before touching down.

The troops attacking the Dieppe positions were effecting a seaborne landing. No nation has had greater experience in this type of operation than Great Britain, so its hazards should have been fully understood. Those who planned the operation did not need to go far back into history to inform themselves about the risks and possible course of events. The Gallipoli seaborne operations of 1915 are fully described in official histories and in many personal accounts. The landings and withdrawals in Gallipoli, in face of an enemy in position, were similar enough to what was planned for Dieppe that the planners should have known the heavy price that would have to be paid for a withdrawal in daylight of such a considerable force.

I recall also that soon after I had arrived with the 4th Canadian Armoured Brigade in England, in October 1942, I had a brief talk on the subject with Worthington. He was severely critical of the selection of the landing place for the tanks, which required them to advance through the town of Dieppe if they were to reach their objective. It had become one of the standard rules of tank tactics *not* to commit tanks to fighting in towns and villages, where they would have no room for manoeuvre, and would be vulnerable to ambush by stout-hearted infantry (or guerillas) who could issue suddenly from cover and attack them with Molotov cocktails or short-range bazooka-type weapons. However, Worthington concluded the talk by warning me that I should avoid criticism or even discussion of the operation, because this would not be at all popular with the higher-ups.

With all the adverse conditions mentioned, it is surprising that the planning staffs in the Canadian formations and in Combined Operations H.Q., and those commanders who authorized the Dieppe operation in its final form could have hoped that it would succeed. Some of them must have known of the conditions which World War I had shown were required if a large-scale raid was to attain its object.

Field-Marshal Montgomery comments on the Dieppe raid in his memoirs. He had been in charge of the army side of the planning and preparation at an early stage, when the attack was to take place in the first week of July. It had to be cancelled, owing to bad weather. He thought it was finished for good. However, he records that Combined Operations Headquarters decided to revive the scheme and got it approved by the British Chiefs of Staff. He "was very upset" by this news, and wrote to the Commander-in-Chief Home Forces, recommending that the raid on Dieppe should be considered cancelled "for all time." But his advice was disregarded, and soon he was on his way to the Western Desert with no further responsibility in the matter.

In summing up the affair, he writes:

> Without doubt the lessons learnt there were an important contribution to the eventual landing in Normandy on the 6th June 1944. But the price was heavy in killed and prisoners. I believe that we could have got the information and experience

we needed without losing so many magnificent Canadian soldiers.[12]

According to the official Canadian history, 907 were killed and died of wounds of a total of 3,369 casualties suffered by less than 5,000 men engaged.

The Dieppe tragedy has been fully discussed in several books from many angles. One obvious reason for taking the risks of tactical failure, which must have been apparent, was the need to do something in response to Russian pressure (supported by left-wing elements in England) for a "Second Front."

The final judgement on the Dieppe operation has yet to be delivered, in my opinion. More explicit statements of the decisions of the responsible authorities, and the information which they had on which to base those decisions will have to be published before final judgement can be made—if it ever will be.

It had been decided, in the planning for the Normandy invasion, that the 3rd Canadian Division should be one of the assault divisions. The role of the 2nd Canadian Division would be in the follow-up of the initial assault and the break-out battle which would then take place. This decision set the pattern for the training of the division during the period I was in command. Most of the remainder of the year was spent in Sussex, exercising mainly in the break-out battle from a beachhead. The 3rd Canadian Division carried out similar exercises related to its assault role. In these exercises, infantry-tank co-operation was practised, and in some of them the infantry advanced, following concentrations of fire with live shells by the field artillery. The whole training programme of the Canadian forces still in England had been made more realistic and intensified. Besides these large-scale exercises, there were special training establishments in which street fighting and other specialties were taught. Many exercises were carried out at night, to accustom the troops to operating in darkness.

While I commanded the 2nd Canadian Division one of my main concerns was the training of the troops in the use of their weapons; especially training the infantry in firing the rifle, sub-machine guns and machine guns. I aimed to ensure that no men should go into battle without knowing how to use their weapons, as mere cannon-fodder. This emphasis on weapon-training came from the hard lesson I had had in the Battle of Vimy. When later I was commanding the Canadians in Italy, I tried to see that no reinforcements should join the fighting units until they had been checked on their ability to fire their weapons—and hit a target. It doubtless will surprise the lay reader that any soldier armed with a rifle and expected to use it in combat could reach the battlefield without being trained to be fully proficient in its use. The fact is, this did happen. "Small-Arms Training" was mostly of the theoretical and indoor kind, which should have been only preliminary to extensive practice on a range, shooting at realistic targets. But unfortunately it was not easy to arrange for these firing exercises; it was hard to find ground for ranges, and small-arms ammunition for training, even in 1943, was not plentiful. But the staff, given direction and purpose, often overcame these difficulties. I obtained a rifle for my personal use, and occasionally when visiting units doing range practice, I fired a series myself. Whether this inspired officers and men to take their weapon training more seriously, I don't know. They were interested, as evidenced by their very audible comments if I did not at least get an inner.

All infantry were supposed to be "battle inoculated"; they carried out a training exercise, usually on the platoon level, in which they were subjected to the sounds (if not the sights) of the battlefield. Machine guns fired over their heads from the "enemy" direction, and not so far over their heads either. Artillery fire was simulated by explosive charges; smoke would be loosed. All this helped a great deal, but as Colonel Stacey comments: "There is no doubt that training can do just so much, and no more. There is no umpire, and no instructor like the bullet." He goes on to say that the Canadians did well in Normandy, and would have done even better had they not been fighting their first battle, and learning as they fought.[13] All this is very true.

Somewhat prejudicial to the efficiency of the Canadian Army were the frequent changes of command necessitated by its expansion from the two divisions contemplated in the mobilization plans of 1939 to a total of an Army headquarters, two corps headquarters, three infantry and two armoured divisions, two independent armoured brigades, and a mass of corps and army troops. There were in addition changes of commanders necessitated by age or ill-health. On the average there were changes of command every year in corps and divisions.[14] If it was not possible for the Canadian formations to enter the decisive phase of the invasion of Normandy with experience of war, it would have been an advantage if they had entered it with generals and brigadiers who had held their command long enough to train them in the operations they would have to perform, and to become acquainted with the abilities of their subordinates. I expected to command the 2nd Canadian Division in the "Overlord" invasion, and hoped to be able to prepare and lead it so that it would fufil its appointed tasks with credit and honour. It certainly did this under General Charles Foulkes, who succeeded me in command.

# To Italy

Shortly before Christmas 1943, I was told that I was to go to Italy as General Officer Commanding 5th Canadian Armoured Division. Guy Simonds had assumed command when the division had assembled in the theatre in November, but he was to come back to England to take over command of the 2nd Canadian Corps. The idea behind switching him from the command of the 1st Canadian Division, in which he had been outstandingly successful, was to give him experience in handling an armoured division, prior to taking over a corps command. As the succeeding pages will show, circumstances were to prevent his getting any fighting experience with the division.

The invasion of Sicily, and then the firm lodgment of the allied armies on the mainland was soon followed by the overthrow of Mussolini, and the conversion of Italy from enemy to "co-belligerent." The aspect of the war had completely changed. The Germans had suffered a heavy defeat in North Africa, and the Russians were advancing relentlessly on the eastern front. Many people thought the war in Europe might be ended during the summer of 1944, and that the invasion across the English Channel would be nothing more than a takeover by occupation forces. Indeed, plans were being made for such an operation in the case of there being little or no opposition. If the plot against Hitler had succeeded, if the briefcase containing the explosive had been a little closer to him, the war in the West might indeed have ended in that way. In view of this possibility, the Canadian authorities thought that the Canadian

Army's role in the war would look pretty meagre, in spite of all the effort to build it up as a fighting formation, if the only Canadian troops to have engaged in active operations were to have been the 1st Division and the Armoured brigade.

Accordingly, it was decided in the autumn of 1943, after difficult negotiations, that the Canadian forces in Italy should be increased to a corps. This would be done by sending the 1st Canadian Corps Headquarters, the 5th Canadian Armoured Division, and a number of corps and army troop units to join the 1st Canadian Division, the 1st Canadian Armoured Brigade and other Canadian units already in Italy, the whole to be under the command of Lieutenant-General Crerar.

The plan to send the 1st Canadian Corps to the Mediterranean Theatre had to contend against a good deal of opposition, both in the War Office and in the headquarters of the various higher commands in the Mediterranean.[1] Eventually the pressure by the Canadian Government persuaded Prime Minister Churchill to agree to the arrangement, and the War Office, presumably with some reluctance, put the necessary movements in hand. That the higher British commands and staffs should have been against the idea was not due in any sense to prejudice against Canadians, or mere bloody-mindedness (to use a British expression). The switching of Canadian formations from England, where their planned task would have been with the forces allotted to the Overlord invasion, required altering plans and providing scarce sea transport—an unwanted problem for the War Office and the Royal Navy. But when a more detailed study of what really would be involved was made, it was concluded that the effect on the build-up for Overlord would be negligible.

General Eisenhower, Commander-in-Chief of Allied forces in the Mediterranean when these exchanges were taking place, said in a message:

> While the arrival of these troops at this time is likely to cause us considerable embarrassment . . . General Alexander advises me, and I agree, that appreciating the political considerations which may be involved, we accept the Canadian Corps Headquarters, Armoured Division, and non-divisional troops. In view of our total build-up, we shall eventually be glad to have this HQ.[2]

General Alexander's previous comments in a cable to the Chief of the Imperial General Staff showed that his consent was reluctant. He had said:

> We already have as much armour in the Mediterranean as we can usefully employ in Italy. I should have preferred another Canadian Infantry Division. . . . I do not want another Corps Headquarters at this stage. I shall be grateful if I can be consulted in future before matters of such importance are agreed upon.[3]

It is quite understandable why General Alexander did not want another corps headquarters. There would be more corps H.Q. already there than would be required to control the British and Dominion divisions which would be left in the Mediterranean after the drafts for Overlord had been levied on his forces. Furthermore, the Canadian Corps headquarters would be quite inexperienced in battle. It must be allowed that our operations in the Liri Valley in May-June showed our inexperience. Adding the Canadian Corps H.Q. to the formations in Italy would mean that one or more of the British Corps H.Q. would become redundant, although they had had battle experience. Officers on the various staffs would not unnaturally contrast their hard-won "know how" with the greenness of Canadian officers who might hold posts of equal or higher rank.

Reflection on this leads one to think that the path of the Canadian Corps in Italy (and perhaps the Canadian forces in Western Europe) might have been smoother if it had been possible to send a Canadian formation to fight in the Western Desert, as had tentatively been suggested at an earlier stage.

When I heard that I was to command the 5th Canadian Armoured Division, I recalled various bits of information which indicated that there had been certain inadequacies in its training—as there were in the training of all Canadian formations. This was due probably more to the lack of well-defined doctrine on the tactical role of the armoured division in Europe, to which I have referred previously, than to the fault of its commanders, much less the fault of the units and the men in them.

> . . . when it left to join the 1st Division in the Mediterranean, the 5th had made much progress, but still had something to learn about armour in battle.[4]

This was a considerable understatement, as I think most of the officers and men in the 5th Canadian Division who arrived at the fighting front in the winter of 1943-4 would agree.

It seemed clear, owing to this state of affairs, when I took over command my first problem would concern what additional training should be given to the division to improve its fitness for battle. Up to that time (early January) it had not seen action. In order to gain some authoritative guidance, I sought an interview with General Montgomery who had just returned from commanding the Eighth Army in Italy, to take over as commander of the Normandy invasion in its first phase. He kindly agreed to see me. After preliminary greetings, I asked him what advice he could give me as to preparing the armoured division for its role in Italy. He then made the very negative and rather dismaying pronouncement: "There is no role for an armoured division in Italy!"

Naturally I was a little taken aback by this. I said, however, that the 5th Division was there and I was appointed to command it, and it would be necessary for me to have some guidelines for the last stages of training before it entered battle. (I would no less need guidelines for myself, although I did not think this needed mentioning.) After reflecting a moment, General Montgomery advised me to find out what training Simonds was giving them. "Simonds is first class," he observed.[5]

When I arrived in Italy and met Simonds, I found that he had not been able to do much towards organizing the final preparation for battle of the 5th Armoured Division. He had taken over command of the division on November 1, 1943 before the bulk of the troops had arrived in the theatre. November and December had been occupied in struggling to get the division fitted out with transport, guns, tanks and other fighting and logistic equipment. When the move of the division to Italy had been decided, it had been planned that it would take over all this equipment from the famous 7th Armoured Division — the "Desert Rats"; thus economizing on sea transport. Unfortunately the equipment, including the tanks, was in very poor state, due to the long desert campaign and rough roads from Alamein to Tripoli. I recall before I left England telling an Eighth Army tank brigadier who had returned with General Montgomery about this plan for swapping equipment. He grinned in a sympathetic way and suggested that we would find the

7th Division transport "pretty ropy." This was a typically British understatement. In the end, after great difficulties, the 5th Division was equipped with serviceable and mostly new vehicles. It was three months after the division had landed in Italy that I assumed command, and when I talked to unit commanders their greatest problem was still the state of the "used" transport they had taken over.

In the latter part of November, the division moved from its assembly area in Naples to the area around Altamura, a town about twenty-five miles southwest of Bari, on the Adriatic coast in Southern Italy. No doubt General Simonds' time and energy had been fully occupied in the administrative difficulties just mentioned. Added to this must have been the preoccupations caused by his impending transfer back to England, to take over the 2nd Canadian Corps. In any case, I did not gather from my conversations with him that he had thought out what the role for the division was likely to be in the fighting that lay ahead, nor made plans for any very specific programme of training (or retraining) the division for it. The only piece of advice I recall his giving me was that during the Sicily operations he had tried going forward in an armoured command vehicle he had had fitted up, when moves at night did not seem to be going according to his plan – and had found that he merely became enmeshed in traffic jams himself and was unable to do anything to straighten them out.

Just before I reported to General Crerar in Italy, the 11th Canadian Infantry Brigade of the 5th Canadian Armoured Division had fought its first action. While this took place before I had responsibility for the division or its operations, some comments on this initiation of the brigade into battle may not be out of place.[6]

Early in December General Simonds had informed General Crerar that the 11th Infantry Brigade was going ahead well, and that he would like to send it forward about the end of the month, to get experience in contact with the enemy. On January 4, orders were issued for the brigade to relieve the 3rd Infantry Brigade of the 1st Canadian Division on the eastern sector of the division's front. It appears that originally the intention was that it should only have a defensive tour in the line, during which it would learn what enemy shell and mortar fire was like. However, within a few days the brigade found that instead of gradually accustoming itself to facing the enemy in a defensive role, it was to carry out an attack. The objectives were the enemy positions on the opposite ridge, and after seizing these the advance was to continue to the Arielli River. The attack was to be on a front of a little over 1,000 yards, with a depth of advance of about 3,000 yards.

This attack was mounted because the higher command considered it was necessary to maintain offensive activity on the Eighth Army front on the Adriatic, in order to prevent the enemy from transferring troops to the western side of Italy. The 10th Corps (British) under the Fifth (U.S.) Army had effected a crossing of the Garigliano River on January 17; an attack on Cassino was to be mounted about January 20, to be followed by the landing at Anzio on the 22nd of January. It was hoped that these consecutive operations would dislodge the enemy from the "Gustav" position,[7] and force him to retreat beyond Rome.

General Sir Oliver Leese, who had succeeded General Montgomery in command of the Eighth Army, issued an instruction which called on the 5th (British) Corps, using the 1st Canadian Division reinforced by the 11th Brigade, to "make every effort to gain the high ground east of the Arielli River." It went on to direct that "heavy casualties are *not* to be incurred, and if the Corps Commander decided that this cannot be done without incurring heavy casualties the matter is to be re-referred to the Army Commander." The date for this operation was set by the 5th Corps for about the 16th of January.

It is generally recognized that it is much to be desired that when a new formation is being "broken in" to actual fighting, and especially for its first offensive operation, it should be given a task – such as a large raid against weak enemy forces – in which its chances of success are good. If the first offensive action goes well, it will give officers and men confidence in undertaking more difficult operations later. If, on the contrary, it meets with a more or less severe check and does not accomplish the task set for it, the effect on morale is the opposite, and it often takes some time for the formation to get over this and reach its full effectiveness. However, the "blooding" of new formations with an easy and successful offensive operation was an ideal which was seldom attained.

*The Canadians in Italy* lists a number of factors which contributed to the failure of the 11th Brigade's first offensive operation. The successive attacks by single battalions allowed the enemy to concentrate fire on the narrow front of each attack. Also, two green Canadian battalions were attacking two battalions of experienced German troops, belonging to the 1st Parachute Division, which had the highest fighting reputation of any enemy formation in Italy. To these disadvantages I would add that the attack called for the Riccio stream to be forded, and after that an advance up a steep hillside, against positions which the enemy had held for some time and where his defences could have been expected to be well organized. An attack on a one-brigade front, with two battalions up, could hardly have impressed the German command as a serious threat of a continued offensive. It was aimed at no important strategic objective. World War I should have taught the lesson that attacks on a narrow front enabled the enemy to concentrate his artillery fire against them, and so were seldom – if ever – successful.

It would be wrong to suggest that this initial failure had a prolonged depressing effect on the 11th Brigade. But it certainly was not the best of initiations. The operation did not even achieve its intended effect of simulating a serious offensive. The higher German commanders assumed correctly that the attack was by troops new to battle, and presaged no serious threat to their positions. The Canadian casualties in this Arielli action amounted to sixty killed and about ninety wounded, with twenty-eight taken prisoner.

On the credit side of the 11th Brigade's abortive attack, and another of the same kind carried out farther to the west by the 3rd Canadian Infantry Brigade on January 30, is the fact that the German command did not feel free to move any division from the Adriatic side to the aid of the hard-pressed formations on the Cassino and Anzio fronts until mid-February. The Allied offensives did not win the success hoped for at this time. Nevertheless, the bridgehead across the Garigliano and the beachhead at Anzio were won, and were indispensable to General Alexander's strategy in the battles of May-June, which brought about the liberation of Rome.

While the 11th Brigade of the 5th Canadian Armoured Division was not introduced into battle in circumstances which added to its confidence, the 1st Canadian Division had been more fortunate in this respect, in its landing in Sicily and subsequent advance through the island.

The actual landing succeeded quickly and easily against low-grade Italian garrison troops. In the division's subsequent advance, contact was soon made with German formations of very good quality. The fighting became harder, with increasing casualties, and in increasingly difficult country. But the division was successful in taking all the objectives assigned to it, and drove back the experienced German troops in a number of brilliant attacks, in which the long training in England, and especially in night operations showed its value. The division never looked back from this auspicious beginning of its fighting experience, and by 1944 had won the reputation of being the best infantry division in the theatre.

In the late autumn of 1943, however, the 1st Division had a period of hard bitter fighting in abominable weather conditions, which tried the hardihood and resolution of every officer and man in the formation. From the crossing of the Moro River on December 5, 1943 through the capture of Ortona until the line of the Riccio was reached on January 3, it was essentially a soldier's battle and victory. The successive attacks which eventually broke the enemy resistance and drove him back to beyond the Riccio were mostly carried out by only one or two battalions. And the battalions were fighting the weather as well, as might be expected at the time of the year. In the advance across the Moro River on the 1st of January:

> . . . one company of the Seaforth battered its way through the mud of deeply ploughed olive groves in an attempt to secure the ridge on the near side of the Gully. . . The boggy ground, saturated by the previous night's rain, hampered the movement of supporting Ontario tanks. About 45 infantrymen struggled up the muddy slopes to the objective. . . .[8]

After the capture of Ortona:

> The Eighth Army's winter offensive had ground to a halt. Heavy fighting and the additional strain imposed by the hostile weather had exhausted the troops. Against a determined enemy, strongly emplaced, the infantrymen had carried the weight of the fighting, for the soaked ground had nullified the Allied superiority in

> armour, and the continual rain and overhanging cloud had drastically curtailed flying operations. . . . General Montgomery realized that to continue to attack in conditions so unfavourable to the infantry might seriously prejudice his Army's ability to launch a balanced offensive when the return of good weather should again allow effective employment of armour and air power.[9]

General Montgomery might have been thinking of the lessons of Passchendaele and the spring of 1918.

One wonders why the battle for Ortona had to be fought in that month of December? The weather on the Adriatic had been very bad in November; it could be expected to be worse in December.

> The weather began to break up at the end of October and very heavy rain descended on us. The rains continued and by the 9th November the whole country was completely waterlogged, the mud was frightful, and no vehicles could move off the road, which was covered in "chocolate sauce."[10]

The answer to the above question depended on plans made in the early autumn of 1943, after the surrender of Italy. The Eighth and Fifth Allied Armies had established themselves from Bari to Salerno, and it was concluded that the Germans would probably withdraw under pressure to a defensive line in the north, from Pisa to Rimini. The liberation of Rome would be a most important political success, and would seem to be within the powers of the Allied Armies. About the end of September, General Alexander, Commander-in-Chief of the Allied Armies in Italy, gave a directive which called for a two-pronged thrust up the peninsula; the Eighth Army to advance up the Adriatic coast to Pescara, whence it would turn southwest towards Rome, while the Fifth Army advanced on Rome up the western coastal corridor through Naples.

Only as the advance progressed and the German resistance became stronger was it realized that the enemy had no intention of giving up Rome, but had determined to stand and fight on the Gustav Line. Field-Marshal Montgomery, in his memoirs, complains bitterly of the inadequacy of the logistic arrangements for the operations he was expected to carry out.

Eventually he realized that to attempt to continue the offensive in the conditions of November and December would merely cost the lives of good fighting men, without bringing any significant advantage over the enemy. General Alexander in turn was persuaded of the facts, and decided to halt the offensive on the Adriatic except for the two holding attacks already discussed. The Anzio landing and the crossing of the Garigliano went ahead, however. No doubt the higher command weighed the merits of postponing these operations until better weather came. The decision that they had to be undertaken in winter was probably because the Allied forces and landing craft in the Mediterranean Theatre were soon to be depleted in the build-up for the invasion of Normandy. So the question ascends into the higher reaches of strategy, and goes beyond the scope of this book.

In the month's fighting, from the Moro to the Riccio, an advance of about four miles, there were 2,339 Canadians killed, wounded or missing. In addition, the strength of the division was depleted by 1,617 sick; most of them victims of the weather.

What General Montgomery has written in his memoirs and the extracts from *The Canadians in Italy* quoted above are testimony to the formidable power of "General Mud," especially in the Italian campaign. As we shall see when the narrative reaches the events of September-October, 1944, officers and men of the Canadian formations remembered their experiences of the late autumn and winter of 1943.

After the Adriatic operation the 11th Brigade was drawn into reserve for a short rest, and three days later took over a sector from a brigade of the 4th Indian Division northeast of Orsogna. Then, on February 1, the 5th Canadian Armoured Division, which by this time had completed its concentration in the forward area, relieved the whole of the 4th Indian Division on the front it had been holding. I had taken over command of the division from General Simonds on the 30th of January. On the night of February 8-9, the division sideslipped to the right, occupying the front previously held by the 8th Indian Division. At the same time we came under command of the 1st Canadian Corps, thus bringing a complete Canadian Corps into line facing the enemy for the first time in the war.

When I found myself actually in command of a Canadian division in a theatre of active operations, my mind went back to 1918 when as a Lieutenant and staff-learner I had served on the 3rd Canadian Division Headquarters. Then I had watched General Lipsett and General Loomis from a respectful distance, while the division was engaged in the hard fighting from the end of August to October – from Arras to Cambrai. Those Generals had risen to their divisional command after successfully commanding battalions and brigades. In 1942-3 I had commanded an armoured brigade and a division, but only in the training phase in England. How would I succeed in the hard test of war? However, I did not spend much time in considering my own position. I was there, I had my job to do, and, as I saw it, the main part of my duty would lie in preparing the division for the offensive action which clearly lay ahead of it and the rest of the corps in the coming spring and summer. I have mentioned the lack of doctrine on the methods of operation of an armoured division in Italy. Fortunately we were soon to have directions on tactics from the Eighth Army, drawn from the lessons of the campaign.

The division's tour in the line in February was generally uneventful, with the rain, snow and mud giving all ranks more to worry about than did the enemy. Throughout this February it snowed nearly every day on the 5th Division front – an unusually bad spell of weather. During the day the snow would melt, or turn to rain, and everywhere the troops went there was the depressing struggle against mud. The forward troops

> . . . found themselves forced to spend the day in cramped slit trenches, with anything approaching normal movement only becoming possible at night. . . . "The slit trenches are full of water, the ground is deep in mud, and temperatures at night are below the freezing point," an officer reported.[11]

"Come to Sunny Italy for your holidays," became a favourite gag.

The main activity of our infantry was patrolling at night, chiefly with the object of capturing a prisoner, and thus identifying the formations which were opposing us. The division's first success in this was scored by the Cape Breton Highlanders, who grabbed a German in daylight from across the Arielli River. The Cape Bretons became rough and tough fighters, although previously they had been something of a problem in the disciplinary matters — as many tough fighting units tend to be in "peacetime," when not engaged in actual operations.

The 5th Division remained in the sector west of Ortona until March 7, when its withdrawal to reserve commenced. During this period an important conference was held by the Eighth Army H.Q. in Lanciano, as I recall, during which there was an exposition and discussion of the battlefield tactics in which the troops should be trained, in preparation for the offensive. The main theme was close co-operation between infantry and tanks and the problem discussed was how to effect this; how the two arms could best communicate during the battle.

I remember being told, during one of my first conversations with Canadian commanders in Italy, that it had been found that the infantry always needed to have tanks with them — when on the defensive quite as much as when on the offensive. They wanted tanks with them during defensive phases for protection against an enemy tank attack. The infantry had their own anti-tank weapons, from 6-pounder guns to PIAT's (Projectile, Infantry, Anti-Tank); and there was in the division an anti-tank regiment of artillery with more powerful guns. But these defensive arms might not be in the right spot when needed, were more or less static and could be put out of action by small arms and mortar fire. The tank, on the other hand, could be in a hidden position slightly in the rear of the forward infantry, able to move quickly to any point where enemy attack developed.

But the tank-infantry partnership was two-way; tanks operating by themselves at night, or in country where there was cover in which enemy infantry could conceal themselves, were vulnerable to stealth attack by stout-hearted opponents with infantry anti-tank weapons — the German weapons corresponding to the above-mentioned PIAT. Therefore they had to be accompanied by infantry which would post themselves so as to prevent the enemy infiltrating to where they could use their weapons against our tanks. Also, infantry advancing ahead of and supported by tanks could spot where anti-tank mines had been laid, and give warning to keep clear of them until they could be lifted.

Co-operation between the infantry and the artillery was equally important, and had to be adapted to the flexible infantry-cum-tank tactics. No longer did infantry, deployed in a more or less straight line, advance behind a linear timed barrage; instead, concentrations of shelling were brought down on selected points or areas where enemy resistance was suspected or detected. A programme of such concentrations would be drawn up, and timed to phase with the anticipated rate of advance of the infantry and supporting tanks. But with the improved radio communication at the disposal of both infantry and artillery, it had become possible in favourable circumstances for the forward infantry, if delayed in their progress or held up, to call for supplementary concentrations of fire to be brought down on the enemy points of resistance. Forward artillery observation officers with efficient radio communication were often able to work directly alongside company and battalion commanders and call down prompt fire support when needed. While this sort of co-operation was technically practicable, in an actual battle many things could happen to prevent it working as smoothly as in training. The forward infantry company commander might not be able to locate exactly where the fire which was impeding his men was coming from; his signaller with the radio might become separated from him, or the set might choose that particular time to go out of order, and so on. But by and large, the possibilities of infantry-artillery co-operation on the battlefield were immensely improved by the development of portable two-way radios.

After the conference, which had been attended by many commanders and staff officers, the 5th Canadian Armoured Division had an opportunity to carry out small exercises with live ammunition fired by both infantry and tanks, in which the principles of the tactics decided upon were practised. Unfortunately, time was too short for as much training to be carried out as was desirable, before the division found itself in active operations.

I had left the armoured division on March 19, and had taken command of the 1st Canadian Corps on the following day. I had not anticipated this appointment, and was still adjusting my thoughts to commanding a division in a theatre of war. It was a great surprise when General Crerar broke the news to me. General Crerar himself was going back to England to become commander of the 1st Canadian Army in place of General McNaughton. He said he had selected me, rather than other divisional commanders, because he judged that I had greater capacity for foresight and planning ahead than other possible candidates – though others might possess more dominating personalities and perhaps be better at fighting a division in a tight situation. He considered it essential that the commander of a corps should have the ability to look forward to the next operation and the one beyond that. I suppose he had decided that I had the necessary qualifications, as he had got to know me well during the lengthy period I had worked under him in the early years of the war as a staff officer, and during 1942 and 1943 as commander of the 4th Canadian Armoured Brigade, and then the 2nd Canadian Division, within the 1st Canadian Corps.

I found it a little hard to believe that I had been appointed to this very responsible post. I contrasted myself with the formidable personality and person of General Currie, whom I had seen at close hand during his fairly frequent visits to the headquarters of General Odlum, for whom he had a special regard. Again, I regretted having come into high command without working up through lower echelons, in actual fighting. But regrets and self-doubts did not concern me for long; I had been given the job by my superiors with the approval of the Canadian Government, and it was up to me to do it as best I could.

It was not only the British higher command and staffs which had little enthusiasm for the coming of the 1st Canadian Corps to the Italian Theatre. Not a few officers in the 1st Canadian Division and the 1st Canadian Armoured Brigade took a dim view of being placed under the command of fellow Canadians who had come to the battlefield over half a year after the vanguard had waded ashore on the Sicily beaches. The feeling was not unnatural; the first contingent of Canadians in the theatre had had seven months' hard fighting, and had been consistently successful up to and including the capture of Ortona. There was a certain disposition to assume that the history of modern warfare had begun on July 10, 1943, and that only the lessons which had been learned after that date had any relevance to the way the war in Italy ought to be fought.

However, the tendency to look on the 5th Armoured Division and the corps staffs as Johnny-come-latelys disappeared after the battles in the Liri Valley and the subsequent advance towards Rome, especially when commanders and staff officers were transferred from the 1st Division to the 5th and to the corps staff.

On my promotion to command the corps, Brigadier-General Hoffmeister moved up from the 2nd Infantry Brigade to command the 5th Canadian Armoured Division and was promoted to Major-General. General Crerar had asked me to recommend a successor for command of the division, and had mentioned several possibles among the brigadiers. I had recommended Bert Hoffmeister, although at that time I did not know him well. However, I had seen and talked with him since coming to Italy, and I remembered the strong impression he made on me from the early days of training in England. He had distinguished himself in the Sicily campaign in command of the Seaforth Highlanders, and as acting Commander of the 2nd Brigade.[12] I had no cause to regret this recommendation. General Hoffmeister commanded the 5th Division with great competence and success throughout the Italian campaign. When the war ended in Europe he was selected from all the divisional commanders to command the Canadian Division which was intended for the war in the Pacific – a strong testimony of his superior ability.

In the last weeks of March the various elements of the 1st Canadian Corps had begun to move to the western part of Italy, as part of the strategic regrouping in preparation for General Alexander's new offensive which would liberate Rome and drive the German armies another 150 miles to the north, beyond Florence. But the 1st Division remained in the line in front of Ortona until April 23, under the command of the 5th Corps.

It was while the Canadian Corps Headquarters was at Larino that an amusing episode occurred. One night when the "A" Mess was seated at table, we were startled by a sudden loud noise, a kind of inarticulate yell. I asked what in hell that was. After a brief embarrassed silence, John Bassett, who was my Military Secretary and who also ran the mess, said that it was a goose. These creatures had been acquired to be kept on reserve as eventual *pièces de résistance*, to relieve the monotony of army rations on which we normally subsisted, or to grace the table if we should be visited by some Very Important Person.

In keeping livestock for this purpose, the corps mess staff had imitated Eighth Army Headquarters, which had quite a farmyard: a sheep, a turkey, geese and chickens. Perhaps they had been brought over from Africa, as there were strict orders that the Allied armies in Italy should not purchase food from the civilian population. (This was due to a great shortage of food, particularly proteins, owing to the years of war.) It seemed to me that corps headquarters should set an example in obeying this rule, so I ordered the immediate return of the goose to where it had come from. Its voice was heard no more around our camp, but whether it was in fact returned to its previous domicile, I can't say. Geese saved ancient Rome by their cackling, and our goose by a well-timed "Honk" saved its own neck – for a time at any rate.

It may not have been very consistent, but I never objected to the appearance of eggs on our breakfast table, and these certainly didn't come with the rations. They were procured from the farmers here and there. Payment was usually made in cigarettes, of which we had plenty, unlike the poor Italians. I thought that this particular barter probably made for the happiness of both parties.

Later, as an aftermath of battle, we had complaints from farmers that some of their cows had provided barbecues and stews for our troops, and that the animals' demise had not been caused by German shellfire, but by well-directed Canadian bullets. This was not improbable, but it did not seem feasible to determine who were the guilty beef-lovers among the front-line troops. After all, when one has recently escaped sudden death, and is hungry as well, property rights – particularly those of ex-enemies – hardly seem sacred. I hope the farmers were eventually given satisfaction by the claims commission of the Allied Military Government.

About mid-March I was given the opportunity to visit the Cassino-Garigliano front, and to watch the attack being carried out by the New Zealand Division and an Indian division against Cassino and the famous monastery. The spectators, among whom were other senior officers, had a gallery view from the heights to the south of Cassino, but as usual in battle little could be seen except the shell-bursts, ragged smoke screens and perhaps an occasional tank. The infantry were invisible, except for a few figures now and then. But it was clear, from what we could see and the reports that came in belatedly, that in spite of the most gallant efforts the German position on the heights below the monastery was holding firm, although the ruins of Cassino fell into our hands. No one, I think, who stood in the lower ground could fail to be impressed by the dominating position of the monastery, which we naturally assumed would be filled with German fighting troops and observers. Advance up the Liri

Valley, on the axis of the road to Rome, could hardly be achieved while the Germans held this commanding position. Therefore the blasting of the monastery by the U.S. heavy bombers which General Alexander ordered – and which has since the war been criticized because of the resultant destruction of a building of unique historical and religious character – certainly met no objection. On the contrary, it received hearty approval by the troops on the ground who had to carry out the offensive towards the north.

When the grand strategy for the year 1944 was being planned at the Quebec Conference in August 1943, it was decided, and subsequently confirmed at other inter-Allied conferences, that Overlord – the code name for the cross-Channel invasion of Normandy – would be supported by an invasion of Southern France mounted from Italy (which would be given the code name "Anvil"). These operations were to take place about mid-May. But it had been assumed that the Allied offensive in Italy would have progressed beyond Rome and far to the north, to the Pisa-Rimini Line which the Germans were known to be preparing for defence. However, the Allied forces were held on the Gustav Line. The Anzio operation was an attempt to outflank the Gustav Line by a seaborne landing, and so to force the German formations manning it to retire and keep on retiring until they had to evacuate Rome. But after the initial landing and advance inland, which took the Germans by surprise, they recovered quickly and managed to seal off the beachhead. Indeed, at one point they threatened to throw the Allied troops back into the sea.

When this situation of stalemate was appreciated, about mid-February, General Maitland ("Jumbo") Wilson, who had succeeded General Eisenhower as Allied Commander-in-Chief, Mediterranean Theatre, recommended to the Allied Chiefs of Staff that first priority should be given to operations linking up the Allied forces south of the Gustav Line with those on the Anzio beachhead, after which they would advance together to drive the Germans out of Rome. The Anvil operation would be postponed. This alteration in plans was approved by President Roosevelt and Prime Minister Churchill, and preparations for the operations were put in hand accordingly.

In the regroupings for the forthcoming offensive, planned to begin about May 10, the Fifth (U.S.) Army was to concentrate from opposite the junction of the Liri River with the Gari to the Mediterranean coast; while for about ten miles to the east of the Fifth Army's front would be deployed the Eighth Army, comprising the 13th Corps, the 2nd Polish Corps and the 1st Canadian Corps (in reserve), totalling eight divisions and three armoured brigades.

In order to mystify and confuse the enemy as to the Allied intentions, an elaborate deception exercise carried out by means of false radio traffic was put in hand. The general idea was that false messages from a skeleton radio network would give the impression that the 1st Canadian Corps and an American division had concentrated in the Salerno area, where a landing exercise would be simulated. The whole was intended to cause the Germans to believe that the Allies were preparing a seaborne landing near the port of Civitavecchia, sixty kilometres northwest of Rome.

The deception worked admirably, and fear of an outflanking seaborne landing induced the German commander in Italy, Field-Marshal Kesselring, to keep several divisions along the Tyrrhenian coast north of Rome. When the attack on Cassino and across the Garigliano developed he delayed moving them south until the Allies had made a considerable advance and broken up the organization of the German defence. It is an interesting reflection that without firing a shot the officers and men of the Royal Canadian Corps of Signals made a considerable contribution to the successful battles that liberated Rome.

# The Liri Valley and the Hitler Line

The 1st Canadian Corps and the 5th Canadian Armoured Division were about to have their first test in battle in the offensive which would begin on May 11, and which was intended to drive the Germans back from their winter defences and out of Rome.

The Liri Valley and the Sacco Valley which extended it to the west formed a natural avenue of approach to Rome. Through them ran the Naples-Rome railway and Highway 6, which followed the line of the ancient Via Casilina. The Liri Valley is from four to seven miles wide and about eighteen miles long, from the Liri River's junction with the Gari to its junction with the Sacco, near Ceprano. It is bounded on the north by the mass of Mount Cairo, on a spur of which the Cassino monastery stands, and on the south by the Aurunci and Ausoni mountains. The valley floor could be described as close country; that is, affording little observation in any direction, owing to cultivated fields and orchards in the part near the Garigliano River, and scattered woods more to the west.

The Germans had built strong fortifications to block this approach. The first complex was the Gustav Line proper, running from Cassino along the west bank of the Garigliano River. This was a very strong position, especially because of the tank obstacles constituted by the river and the steep mountain sides north of Cassino. But the German staff, following their usual practice, had also constructed another line of defence, some seven miles farther west. This ran at an angle from behind Monte Cassino, in front of the villages of Aquino and Pontecorvo, and then in a southwesterly direction through the Aurunci mountains to the sea. It was first called the "Fuehrer Riegel" (Riegel meaning switch); but apparently when Hitler himself heard of this nomenclature he thought that it would not improve his image if a line with his name on it should be broken through, so he had it officially renamed "Senger Riegel" – after the Commander of the 14th Panzer Corps. But the Allied Armies continued to call it, inexactly, the Hitler Line. The Germans, with the aid of specialist fortification units and forced labour, had been working on this line ever since December 1943 – five months. Concrete underground shelters connected to machine-gun emplacements with all-round fields of fire; and formidable anti-tank defences consisting of Panther tank turrets on concrete emplacements at ground level, with a capacity to fire in all directions (in other words a kind of dug-in tank) were the principal features. Besides these specially strong defensive constructions, there were also more shelters, trenches, small pillboxes and of course thick barbed-wire obstacles and extensive anti-tank minefields. The work was not complete when the 1st Division assaulted and it was not garrisoned by the full number of troops for which it had been designed. Moreover the German units which did man it had been roughly handled and had lost many men in previous engagements. Otherwise the break-in would have taken longer and have been costlier in lives than the actual event, hard and bloody as that fighting was.

After the Hitler Line there were no more fortified defensive lines on the road to Rome, until Valmontone, some seventy miles farther to the northwest.

General Alexander's operation order of May 5 – which confirmed preliminary directives given at conferences during the preceding month – called for the three corps on the left of the Eighth Army to drive up the Liri Valley and along Highway 6 to Rome. The *Corps Expéditionnaire Français* and the U.S. 2nd Corps under the U.S. Fifth Army, would advance across the Aurunci mountains, to the south of the Liri River, in a direction roughly parallel to that of the Eighth Army. It was hoped that these strong attacks would cause the German command to throw in their reserve formations, thus opening the way for the U.S. 6th Corps (comprising two U.S. and two British divisions) to strike out from the beachhead at Anzio in a northeasterly direction. If this advance from Anzio were rapid enough it could cut off the bulk of the German forces south of Rome.

The plan of operations of the Eighth Army was given out at a series of conferences held by General Sir Oliver Leese in April and early May. It was not the Eighth Army's practice to issue full operation orders, but instead to work by short directives to corps commanders. General Leese directed that the Polish Corps should strike through the hills, outflanking the Monte Cassino monastery position, and advance on a line which would bring it to a junction with the 13th Corps, in the valley. The 13th Corps was to attack across the Gari River[1] and advance westward, parallel to Highway 6. If the 13th Corps should succeed in advancing rapidly and breaking through the Hitler Line, the Canadian Corps, at first in reserve, was to be prepared to pass through and exploit up Highway 6 towards Rome. If, however, the 13th Corps encountered such heavy opposition as to make doubtful whether it could break through quickly, then the Canadian Corps would come into action on its left, to carry on the advance through the valley in parallel with it. This second alternative General Leese considered the more likely one, and this, in fact, was what happened.

Assisted by my staff, I had now to try to forecast how the corps could carry out the tasks that had been laid out for it, and make tentative plans. Apart from speculation as to how the operations of the 13th and Polish Corps would succeed, the forward look mainly involved a study of the terrain over which we might operate. For this we had maps and air photographs, plus a view of the panorama of the valley from the isolated peak of Mount Trocchio (which stood east of the Gari River, something like a stopper opposite the bottleneck of the lower Liri Valley). If the corps' task should be the first, or pursuit alternative, the main decision to make was whether to operate on the northern side of the valley, along Highway 6, or on the southern side, parallel to the Liri River. The northern side seemed to be the likeliest; mainly because the country appeared less enclosed, and the watercourses which ran across the valley seemed less of a tank obstacle than on the lower southern side where they flowed into the Liri. Hence the northern side looked more favourable for tank operation. The corps' main advantage over the enemy formations which might oppose it was in the number of tanks at our disposal — the Armoured Brigade of the 5th Canadian Armoured Division and the 25th Army Tank Brigade which we could expect would co-operate with the 1st Infantry Division — involving between 350 and 400 tanks in all.

There was another reason which made it seem that the north side would be more favourable. An advance on either side could not be sure and rapid if the enemy held the high ground rising to the mountains on the flank. If they held firmly to such vantage positions, they could unmercifully harass our troops in the valley with artillery, and even counterattack. We expected that the drive of the Polish Corps over the Cairo mountain combined with the 13th Corps push up the valley would throw back the enemy on this flank more quickly than the *Corps Expéditionnaire Français* could advance over the very rough and almost trackless area of the Aurunci mountains. The C.E.F. was at that time an unknown quantity. It was the first French formation to meet German troops in Europe since the unhappy days of 1940, and consisted largely of Algerian and other colonial troops. How well could they succeed against the battle-hardened Germans they would be facing?

The alternative task for the corps, to deploy in the valley on the left of the 13th Corps and to break through the Hitler Line, would clearly mean that we should have a hard fight. We had enough intelligence about the fortifications described above to appreciate the difficulty of this. However, the pattern for the kind of battle it would be was well-known: a break-in to a fortified defensive position, followed by break-out of armoured formations and exploitation. This had been set in the Battle of Alamein and those which followed it in the campaign which cleared North Africa of the enemy. Commanders and staffs all had a general knowledge of what had to be done; first an infantry assault, usually at night, supported by strong artillery fire, to clear a way through the minefields and barbed wire; then the elimination of the defending enemy in his defensive zone. When a sufficiently wide gap had been cleared, armoured formations would pass through. These were to drive into enemy territory, to break up his command and logistic organization, and if possible to cut off the retreat of the enemy troops which had been holding positions on the flanks of the point of break-through. This was the general scheme; the break-in part had worked in North Africa, but the pursuit and exploitation had never been entirely successful until the final battles in Tunisia, where the Germans and Italians, pinned against the sea, could retreat no farther and had to surrender.

It would have been better if both divisions of the corps could have had more training in this type of operation. Such bulletless rehearsals can greatly improve chances of success by familiarizing all ranks with the tasks they would have to carry out in the face of the enemy.

In spite of the fact that the forthcoming battle would be the first for the 5th Division and for the corps staff, I had no doubt that we should accomplish our task, and this confidence, I suppose, stemmed from my experience in World War I. Even in the mud of the Somme and Passchendaele, the Canadians had always taken their objectives in the end, although at the cost of much blood and with occasional setbacks. However, I did not let this general confidence blind me to the fact that in battle against such an enemy as the Germans, victory could never be taken for granted; his reaction, and the many unexpected possibilities of combat could upset the best-concerted plans. I conceived it my duty, in working out a plan and putting it into operation, to try and foresee where it could go wrong, and then to try and ensure that it did not. Naturally I talked over such possible mischances and how they should be guarded against with the divisional commanders and other subordinates. This may have created an impression, I realize now, that I was fundamentally pessimistic – which I am not. However, my habit of mind is generally to think of the misfortune which can happen and be surprised by unexpected good luck, rather than vice versa. In short, I tried to leave nothing to luck, although of course I didn't succeed in eliminating all mischief.

Before we entered the battle General Leese visited the Canadian formations, and gave groups of officers the sort of "pep talk" for which General Montgomery had set the pattern. These brief speeches appeared to make a good impression: the general theme was that the Eighth Army, together with the Fifth, was about to deliver a terrific blow against the enemy, and if we all did our utmost we could expect to drive him out of Italy, and perhaps, together with the Allied forces on other fronts, win final victory in 1944. To hearten the troops before battle by telling them that shining victory could be won by their bravery and constancy is a proven technique.

The only doubt I had as to what was said on this occasion was as to what the effect might be if, in fact, final victory in Italy and in the whole Western Theatre should *not* be won in 1944.

I remember that General Freyberg, Commander of the New Zealand Corps, took another view of the chances of success of the Eighth Army offensive. In a private conversation he surprised me by asking whether I really thought the assault on Monte Cassino and across the Gari would come off. He himself had unhappy doubts. I expect that these doubts were due to the check which his own New Zealanders and the Indians had met in March – the attack on Cassino and the monastery which I have mentioned. General Freyberg was a legendary figure; winner of the VC and several bars to the D.S.O. There was, I suppose, no personally braver man in the British and Dominion Armies. Furthermore, he had led the reinforced New Zealand Corps in one of the most successful operations in the North African campaign – the outflanking of the Mareth Line in Tunisia, in March 1943. Yet on this, and on some other occasions, I found that he seemed dubious of offensive actions planned. The New Zealanders had only a secondary role in the Eighth Army offensive. They were in the 10th Corps, which held a wide front in the mountains to the north of the area of the main Eighth Army thrust, and their task was to try to convince the enemy facing them that an attack on that front was threatened also – and so to prevent his withdrawing formations to reinforce the main battle area.

At eleven-forty-five p.m. on the night of May 11 the 4th British and 8th Indian Divisions of the 13th Corps launched their assault across the Gari River against the Gustav Line defences. It had been preceded by an intense bombardment and counter-battery programme by the 1,060 guns massed on the Eighth Army front; simultaneously with similar artillery action of the Fifth Army front to the south. The Canadian artillery of both divisions and corps troops took part in this bombardment, and the 1st Canadian Armoured Brigade was taking part in the assault under command of the 8th Indian Division. They played a decisive role, supporting the Indian infantry, in establishing and expanding the bridgehead.

The bridging of the deep and fast-flowing river was the key in moving the tanks to the west bank, and great gallantry was shown by the Indian engineers under fire, in building a Bailey bridge at one point. This enabled most of the Ontario Tank Regiment to cross. An ingenious method of launching a bridge on the back of a tank, pushed behind by another, was developed by Captain H. A. Kingsmill of the Royal Canadian Electrical and Mechanical Engineers detachment of the Calgary Regiment. This allowed four Calgary tanks to cross, but an unlucky shell put it out of action. By nightfall nearly five squadrons of Canadian tanks had crossed, in spite of heavy fire and the additional obstacle of soft muddy areas on the west bank which bogged many down temporarily. By the end of May 12 the Eighth Army had not progressed far towards the planned first objectives, but early on May 13, another bridge was completed between Sant' Angelo and Cassino, enabling tanks of the British 26 Army Tank Brigade to cross, and they and the 4th Division infantry drove back the opposing Germans. The tanks of the Ontario Regiment played a very effective part in the capture of Sant'Angelo, the village on the west bank of the Gari which had been the strongest centre of resistance to the attack on the 13th Corps front. Further to the south, the Calgary Tank Regiment combined with a brigade of the 8th Indian Division to capture Panaccioni. These actions proved the worth of joint training exercises carried out by the Indian infantry and the Canadian tanks in rear areas during the preceding weeks.[2]

Hard fighting went on during the next two days, and by nightfall on the 15th the British and Indian divisions were in possession of the lateral road from Cassino through Pignataro to the Liri River. However, the Cassino monastery and surrounding defences had resisted the gallant attacks of the Polish Corps. South of the Liri River, after a hard fight on the opening day of the offensive in which little ground was gained, the *Corps Expéditionnaire Français* suddenly surged forward over the rugged Aurunci mountains, and by May 15 had reached the defile south of Esperia and San Giorgio on the banks of the Liri. The German command was thrown off balance by this sudden thrust, together with the powerful advance of the 13th Corps in the Liri Valley, and by the evening of May 16 Kesselring had issued orders for withdrawal to the Hitler Line.

On the evening of May 15 General Leese directed the Canadian Corps to relieve the 8th Indian Division in its sector of the 13th

Corps front, and to continue the advance westward. In accordance with my plans for such an eventuality (the second of General Leese's alternative tasks for the Canadian Corps) the 1st Canadian Division was given this task. General Vokes had made preliminary arrangements with the General Officer Commanding of the 8th Indian Division, and on the night of May 15-16 the 1st Canadian Infantry Brigade relieved an Indian brigade. On the next night the 3rd Canadian Infantry Brigade took over the right brigade sector, and on May 17th the division began its advance to the Hitler Line. The Royal 22nd Regiment, supported by the Three Rivers Regiment tanks, captured a bridgehead over the Forme d'Aquino. This had been a serious anti-tank obstacle running in a southeasterly direction across the line of advance of the division, from the village of Aquino to the Liri River, about one and a half kilometres west of San Giorgio. The successful co-operation of the battle-experienced tankmen of the 1st Canadian Armoured Brigade with the infantry of the 1st Canadian Division was an example of what might have been achieved if these Canadian formations had been allowed to fight together during the rest of the 1944 campaign.

On the night of May 17-18, the 1st German Parachute Division retired from Cassino and the north of the Liri Valley, to the line Piedimonte-Aquino. We hoped that it might be possible to crash through the Hitler Line before the Germans had time to occupy it effectively. However, an attack on May 19 by the 78th Division on Aquino and another by the 3rd Canadian Infantry Brigade directed midway between the Forme d'Aquino and Pontecorvo came up against resistance which was too strong to overcome with the limited artillery support available. General Leese decided that to break through the Hitler Line a set-piece attack would be necessary, and he issued orders on the morning of May 20 for the Canadian Corps to mount it in the general area where the 3rd Brigade attack of the previous day had been halted. The 13th Corps was to "maintain pressure" on Aquino and to concentrate forward, ready to resume the advance when the breakthrough had been achieved.

The front to be attacked was about 5,000 yards in width, and was held, on the day of attack, by four battalions of the 90th Panzer Grenadier Division, the 44th Ersatz (Reinforcement) Battalion near Pontecorvo, and the 334th Engineer Battalion in Pontecorvo itself. The 1st Parachute Division, old opponents of the 1st Canadian

Division, were in and around Aquino, on the right of the Canadian sector, but they intervened with telling effect from this flank when our attack was launched. The measures to "maintain pressure" by the 13th Corps were not sufficient to prevent this.

General Vokes decided to make his assault with two battalions of the 2nd Brigade, on a front of about 2,000 yards running south from the divisional and corps boundary, which at that point ran through the junction of the Forme d'Aquino and the Hitler Line. The attack would be supported by a heavy barrage, and the infantry battalions would each be supported by a regiment (about fifty) of Churchill tanks of the 25th Army Tank Brigade. Vokes selected this line of approach because it seemed more open and better suited for tank operations than the ground farther to the division's left, towards Pontecorvo.

I had agreed to his plan, but it was quickly pointed out to me by General Leese that the front of attack was too narrow and should be extended by at least one more battalion frontage. This conference was held at his advanced H.Q., and General Kirkman, Commander of the 13th Corps, was also present. I saw at once that I had been wrong in agreeing to General Vokes' first plan, and immediately told him of the required extension. He was not too pleased at having to alter his arrangements but it is indeed fortunate that this was done, for the break-in was made by the Carleton and York Battalion of the 3rd Infantry Brigade on the extended front while the 2nd Brigade was held up by fierce resistance on the originally planned front of attack.

The rapid advance of the *Corps Expéditionnaire Français* on the south of the Liri River and over the mountains has been mentioned. By May 20 the right division of this corps, the 1st Motorized Infantry Division, had reached a point beyond Pontecorvo. One day I was invited to a *Prise d'Armes* which was to be held by the French Corps. This is a ceremony at which decorations and honours are presented to units and individuals who have distinguished themselves in battle. It was held at San Ambrogio, a little village a kilometre or so to the west of the Garigliano River. It was a bright sunny day, with a brisk wind which snapped the tricolour flags and pennons. General de Gaulle was there to make the presentations, together with General Juin, the Commander of the corps. For me it was a most memorable occasion, marking the revival of the power and honour of the French Army, long in eclipse after the lamentable events of 1940. As the tough-looking colonial officers and men came forward to receive their honours, I shared their emotion; victory had come again to illumine the standards of France.

After the ceremony I had a brief conversation with the two generals. They were interested to know what the Canadian Corps was going to do. I told them we were going to break through the Hitler Line, and were now moving up to position for the assault.

General Juin was very professional and did the talking while General de Gaulle listened. He was already a legendary figure, the symbol of the indomitable spirit of France. Austere, proud and authoritative even in his silence, he seemed to tower above the rest of us, morally as well as physically. As I left the group I heard him say that I spoke French pretty well; quite a compliment coming from him!

The advance of the French Corps south of the Liri River, and on the heights beyond seemed to open up the possibility of outflanking the strong defences of the Hitler Line north of Pontecorvo. The French 1st Motorized Division, which had been pushing ahead along the south bank of the river had had some co-operation from the 1st Canadian Infantry Brigade and our artillery. On May 21 prisoners were taken by the Princess Louise Dragoon Guards (the reconnaissance regiment of the 1st Canadian Division) from the 44th *Feldersatzbataillon.*[3] These men seemed of poor fighting quality. General Vokes had Brigadier Spry visit the French divisional commander to see whether the 1st Brigade could move through the French division's sector, and attack northwards across the Liri River, outflanking Pontecorvo and the Hitler Line defences, and using assault boats to cross the river. But the German defences were found to extend along the north shore of the river, which moreover was a difficult obstacle with high embankment walls. So this alternative was ruled out. General Vokes nevertheless thought that the resistance in the 1st Brigade sector might be weak, and the defending troops poorly organized. He therefore proposed to send in the 1st Brigade to attack towards Pontecorvo to try to break through on this portion of the front. I agreed to this operation although I was not very happy about it. It would mean that attention could be distracted from the preparations for the three-battalion attack on the front running south from the Forme d'Aquino, planned to take place at six a.m. on the

23rd of May. The 1st Brigade thrust towards Pontecorvo was to be on the 22nd of May.

I decided to go forward and try to see how the 1st Brigade attack got on. It was to start about mid-morning. I had a staff officer with me, and a radio vehicle from which I could speak to the main corps headquarters by telephone. There was a covered approach and I was able to reach a small hill from which I could view the road to Pontecorvo, which was the axis of attack. It was about 1,000 yards or less to the advancing tanks which could be seen quite clearly through binoculars. A few infantry were in view, but, as usual, attacking infantry that know what they are about do not show themselves much on the battlefield. After some supporting artillery fire the tanks advanced, and in rapid succession two of them were hit and set on fire – a grim sight. After watching this attack for some time, and weighing all the possibilities, I concluded that it was not going to succeed. To persist in it would not achieve the rapid breakthrough that the Eighth Army and the higher command had laid down as the task of the Canadian Corps. A continued advance on this line would have brought the troops into Pontecorvo, and fighting to clear a town or village which was resolutely defended could be a long and hard business – as many examples from World War I and the experience of Ortona more recently had shown. Accordingly I telephoned back to Brigadier McCarter, the Brigadier, General Staff at corps headquarters, to inform General Vokes that the push on the left flank did not seem likely to succeed, and to go ahead and put the whole weight into the three-battalion front attack as previously planned. It was not until five p.m. that the regrouping of the brigades to carry out this assault was under way.[4] This was because Vokes had held back the 2nd Brigade, intending to use it to follow through on the left flank if the attack of the 1st Brigade had been successful. He had been intending to ask permission to do this,[5] but I was not aware at the time that this alternate plan of his was delaying the deployment for the main planned attack.

The 2nd Brigade battalions and supporting tanks had been delayed in taking up their positions for the assault. This left them insufficient time for reconnoitring approaches to the Hitler Line fortified zone, and especially little opportunity to lift mines to allow clear passage for the tanks. This contributed to the early check of the advance of the Princess Patricia's Canadian Light Infantry and the

Seaforths. On the front of the Carleton and York Regiment, the third battalion designated for the assault, the luck of battle was in our favour. This battalion had staged a diversionary attack on May 22, intended to draw attention from the 1st Brigade's thrust on the left. They had succeeded in getting their leading platoons into the wire obstacle. "The information which they gained about the enemy's defences was to serve in good stead next day."[6]

Looking back, it seems I should have not agreed to Vokes' idea to get round the Hitler defences by the Pontecorvo flank. However, the rapid advance and weak resistance met there on the 21st did give colour to the idea that the Germans might be pulling out. Their right, south of the Liri, had been penetrated deeply by the French advance, and they had suffered heavily in the battles since the 11th of May. If indeed they were retiring from the heavily fortified Hitler Line there would be no point in incurring the heavy losses which an assault on it would be bound to cause. It was only when I saw that the progress of the 1st Brigade attack was checked, that I decided that the originally-planned break-in should go forward.

When he orders an attack against an enemy in position, a general knows that some of the men he sends forward are going to be killed, and more will be wounded. Sensitive civilians may wonder how any man can give such an order without a terrible sense of guilt, and may feel that if the general does not have such a guilt-feeling he must be a heartless brute. It would be idle to deny that professional training and temperament has given most successful generals a capacity to shut their minds to the inevitable "butcher's bill."

A soldier who has reached the rank of general and commands a fighting formation is probably a fighter by nature. If he has no stomach for fighting he will not long remain in his post. Cases have been known where the responsibility of command has given very senior officers a real and severe intestinal malaise. It is an extreme case of the "butterflies in the stomach" before a football game, a speech, a theatrical performance, or other such event which vulnerably exposes any individual or group.

A general has spent most of his life training himself for the moment when he must make decisions — especially the decision to attack and destroy the enemy when the occasion is favourable. He has done it in the various tactical exercises which have prepared him for the real thing. So he will take the action which he has been trained to take, his mind will be concentrated on victory, and he will hope that casualties will be few. His object is to inflict the maximum of loss on the enemy, while suffering minimum loss in his own troops.

Also a general has usually experienced battle when he held lower rank – perhaps as a junior officer. Having taken his own chance with wounds or death, he will be less likely to feel guilt about ordering his present subordinates to do so.

Finally, he has been directed by his country to obey the orders of a higher command under which his formation serves. If that higher command orders him to attack with his formation, it is his duty to obey, as a link in the chain of command. The responsibility comes down from above, from the government of his country which has decided to go to war. As its military servant he is expected to do his part and see that those under him do their part to defend the country's vital interests.

The responsibility which a general cannot escape, in my view, is to strain every nerve to ensure that the action is planned and prepared to give the very best chance for success, success without paying a heavy price in blood.

Once the thunder of the preparatory bombardment, followed by the barrage that precedes the advance of the infantry and tanks is heard, there is little that can be done at corps headquarters until information comes back as to how the attack is going. And that information comes slowly; it came very slowly and unsurely in World War I, and in World War II, in spite of the improvement in radio communication which I have several times mentioned, as a rule it was several hours before any firm information came back. The duty of corps and divisional headquarters should have been done before the guns began to fire: detailed planning, orders, and supervision to see that moves were made on time and obstacles to movement prevented, that engineering work was completed, that the required quantities of munitions were deposited where they were needed. When the artillery fire marking the assault began, one could only look at one's watch and pray: God help the men in the forefront.

The concentration of artillery in the fire plan was the heaviest utilized by the Allies up to this stage in the war. Eighteen heavy batteries, firing pieces from 7.2-inch to 9.6-inch, eleven medium regiments (mostly 5.5-inch pieces) and twenty field regiments – 810 guns in all – took part. And the attacking infantry had the whole of the 25th Army Tank Brigade supporting them, as well as part of the Three Rivers Tank Regiment.

Zero hour for the assault on the Hitler Line was six a.m. It was well on in the morning before there was enough information to form a clear pattern. At first it was not at all encouraging; the Princess Pats and the Seaforth were in trouble, and so were the tanks accompanying them.[7]

General Vokes and I talked by phone throughout the day. Until noon it did not become clear that the two right attacking battalions, in spite of much individual gallantry, had been pinned down by the fire of the Germans from their concrete machine-gun and anti-tank emplacements. The situation was especially serious on the P.P.C.L.I. front, owing to the flanking fire from battalions of the Parachute Division across the Forme d'Aquino, on the 13th Corps front.

But in the sector of the Carleton and York Regiment, the first objective – roughly the line of the Pontecorvo-Aquino road – had been taken with comparatively light losses. General Vokes' plan had called for the advance by all three battalions, after the first objective had been taken, to the second objective, which was the lateral road leading north from Pontecorvo, some 1,200 yards to the west of the first objective. His problem was whether to order the 3rd Brigade to advance to the second objective while the 2nd Brigade had not yet reached the first. We discussed this together, and with my advice and agreement he took the bold course of exploiting the success on the left. The second phase of the 1st Division's battle was led by the West Nova Scotia Regiment, supported by two squadrons of the Three Rivers Armoured Regiment. (The squadrons of the British 51st Army Tank Regiment had suffered very numerous losses during the advance through the fortified zone and the subsequent halt between phases of the operation.) The advance began at four-fifty p.m. and soon after six p.m. the assaulting troops were on the final objective. An attempted counterattack by one of the Panzer Grenadier regiments was broken up, after a slight initial success.

Next, the Royal 22nd Regiment passed through the breach in the line, wheeled to the north, and after some fighting reached a position about 1,200 yards north of the right flank of the West Novas, where it consolidated for the night. This completed the primary task of the 1st Division, as it had been planned – to open a breach in the Hitler Line through which the 5th Armoured Division would pass to exploit the advantage.

When the 3rd Brigade moved to advance in the second phase, Vokes telephoned me in some apprehension over reports that the 26th Panzer Division was in the area behind the Hitler Line. He feared that this formation with numerous tanks might counterattack the 3rd Brigade units and put them in grave danger, as most of their supporting tanks had been knocked out. I pointed out that besides the Three Rivers Regiment, which had not suffered many losses, the whole of the 5th Division armour was close behind, placing themselves in position to pass through the hole his troops had punched. Taking the point, General Vokes drove on, and an hour or so later telephoned me again to report the success of the 3rd Brigade attack and capture of the second objective. "This is the proudest day of my life!" he blurted out. Indeed, he had every reason to be proud of the brilliant and gallant fighting of the men he commanded, and of the will and resource he himself had shown on that historic day.

One episode of the fighting has stayed in my mind as the most memorable on the day it came to my notice when its hero was recommended for a Distinguished Conduct Medal. Two soldiers of the Seaforth Highlanders constituted an anti-tank team, armed with the P.I.A.T. – the infantry anti-tank weapon. Spotting an enemy tank in the Hitler Line zone where the Seaforth had penetrated, they stalked it through trees and undergrowth, and got within range, without the tank crew having observed them. Then – and this is the point which impressed me particularly – the leader took off his spectacles, wiped them carefully so he could see clearly, then aimed, fired, hit and destroyed that tank. But this is only one of the many acts of bravery and endurance by Canadian troops that day.

The part played by the 1st Brigade on the left flank of the division should not be forgotten. Although their attempt on the previous day to get through the line near Pontecorvo had been checked, they had made a limited penetration into the defended zone. Their role in the main attack on the 23rd was to keep up pressure on their front, so the enemy could not concentrate all his resources on the front attacked by the 2nd and 3rd Brigades. With the aid of a fresh squadron of the 142nd Royal Tank Regiment, the 48th Highlanders and the Hastings and Prince Edward Regiment succeeded, in a day of stiff fighting, in capturing Point 106, a hill about a mile northeast of Pontecorvo, lying between the defended zone and the lateral Pontecorvo-Aquino road. Early the next morning the Royal Canadian Regiment entered Pontecorvo and captured the surviving garrison.

The 1st Canadian Division had suffered heavy losses in its breakthrough: 880 officers and men killed, wounded and missing. But they had inflicted heavier losses: 700 German prisoners had been taken, and four German battalions wiped out – according to the enemy's records. Many of the German losses were due to the powerful artillery support; the 810 guns I have mentioned were concentrating their fire on little more than 3,500 yards – about one gun for every four yards of front. The Royal Canadian Artillery and the gunners from other formations had done a fine job in protecting the hard-fighting infantry and tankmen.

The corps plan had provided for the 5th Division to advance through the gap as soon as it had been punched out by the 1st Division. Before the attack we hoped this would have been achieved in the morning of the 23rd, but, as we have seen, the uneven fortunes of the battle delayed the final success until the evening. (When I saw General Leese, who again had General Kirkman with him, they congratulated me on the 1st Division's success, and I detected some surprise that it had been as rapid as it was.)

General Hoffmeister had his leading troops lined up on the Forme d'Aquino, and kept in touch with the progress of the battle through 1st Division and corps headquarters. About five-thirty p.m., when the success of the 3rd Brigade seemed confirmed, Hoffmeister phoned me that the situation seemed ripe for his armoured brigade's advance, and I told him to go. But as the armoured brigade had been deployed so as to move through a gap on the right of the 1st Division's front, they had to shift left; and because of this some confusion and delays occurred. Delay was increased by rain which fell during the afternoon and turned the sandy tracks bulldozed along the valley into mud. This slowed the tanks up. By eight-thirty p.m. it appeared to Hoffmeister that he could not get his troops away in proper order that night, so the break-out was postponed until the following morning.

General Hoffmeister had given to the 5th Canadian Armoured Brigade, commanded by Brigadier J.D.B. Smith, the difficult task of crossing the Melfa River, some four and a half miles beyond the Hitler Line. The brigade had with it the Westminster (Motor) Regiment, and the Irish Regiment (from the 11th Brigade) together with detachments of artillery and engineers. The divisional reconnaissance regiment,[8] the Governor-General's Horse Guards, operated on the flanks of the two fighting groups into which Brigadier Smith had organized his force.

Smith's plan was simple and effective. The B.C. Dragoons, commanded by Lieutenant-Colonel Fred Vokes (Major-General Chris Vokes' younger brother) moved up with the Irish Regiment and took position in a large farm called Mancini. They thus guarded the flank of the advance against action from the Germans who still occupied Aquino and ground westward on the 13th Corps front. Vokes' group, passing the start line of the Aquino Pontecorvo road at eight a.m., had occupied Mancini by midday, fighting successful actions against the remnants of one battalion of the 90th Panzer Grenadier Regiment on the way. It had also chased off a detachment of Panther tanks, destroying three of them — the first encounter of Allied troops in the west with this new and powerful type of tank.

The second group consisted of the Lord Strathcona's Horse (whose Commanding Officer was Lieutenant-Colonel P.G. Griffin) and the Westminster Regiment. Their task was to drive forward and seize a bridgehead over the Melfa River. About three-thirty p.m. the

Melfa was reached by the reconnaissance troop of the Strathconas, commanded by Lieutenant E.J. Perkins. Under his skilful and courageous leadership, the troop made the difficult crossing and seized a small bridgehead on the west bank, around a defended house whose German occupants they had captured. This exploit earned him an immediate D.S.O., a rare award to a subaltern. Soon the "A" squadron of the regiment arrived at the road some 400 yards east of the river, and became engaged in a battle with Panther tanks and self-propelled guns which had appeared from the direction of a ford about half a mile farther south, where the Germans seemed to have expected an attempt to cross and had prepared defences against it. In about an hour the German tanks had been driven back across the river, but the tank fight continued from the two banks. Seventeen tanks were lost by the Strathconas, while they destroyed five enemy tanks and eight self-propelled guns.

While the tank battle was going on, "A" Company of the Westminsters had arrived on the east bank, and on orders of Lieutenant-Colonel Griffin, began to cross the river and extend the precarious hold of Lieutenant Perkins' troop. "A" Company widened the small bridgehead and clung to it for the rest of the day, under constant artillery and mortar fire, and several attacks by tanks and infantry. Major J.K. Mahony, Commander of "A" Company, was the inspiration of the defence, exposing himself fearlessly wherever danger threatened, continuing to command although twice wounded. For this fine performance — of great importance in the development of the whole of the 5th Armoured Division's operation — he was awarded the Victoria Cross. It was not until after nightfall that another company of the Westminsters crossed the river, and joined Mahony's company to make the bridgehead safe.

Next morning, May 25, after artillery to support the attack had been moved into position, the Irish Regiment, which had come up during the night, supported by the B.C. Dragoons from the east bank, crossed the river. Together with the Westminsters it advanced to the lateral road about a kilometre west of the river. The remainder of the 11th Brigade crossed during the afternoon, and extended the advance, gaining positions for a further advance on the following day.

The 5th Division had gained a big success on their first day of battle. Their advance had by no means been a walkover or merely the following of a retreating enemy — as our tank and infantry losses attested. The Germans had intended to hold a line three miles behind Pontecorvo with remnants of the 90th Panzer Grenadier Division (from which many prisoners were taken). Then they had defended the Melfa Line with a strong force of tanks and self-propelled anti-tank guns, including many of the deadly 88's.[9] The orders from the Fuehrer to the commander of the 51st Mountain Corps were to hold the Melfa Line for several days. But he no longer had the infantry to do so, in face of the vigorous push of the 5th Division's armour and infantry.

While the 5th Division was driving for the crossing of the Melfa, a composite force of the 1st Division was advancing along the road running north of the Liri River, from Pontecorvo to the junction of the Melfa and the Liri. This force consisted of its reconnaissance regiment (the Princess Louise Dragoon Guards, commonly known as the "Plugs"), two squadrons of the Royal Canadian Dragoons, the Corps Armoured Car Regiment, a squadron of the Three Rivers Tank Regiment, and the Carleton and York Regiment, all under the command of Lieutenant-Colonel F.D. Adams of the P.L.D.G. Enemy elements resisted their advance, and by nightfall on the 24th, Adams force was still east of the Melfa. Next morning, May 25, Carleton and York's company crossed by surprise about 1,000 yards above the river junction. Heavy shelling along the line of the river and west of it delayed the build-up. However, by the end of the day much ground had been gained and the Carletons had linked up with the 5th Division on the right.

On the right of the Canadian Corps, the 6th (British) Armoured Division began to move on May 25 towards Roccasecca Station on Highway 6. The advance had been planned for the previous afternoon, but as the enemy still held Aquino, the Eighth Army decided that the 6th Armoured Division should make an outflanking move through the Canadian Corps sector. This was delayed, first by the 5th Canadian Division's troops not having cleared the Forme d'Aquino crossing until nine p.m., and on the following morning by mines. The 6th Armoured Division advance guard reached the line of the Melfa by late afternoon May 25, but was not able to make good a crossing. On the right, the 78th Division and the 8th Indian Division were pushing forward, supported by tanks of the Calgary and Ontario Regiments.

On the Anzio front, on May 23 shortly after the assault on the Hitler Line had begun, the 6th U.S. Corps had broken out of the bridgehead, and were advancing towards Valmontone, taking the enemy completely by surprise. The U.S. 2nd Corps were advancing north of Highway 7, along the coast, while the C.E.F. attempt to move from Pico on Ceprano was held up by the Germans. By the night of May 25 the advance of the 6th U.S. Corps had placed the German troops facing the Eighth Army and the right flank of the Fifth Army in danger of being cut off and hemmed in against the central range of mountains. The German high command decided to fall back to the planned defensive line through Valmontone. Their retirement in front of the Eighth Army would be by withdrawal through successive lines on which rearguard actions would be fought. The first of these west of the Melfa was to run through Ceprano and along the west bank of the Liri River, as it turned north into the mountains. Another, running more or less at right angles to Highway 6, was east of Frosinone, and another through Ferentino, both of which towns were on the Canadian Corps' axis of advance. The task of the Canadian Corps, on the left flank of the Eighth Army, was to pursue the greatly reduced German formations on this front, to press and harry them so that they could not disengage at will, and of course to inflict as much further loss on them as possible. This pressure by the Eighth Army was a necessary part of General Alexander's plan to cut off and destroy the bulk of the German Tenth Army, which was holding the southeastern front. To follow up and increase the losses of a foe that has been defeated in a pitched battle and forced to fall back sounds rather easy to the uninitiated, but in fact it is one of the more difficult operations of war, and has become more so when the enemy being pursued possesses modern automatic weapons, tanks, self-propelled guns and motor transport — and stout-hearted men to handle them.

The performance of the Canadian Corps was not as good in the pursuit as it was in the breakthrough of the Hitler Line, and the follow-up and seizure of the Melfa River crossings.[10] In part this was due to the inherent operational difficulty of pursuit, in part to the broken and difficult country in the valley of the Sacco, which gave the Germans good opportunities for delaying tactics. Then too, it was the 5th Armoured Division's first battle. A glance at the history of the war in the desert will show that armoured divisions never achieved brilliant success in their first battles — quite often the reverse. The 5th Armoured Division did very well, I consider, in the light of these factors.

The Canadian Corps headquarters (and I as its Commander) were also fighting a first battle, and there were plenty of defects in our performance. I blame myself for not insisting on a more rapid advance, taking more risks.

Sir Brian Horrocks (one of the most brilliant corps Commanders in the British Army in World War II) comments on the pursuit after the battle of El Alamein:

> . . . It is true that the pursuit started rather slowly. This, however, is a familiar phenomenon in war. Over and over again throughout history the full fruits of victory have been lost because of a failure to pursue the defeated opponent energetically after a hard-fought battle . . . there is always a natural tendency for the victors to relax the pressure: the battle has been won, so, "What the hell?" This is the time more than any other when commanders must go round "driving" and "driving" in order to get the pursuit into gear.[11]

Certainly I didn't drive as I should have done. A commander to be fully effective in his role must be able to apply pressure when it is needed.

The first delay which could have been avoided had the Canadian Corps and the 5th Armoured Division been battle-experienced, occurred during the 26th of May. General Hoffmeister ordered the 11th Infantry Brigade, supported by the N.B. Hussars, to advance on Ceprano and make good a crossing of the Liri River. Below the town the Liri turned north from the point of its junction with the Sacco. The distance was just over four and a half miles and the opposition slight, but the Brigade only reached a position about a mile east of Ceprano by nightfall. Men of the Irish Regiment swam the river during the night and found Ceprano apparently abandoned. The slowness of the advance was due to the inexperience of the infantry— and to undue nervousness about the open flank on the right, where the 78th Division had not yet come level. Also the accompanying tanks had run out of fuel and had had to halt while more came up. On the 27th of May the brigade crossed the river, using assault boats. They were opposed mainly by artillery fire and a few machine-gun teams, elements of the 26th Panzer Division. The brigade was now in position to advance on Frosinone, to which the Germans had retired. Or it would have been, if the tanks had been able to cross the river. The bridge which was being constructed south of Ceprano during the night of May 27-8 failed, owing to excessive haste in the work, and was not fit for traffic until five-thirty p.m. on the 28th of May.

Meanwhile, on May 26 the 1st Canadian Division's "Adams' force" had pressed forward, taking advantage of the progress the French had made on the left flank, and moved a patrol across the Sacco River south of the Ceprano railway station. During the night of May 26-7, the 1st Division Engineers bridged the Sacco. These two bridges furnished a way for tanks to get across the river obstacles. I was not quick enough to appreciate the point that while no tank crossing was available on the right, there was a crossing on the left. There had been a lack of reports on the situation on the front of the 5th Armoured Division. I should have gone up to see for myself how things were when the slowdown became apparent. Vokes had reported the progress made by his troops, and suggested they should exploit. I said no, expecting the 5th Division to be able to push forward over the two-mile wide front of the corps, while I wanted the 1st Division to prepare itself for the next phase, when it would be taking over the advance.

Sometime during the afternoon of May 28, Brigadier Smith sent part of his 5th Armoured Brigade tanks to the left flank to use the crossing established by the 1st Division. However, they were not able to join up with the 11th Brigade until midnight, and consequently the advance on Frosinone did not commence until the morning of the 29th of May.

When it was seen that the 5th Armoured Division's bridge below Ceprano would not be ready until the evening of May 28, the Eighth Army gave the 13th Corps priority in its use, as their advance had been held up at a defile on Highway 6 at Arce. By use of this bridge, and passing through the Canadian Corps sector, they were able to outflank this opposition.

About this time General Leese gave me a "rocket" (army slang for a sharp admonition) because of the slowness of the Corps' advance, and I felt I deserved this. He softened its asperity, presently, by intimating he was passing on the rocket he had had from General Alexander, and saying that it was not only in the Canadian Corps that things had gone wrong. By the time I received this gingering up, the 5th Division was on the move again. The advance towards Frosinone was slow, owing to the rough terrain for tanks, with mines adding to the difficulties of crossing several tributaries of the Sacco. Most of the fighting occurred on the right flank, where tanks and self-propelled guns, protecting the retreat of the Germans along Highway 6, gave the Strathconas a tough time.

Orders had been issued on May 28 for the 1st Division to take over the front, a brigade at a time. The 2nd Brigade relieved the 11th on the night of May 30-31, and General Vokes took over command of the front on the next morning. During the day the Edmonton Regiment captured Frosinone, overcoming the resistance of a small rear-guard. By night, the brigade was established on a position west of the town, overlooking the plain over which ran Highway 6 towards Rome. I had ordered the 1st Division to continue the advance along this axis, and in the next two days it advanced a further sixteen kilometres against light opposition, occupying Ferentino and Anagni. On June 3 a patrol of the "Plugs" met up with the French corps at Colleferro, another sixteen kilometres west of Anagni. This ended the advance of the Canadian Corps, from the Liri Valley, to a point twenty-five miles east of Rome – a distance of forty-five miles in a straight line. We had been ordered to halt when Anagni was reached, and on June 4 the corps passed into Army reserve. Rome was captured that day.

During the corps' fighting, from May 15 to June 4, there had been 789 men killed, 2,463 wounded and 116 missing – 3,368 casualties in all. We had captured 1,400 prisoners; what other casualties we had inflicted on the enemy is not known, but the total, including the prisoners, would probably exceed our own. The advance was made in generally fine weather over dry ground, except for patches of mud bordering stream and river banks. The 90th Panzer Grenadier, the Ist Parachute Division and the 26th Panzer Division had been given a severe mauling, as well as detachments of other troops.

General Alexander's despatches state that, it had been decided that the honour of taking Rome was to go to the Fifth Army.[12] General Leese is said to have issued orders on May 22, stating that the Eighth Army's task was to break through the defensive line which the Germans were organizing, and which passed through Valmontone; and then to exploit northwards to Rieti and Terni. To reach the Valmontone Line, our axis was the Highway Six. I had the feeling that although this was the overall plan of the Allied C.-in-C., General Leese hoped that if his army advanced rapidly enough and broke through the Valmontone Line before General Clark's Fifth Army did, the Eighth Army might at least share in the glory of liberating Rome by having some of its troops enter it from the east and north. This was certainly not an unreasonable wish for the Commander of such a famous force as the Eighth Army, whose victorious advance from Alamein to Tunis had marked the turn in the tide of the war for Britain. Therefore, I felt – or guessed – that the disappointment of that hope may have made him feel somewhat more critical of the Canadian Corps' performance than he would otherwise have been.

# 1st Canadian Corps in reserve: June—July 1944

The Canadian Corps went into reserve on June 4, 1944. The next day, my war diary records, I had a talk with General Leese at Eighth Army Headquarters on the points on which the corps needed to improve to attain greater operational efficiency. I recall that Sir Oliver said that the 1st Canadian Division was the best infantry division in Italy, the 1st Canadian Armoured Brigade the best armoured brigade, and that he expected that the 5th Canadian Armoured Division would be in due course the best armoured division. This praise was very gratifying to Canadian self-esteem – although one must remember that the Canadian formations had been fighting for a far shorter time than had the British, Indian and New Zealand formations; hence were better off in manpower, and less subject to battle fatigue.

While lauding the Canadian infantry and armoured formations, General Leese was not at all satisfied with the performance of the 1st Canadian Corps Headquarters – nor was I, for that matter. He thought that several changes in senior appointments in the staff and engineering structure should be made, and suggested that I should get on with this task immediately. I felt that before going farther in this, or in the reorganization he was asking for, I should know how I stood personally. So I asked him whether he was satisfied to have me continue as corps commander. In reply he asked me what I felt about it myself: Could I do it? I said that I had no doubt that I could. In this interview the question of my fitness to command was left there. My impression, perhaps naive, was that General Leese was prepared to have me carry on. But in fact, he and General Alexander were not at all happy about the presence of 1st Canadian Corps Headquarters in the theatre. The views already referred to, contrasting the experience of the British commanders and corps staff with my own and that of the Canadian Corps staff, had made General Leese " . . . loath to put a British or Indian Division under a headquarters in which he did not have full confidence."[1] The higher command in Italy suggested that the 1st Canadian Corps H.Q. could be broken up, and the divisions and armoured brigade be placed under British Corps. Alternatively, they had suggested replacing me by the best British corps commander they had in the theatre. Neither of these solutions was acceptable to General Crerar, who on succeeding General McNaughton as Commander of the 1st Canadian Army had authority over all organizational and command questions affecting the Canadian troops in the European Theatre. He was very determined that the 1st Canadian Corps should be maintained as a formation, that the Canadian troops in Italy should be under its control, and that a Canadian officer should command it.[2]

One of my reasons for asking General Leese, in our interview of June 5, whether he was satisfied with me as Commander was that if he was not, and intended to ask for my replacement, then the appointments to replace those officers whose performance had not been satisfactory should be made by my eventual successor. But as I understood that General Leese was prepared to have me stay on, I had to proceed with the distasteful task of telling several senior officers that I was obliged to replace them. It happened that they had been officers in the Permanent Force, whom I had known well, and one was a friend of long standing. In another case there was such a clash of personalities between a brigadier and his divisional commander that one of them had to go, for the sake of harmonious and effective command relationship in the formation. The duty of telling a man whom you respect and like that you are obliged to put someone else in his place is a most disagreeable one. But it is the inescapable duty of a commander – duty to those over him, but more particularly to the troops under his command – to replace any subordinate officer whom he does not consider entirely competent or who, for any other reason, may not contribute effectively to the fighting power of his command.

I had been informed that one of the reasons for taking the Canadian Corps out of the line had been to allow us to digest the lessons of the operations which culminated in the breakthrough of the Hitler Line and the pursuit phase which followed. So it became my principal concern during the period in which we were in reserve to determine where the operations and logistics of the corps had not been up to par, and to correct the defects. I issued two instructions which were to be a general guide in the organizational improvements and further training which had to be carried out. These were called, "The 'Set-Piece' Attack, Lessons from the Breakthrough of the Hitler Line," dated July 6, 1944; and "Lessons of the Pursuit from the Melfa to Agnani," dated July 12, 1944. These were issued after a series of conferences with the divisional and subordinate commanders, and after reports by the formations on the operations had been received. The instructions dealt with the two different types of situation which the corps might have to face in the offensive operations which it was clear we should be undertaking after our rest period. The first type would occur when the enemy was in an organized position with fixed defences, and was intending to hold it, with no thought of retirement. The second situation would be generally the same as that after the crossing of the Melfa River, when the enemy was withdrawing from the Bernhard and Hitler positions, holding off and delaying our advance by rearguard actions.

A good deal of the memorandum, or instruction on the "Set-Piece" attack, set forth tactical procedures which had already been developed in the war in the Western Desert.

Looking back to the tactics followed in the breakthrough battle in World War I, and comparing them with those in the second, it was evident that the tanks had become the decisive arm in the assult. Therefore, as the tank breakthrough was the primary object, the action of the other arms had to be planned so as to contribute to this result. In World War I the problem had been to enable the infantry to pass through the barbed-wire entanglements, and to keep down the fire of the enemy machine guns while they did so. In World War II the problem involved getting the tanks through minefields (which were combined with barbed-wire obstacles) or across natural obstacles such as watercourses. Also, the enemy's anti-tank guns had to be neutralized or destroyed. Once a passage of adequate width had been opened the tactics were to push tanks together with infantry through the gap and behind the enemy's prepared defences. They would then turn outwards, on the principle which was called "The Expanding Torrent," to break away the enemy's defences on either side of the gap and force his retirement.

In setting out the principles on which training for another set-piece attack should be carried out, we kept in mind that the enemy had been preparing another strong defensive position, the Gothic Line, which ran roughly from Pesaro on the Adriatic through the Apennines to about fifteen miles south of Spezia, on the Tyrrhenian coast. We thought the corps might well have a battle to break through it to match our battle for the Hitler Line. We did break through the Gothic Line as will be recounted, but the enemy had not had time to build, organize and man it completely. Consequently the corps did not need to set up the rather elaborately prepared type of operation dealt with in the instruction. Nevertheless, the basic tactical principles laid down in it were applicable to all attacks against the enemy defending a position, through all variations of enemy strength and defensive organization.

The lessons brought out in the second instruction, "The Pursuit from the Melfa to Anagni," were more applicable than were those of the "Set-Piece Attack" in the offensive actions which the corps did carry out in the Adriatic Sector.

In the pursuit, success depends mainly on thorough training and high initiative of the battalion and company commanders in the infantry, and the regiment and squadron commanders in the armoured units. Because of the many obstacles — generally watercourses, which the enemy defended because they stopped or slowed down tank advance — the engineers came into the picture for bridging, improving approaches and fords, and removing mines. Covering and destructive fire by the artillery was indispensable. This meant that the elements of all four arms had to work together as a team, and understand, before they got into action, what they had to do and with whom they would be doing it. This in turn meant that for various types of actions — and there were not so many different types — there had to be a drill, or in the term we later adopted from the Americans, a "standard operating procedure."

Of course, in war no two situations are ever exactly the same; topography and the numbers, skill and morale of enemy forces are constantly varying factors. Nevertheless, commanders need to have a framework within which to organize their thinking when they plan an offensive or defensive action; they should have in mind a list of matters which must be dealt with when they issue their orders.

In order to illustrate some of the details of the tactics which the Canadian forces followed during the remainder of the 1944 campaign in Italy, I will cite a few extracts from the "Lessons of the Pursuit from the Melfa to Anagni":

> The object in the pursuit is to overtake and destroy what is left of the enemy's main forces; particularly, his guns, vehicles and administrative echelons. It is, therefore, essential that we advance faster than he can get these clear. Hence, the prime requisite in pursuit is SPEED.
>
> It is essential that all ranks understand the enemy's situation (which calls for good organization for getting intelligence *down*), and that they be determined to drive on and complete the enemy's defeat. In the pursuit, *bold* action – taking risks which in other circumstances might be reckless – is essential for success. Commanders must have it foremost in their minds to maintain contact with the enemy and maintain the pressure on him; cutting off elements of his force whenever possible. Though the advance will be by bounds, the establishment of "firm bases" will only be necessary when resistance is stiff, and counter-attack is possible.
>
> The enemy rearguards will usually take up a position on a tank obstacle. They should be dealt with by immediate and vigorous outflanking attacks by infantry, supported by concentrations of as much artillery as can be brought to bear on the enemy positions.
>
> Whenever possible, armour should lead. Its speed in advance and striking power makes this obvious. When it is held up by ground, infantry must be in position to immediately take over the advance and to push on ahead until contact with the enemy is gained, even without its anti-tank guns or mortars.
>
> When an obstacle is met, the sequence is: infantry get ahead and cover, sappers clear the obstacle, tanks and infantry support weapons follow through and catch up with the enemy.
>
> Night advances proved successful whenever they were carried out during these operations and we should make use of them. This demands a high standard of training.
>
> Counter-battery and counter mortar measures, adapted to fluid operations, must be taken against his guns and mortars; especial-

ly those that may be firing on crossings over rivers. If artillery or mortar fire is brought down on infantry or tanks in the open, the best answer is to continue to advance as rapidly as possible. Frequently, the fire is directed by forward observation officer parties on high ground, covered by only a few infantry, and these will decamp in the face of a determined advance.

Fire by the enemy's tanks and self-propelled artillery must be countered by our own tanks and self-propelled artillery, which should always take up commanding positions as close as they can to obstacles, pending a crossing being made for them.

It is essential to cross on a wide front and to put in hand the construction of enough bridges to allow for delays or failure of one or more of them. Smoke must be used to blind enemy observation and to confuse him as to places where crossings are being carried out. It is to be borne in mind that the object is to get the tanks across as early as possible, as this will usually be decisive in turning the enemy out of his position.

Infantry and armoured troops must NOT depend on the sappers to clear mines on the roads or at obstacle crossings. Unit pioneers should be used, and as many men as possible must be trained to recognize the signs of mining and clear them by use of detector and prodder. Junior officers and senior N.C.O's, in particular, must be thoroughly familar with enemy methods and de-mining. 'Mine paralysis' must be eliminated.

. . . the greatest problem of higher commanders and staffs is . . . to move the fighting echelons of formations forward to where they are to be engaged, while at the same time keeping up the flow of administrative requirements. The first essential is good planning of the route system by the staffs and engineers in conjunction, and that the routes be developed according to this plan under Corps direction; a minimum of effort being devoted to tracks and obstacle crossings required for temporary tactical phases.

. . . A strong centralized system of traffic control on the principles laid down in the official pamphlets must be established. But without proper traffic discipline on the part of drivers, and vigorous correction of all infractions by officers, no system, however well conceived, will work."

Many of the delays in the phase leading up to the assault on the Hitler Line and in the early stages of the pursuit were due to confusion and congestion on the routes through the Liri Valley. Apart from Highway 6, which did not come inside the Canadian Corps boundaries until after we had passed Ceprano, the roads leading in the direction of our advance up the Liri and Sacco Valleys were few and indifferent; and these had to be supplemented by cross-country tracks bulldozed through by our engineers. These tracks were deep in dust in dry weather, and rapidly became mudholes when it rained, which fortunately was not often. My principal staff officers and I realized that for future operations we must have a much stronger and more effective system of traffic control.

A great deal of attention was paid to this problem during the first weeks after the corps came into reserve. Brigadier J.F. Lister, the Deputy Adjutant and Quartermaster-General of the corps (the senior administrative staff officer), with the assistance of specially selected officers, took the matter in hand. Before long we had worked out an organization, set it up and began training exercises with it. Essentially it resembled the "block" system used by railways. The forward and return routes were divided into blocks of several miles in length. At the junctions between blocks, strong traffic control posts were established, each in radio communication with the posts forward and rear, and with the corps traffic control centre. At each control post there was a parking area, or "siding," into which convoys could be "shunted" if the route ahead was blocked or congested, or if it was necessary to give precedence to a convoy coming up from the rear. Convoys were not allowed to go forward from one block to the next unless traffic was moving smoothly and without congestion.

This system worked out very well, and during the Adriatic offensive the corps never suffered the delays and frustrations we had experienced in the advance in the Liri-Sacco Valleys. I was told that General Alexander remarked, when he had been forward in the corps sector on August 26, the first day of the advance across the Metauro River, that he had never seen such a tidy battle area. This was not just administrative staff gadgetry, but an essential for operational efficiency. To control the battle, the higher commanders must be able to get the fighting elements as quickly as possible to where they are to enter into action; and must provide them continuously with the ammunition, fuel and food they need to continue the advance.

Looking over my war diary for the months of June and July 1944, I find many entries of visits to formations and units which were training on various phases of the tactical and administrative operations, making use of the lessons derived from our Liri Valley experience. This period of training greatly increased the fighting effectiveness of the corps. It enabled the troops already distinguished for success on the offensive to achieve even better results, in the Adriatic phase of operations which was to follow.

The most important reorganization of the Canadian troops in the period between the Liri Valley and the Adriatic offensives was the creation of the 12th Canadian Infantry Brigade. It had a relatively short existence, as it was dissolved when the 1st Canadian Corps moved to the West European Theatre in February 1945. But during the time it was in being, it took its place worthily alongside the four more experienced infantry brigades, and fought several gallant and successful actions.

On June 3, I "drew the attention of the Canadian Military Headquarters to the need for two infantry brigades to work in succession with the division's armoured brigade, pointing out that the Eighth Army was providing additional infantry brigades for two of its armoured divisions."[3] As I recall it, Sir Oliver Leese had previously informed me of the intention to add infantry brigades to the British armoured divisions, and suggested that I should recommend that the 5th Canadian Armoured Division should be similarly strengthened. Several proposals for effecting this were considered, without very much encouragement from Canadian Military Headquarters in London or Ottawa. However, the go-ahead was finally given. The plan decided upon was to create the 12th Infantry Brigade from the Westminster Regiment, the motorized battalion already part of the 5th Division, and the Princess Louise Dragoon Guards (which was to be converted to infantry battalion establishment, while the Royal Canadian Dragoons which had previously been the Corps Armoured Corps Regiment would take its place). The third battalion would be made up mainly from the corps' Light Anti-Aircraft Regiment, as its function in defence against enemy air attack had become largely unnecessary because of the complete Allied control of the air in the Italian Theatre. After considerable debate on what the new infantry battalion of ex-gunners should be called, it was decided to name them the

Lanark and Renfrew Scottish Regiment, as the majority of the men in the anti-aircraft regiment had come from these Ottawa Valley counties.

It was a big change in role for the P.L.D.G. and the Light A.A. Regiment, and the majority of the personnel, officers and other ranks of these units did not much relish the idea. Everyone in the other arms admired the infantrymen, and acknowledged that they suffered the most casualties, had the toughest task in battle, had to put up with more hardships, and were therefore deserving of the highest honour. But no gunner, armoured corpsman or other non-infantry soldier wanted to become a foot-slogger. Nevertheless, when it became clear that the job had to be accepted, the units settled down to their training and reorganization with a will, and, as I have said, they became an effective formation in a remarkably short time. In doing so, they notably increased the fighting capacity of the 5th Division and the corps.

I was personally strongly in favour of this reorganization. While the armoured division organized with one infantry brigade and a motorized regiment may have been suitable for warfare in the Western Desert, it was indeed not well-adapted for the sort of fighting that had to be done in Italy. Perhaps this unsuitability in part had inspired General Montgomery's remark to me that there was no role for an armoured division in Italy. I was particularly interested in the matter, partly because I had written an article in the *Canadian Defence Quarterly*, before the war, proposing a basic organization for an armoured division of one armoured brigade plus two infantry brigades.[4]

While the rest of the Canadian Corps was resting, training and in part occupied with the reorganization just dealt with, the 1st Canadian Armoured Brigade continued to fight, taking a very important part in the continued advance of the Eighth Army from the latitude of Rome to Florence. It will be recalled that the brigade had been supporting the divisions of the 13th Corps in the opening stages of the offensive up the Liri Valley. Since that battle began, on only two occasions did any of its units fight along with a Canadian battalion.

In actions during the advance to Florence, with the 4th British Division and the 8th Indian Division, the 1st Canadian Armoured Brigade distinguished itself, and through co-operation with the British and Indian infantry contributed to the success in driving the enemy from the defensive positions he had taken up to the west of Lake Trasimene and west of Arezzo. British commanders paid generous tributes to the fighting qualities of the Canadian tankmen. So did the enemy.

> Kesselring's staff had been indulging in much uneasy speculation regarding the future movements of 1 Canadian Corps . . . intelligence staffs waited for the commitment of the Corps . . . to disclose the centre of gravity of the expected attack. "One of these days," remarked the Chief of Staff of the 76th Corps, "the Canadian Corps is going to attack and then our centre will explode."[5]

Later, when the capture of three members of the Three Rivers Regiment had caused the German intelligence staffs to speculate on what divisions were facing them, the following statement was made:

> My intelligence officer tells me it is the 1st Canadian Division. . . . [He says,] "Only Canadians attack like that."[6]

Perhaps the most sincere tribute to the Canadian Armoured Brigade's effectiveness (though one that I failed to appreciate) was that it was kept detached from the corps during the rest of the campaign in Italy, in spite of my repeated requests for its return. In general the reasons given for refusing this request were that operations of the 13th Corps were at a critical stage, or that something important was going to happen, and that the tactical co-operation between the Canadian tankers and the 13th Corps infantry was so good that it was essential to the success of the operations.

During the Liri Valley and the Adriatic offensives the 25th and 21st Army Tank Brigades (British) supported the 1st Canadian Division. These British tank formations fought alongside the Canadian infantry most gallantly, and general relations were very good. But notwithstanding the good will and mutual respect, the fact remains that Canadians naturally understand other Canadians better than they understand the British, and in the kind of infantry-tank actions which were the staple of the Italian campaign, co-operation would have been easier and perhaps have produced more decisive results if the Canadian tankers had been fighting with the Canadian infantry division.

Towards the end of July, orders were received to send the 1st Division forward to Florence, to come under the command of the 13th Corps. This would mean that more than half the Canadian fighting troops would be detached from the Canadian Corps Command. On the 1st of August I went to Eighth Army advanced headquarters and had a talk with General Leese about this. During this talk, which was continued on the following day, I learned that it was General Alexander's intention to break through the Gothic Line in the Apennines on a front which extended roughly from Dicomano to Pistoia. On the Eighth Army front the British 10th Corps would be attacking on the right, and the 13th Corps on the left. The Canadian Corps would have a static role in the mountainous area to the right of the 10th Corps, taking over part of the front then held by that formation. But it would not be the *Canadian Corps* that would be holding that front; it would be the headquarters of the Canadian Corps commanding an assortment of formations which at that time were not judged fit for offensive operations, but which could well carry out a defensive role. As I recall it, the 5th Canadian Armoured Division would also have been detached from the corps. General Leese explained that he felt that the role proposed for the Canadian Corps H.Q. would allow us to gain further experience in actual operations, enabling us to "shake down" following the changes which had been made after the Liri Valley fighting.

I had come to see General Leese with the intention of urging that the Canadian Corps be reunited as soon as possible for the operations which were in preparation. I explained that I was under instructions from General Crerar that the Canadian troops should be kept together, and that it was the policy of the Canadian Government that, unless in very exceptional circumstances, Canadian troops should fight united under Canadian command. The plan he had outlined appeared to me (though I did not say so) as just a variation on the proposal to break up the corps, which had been made after the Liri Valley fighting. I also pointed out that if the Canadian fighting formations should incur heavy casualties in the forthcoming offensive, as would seem likely from past experience, the Canadian Government and Parliament might raise awkward questions as to why Canadian troops were not fighting under Canadian command. The implication would be — as General Leese grasped without my having to explain — that the Canadians were being used by the British high command as a kind of superior colonial shock troops — which would certainly not be appreciated.

After hearing what I had to say, General Leese told me that I had raised very important questions, and that he did not feel competent to take decisions on them himself. He would therefore arrange for me to see General Alexander, which I did the following afternoon. According to my war diary, I "went over with him the same points that I discussed with General Leese. General Alexander agreed with the arguments I produced and said that after the present operational requirement for the separate use of 1 Canadian Division was over, he hoped that regrouping would be effected."

For the time being the plan for the 1st Canadian Corps to take over the right sector of 10 Corps front was left in force, and on August 3 I went to see Lieutenant-General R. L. McCreery to discuss arrangements for carrying out the relief. The main thing I remember about this meeting was that General McCreery told me that he had taken to reconnoitring his front by flying in one of the small artillery observation planes — the so-called Auster "whizzers" — and had found it very useful. German fighter aircraft were hardly ever seen at this stage in the campaign; therefore it was possible for a corps commander to take a look for himself along the front lines from the air, with very little risk of being shot down. I adopted this practice of General McCreery's during the Adriatic offensive, and found it helped on many occasions to get an early picture of the situation.

The following day I met General McCreery with General Leese and his Chief of Staff, Major-General George Walsh, and learned that the plan of the offensive against the Gothic Line had been changed. Again, to quote my war diary, "1st Canadian Corps, in place of taking over part of the 10th Corps front, as previously arranged, would be kept in reserve for employment later in an offensive role. The 1st Canadian Division [then near Florence] and the 21st Army Tank Brigade [British] would rejoin the Corps for this." More about the new plan of operations would be revealed at a conference to be held with the attendance of the commanders of the 5th and Polish Corps, which were to take part in the Adriatic offensive along with the Canadian Corps.

On July 31, before the moves and changes of plan reported in the previous paragraphs had taken place, the corps had had the honour of a visit from King George VI who was seeing many of the troops in the theatre while travelling incognito as "General Collingwood." According to my diary, the King said that "he was very pleased with the appearance of the troops and their good spirits." His Majesty was also in good spirits, especially during lunch. I recall that he asked why, when the men of the 1st Division had given him three cheers, there had not been a "tiger" – as he had found that to be the Canadian custom. General Chris Vokes replied that King's Regulations and Orders called for three cheers for the Monarch, but said nothing about a "tiger." His Majesty responded, "Then, we shall have to amend the regulations, and put in 'For Canadians, also a tiger.' "

At the rehearsal for the parade which had taken place on the previous day, I had found the troops looking extremely well after their two months of rest and training; drill and formation was excellent, When the parade had marched off I spoke to the officers present to say that we had under us the finest fighting men in the world. Not only their appearance, but their record showed this. It was the duty of every commander and all staff that, when the men went into battle, everything that forethought could suggest should be done, in order to ensure that the troops would have the best chances of victory. Perhaps those who heard me did not need this exhortation. In any event, the successes which were to follow in the next weeks showed that all ranks were doing their duty, and doing it exceptionally well.

# From the Metauro to Coriano

The Allied Armies in Italy, beginning their offensive on the line of the Garigliano River and the Anzio beachhead, had liberated Rome and had advanced beyond Florence to the foot of the Apennines – a great victory. But the enemy was still capable of powerful resistance; the object of destroying his forces or driving them out of Italy had not been achieved. General Alexander, although deprived of more than a quarter of the troops he had commanded at the beginning of the May drive on Rome (seven divisions had been withdrawn to take part in the Anvil invasion of Southern France), was determined to continue the offensive. His first intention was to break through the Gothic Line with a thrust directed on Bologna, on the front roughly from Dicomano to Pistoia. The enemy, whose depleted forces were soon to be reduced by drafts of two divisions to the new front in France, fully expected the Allied attacks to continue, but was not sure on what sector they would fall.

General Leese, when he examined more closely the problems of carrying out an offensive on the line of operation Florence-Bologna, became concerned by the difficulties which the Eighth Army would encounter. Its formations were not especially adapted for fighting in the mountains, and the topography of the sector in which it was to operate afforded many exceptionally strong defensive positions. The Eighth Army's strength lay in the tanks, artillery and supporting aircraft which could be employed to greater effect on the narrow coastal plain between the sea and the mountains bordering the

Adriatic coast. He had put forward these conclusions in a talk with General Alexander on August 4, just before he had informed me that the strategy would be changed.[1]

Convinced by General Leese's arguments, General Alexander changed his strategic plan, and decided to attack on two lines of operations; the main attack, by the Eighth Army, coming up the Adriatic coast, followed by an attack by the Fifth Army through the mountains when the enemy's reserves had been attracted to the Eighth Army front. As he wrote later in his despatches, "We should be able to employ what I call the strategy of the 'two-handed punch,' or more orthodoxly expressed, the strategy of attacking two points equally vital to the enemy [Ravenna and Bologna] either simultaneously or alternatively in order to split the reserves available for the defence."

One of the concerns of Field-Marshal Kesselring, the German Commander-in-Chief in Italy, was to know where the Canadians would be put into action. By this time he had a healthy respect for the offensive power of the Canadian Corps. A deception plan had been set up which was intended to cause the Germans to believe that the Canadians would be operating on the Adriatic Sector (where the Polish Corps had been fighting its way forward with considerable success. Consequently, members of Canadian units were sent over to the area in rear of the Polish Corps, making themselves very visible with their regimental and corps shoulder flashes and "Canada" on their shoulder straps. This was soon observed by spies and reported to the German intelligence staffs. Just as this information was soaking in, General Alexander's plan was changed, and it then became desirable to get the Germans to think that the Canadians were *not* going over to the Adriatic side. It was hoped that such a counter-indication might be given by the presence of the 1st Canadian Division in the Florence area. There was no attempt made to hide this, but somehow or other the German intelligence didn't learn of it. For some time they were in doubt where the Canadians really were, and from where the main thrust was coming. However, when the large-scale movements of troops from the Florence area and about Foligno to the Adriatic Sector got under way,[2] they were soon convinced that a strong offensive in that area was to be expected. Nevertheless, some degree of surprise was achieved. The Germans were certainly not ready to resist the force the Eighth Army was able to assemble when it attacked on the 26th of August.

As soon as I had learned that the Canadian Corps would be called on to attack on the Adriatic side, I began to work on an outline plan for our part in the offensive. My diary shows that from the 5th to the 8th of August I spent most of my time at corps headquarters thus occupied. During this period Lieutenant-General C. F. Keightley, who had recently assumed command of the 5th Corps, came to see me. He was a very fine officer who had distinguished himself in command of the 78th Division in the operations in the Liri Valley and subsequently. We discussed the forthcoming operations, especially boundaries, rates of advance, intermediate objectives – all the points which had to be decided on to ensure the most effective co-ordination of the operations of our adjoining corps. During all the operations up to the Rimini Line, General Keightley and I had frequent meetings. We always found that we were able to agree very readily – a most happy circumstance.[3]

The Canadian Corps was to attack up a corridor or defile, about twelve miles wide, between the sea and the foothills of the Apennine mountains. Up to this time, the Polish Corps had been operating over the whole of this front, and was to continue so up to the Metauro River,[4] on which line the Canadian and 5th Corps would pass through while the Polish Corps would continue forward on a reduced front between the Canadian Corps sector and the sea. The width of the Canadian Corps front, centred on Montemaggiore, would be about four miles. On our left would be the 5th Corps, as mentioned, with the 46th as its right-hand division.

At one point Keightley and I doubted whether the Polish Corps would succeed in pushing the enemy back to the Metauro River, and thought we might have to fight our way forward to this line. The Poles were weak in manpower after their long offensive up from Ortona-Pescara. Most gallant fighters, they never knew from where they could get reinforcements since Poland was a thousand miles away and occupied by the Nazis. But as General Anders, their Commander, liked to say they were the only army in the world that got their reinforcements from in front. That meant that they filled their ranks from prisoners who were Poles and had been forced into the German Army.

My diary for the next week or so shows a number of meetings with General Anders. He was a very brave soldier, an outstanding leader of his countrymen in their exile and a charming person. He has written his own memoirs, *An Army in Exile*.[5] As he spoke no English and I certainly spoke no word of Polish, we carried on our conversations in French, and as his French was not much better than mine we were able to talk without embarrassment. General Leese and his staff officers were also less than first-class linguists, and one of the amusements at the Eighth Army Commander's mess was the composition of sentences and phrases in fractured French – mostly rather improper. "Maison de frappage" is the only one I remember.

General Alexander issued his orders for the offensive on the 16th of August. His intention as stated was "to drive the enemy out of the Apennine positions and to exploit to the general line of the lower Po, inflicting the maximum losses on the enemy in the process." The attack by the Eighth Army, for which D-Day was to be the 25th of August, would be up the Adriatic corridor, aiming to break through into the Po Valley and seize Ferrara and Bologna. Prior to this, the Fifth Army would create the impression that it was preparing for an imminent attack on the axis Florence-Bologna, to distract the German attention from the Eighth Army blow. In fact, their attack would not be launched until later, when the Eighth Army had drawn away the supporting German divisions from the Fifth Army's front – sometime after the 30th of August.

The Canadian Corps completed its move to the Adriatic side and grouped itself around Iesi during the third week of August. On August 24, General Leese gave a pre-offensive pep talk to commanders and senior staff officers of his army in the Iesi Theatre. Supporting the ten divisions of the army, there would be 1,200 tanks and 1,000 guns, and strong support by the Desert Air Force, who were very experienced in tactical co-operation. The essential for success was to drive ruthlessly on, leaving pockets of resistance to be cleaned up by the troops following up. The army, General Leese said, was now larger, better trained and more experienced, and he was convinced it would gain a decisive victory in what might be the last great battle it would have to fight in its triumphant course from El Alamein.

I had issued a preliminary operation instruction on the 12th of

August. Assuming that the Poles would reach the Metauro River as foreseen, the first phase of the Canadian Corps operations, as I saw it during those days of planning, would be getting across the river and establishing bridgeheads on the north side. Since the corps had come into reserve on June 4, the troops had been doing more training on river crossings than on any other type of operations. I was therefore confident that the 1st Division could accomplish this task rapidly and without heavy loss.

The second phase of the operations would be the advance through some twelve miles of broken hilly country to reach the Foglia River, behind which lay the defences of the Gothic Line. The ridge in front of Mombaroccio was about halfway between the two rivers, and was the highest ground to be traversed. It rose approximately 1,200 feet above the level of the river valleys. We expected to be opposed at first only by the weary troops of the German 71st Division, although it was known that the 1st Parachute Division was moving into the zone. The Parachute Division were familiar opponents of the 1st Canadian Division, which had met them at Ortona and at the Hitler Line. It was made up of the *élite* manpower which parachute troops usually attracted in all armies. It came to be a legend in the Italian Theatre, and was even described by some enthusiastic Allied journalists as the best fighting division in any army — Allied or enemy. This became rather a sore point with General Chris Vokes, who used to point out, not without some heat, that whenever his 1st Canadians had met the parachutists the latter had had the worst of it.

The climax of the battle, as conceived before it commenced, would be the assault on the Gothic Line. This was a line of defences which the Germans had begun to construct in the autumn of 1943, largely with Italian forced labour. It ran from about Pesaro on the Adriatic coast to Spezia on the Tyrrhenian Sea. The construction of its defences had gone on at a varying tempo, depending on the ups and downs of the campaign and the estimates of the high German command as to how long the advance of the Allies could be delayed south of it. The defences were intended to be on the same scale and elaborated with the same German skill and thoroughness as those of the Hitler Line. The main features were to be the Panther tank turret emplacements, and the Todt shelters for infantrymen. We had discovered the effectiveness of these to our cost in the Hitler

Line battle. They would be supported by well-sited smaller machine-gun emplacements, rifle pits and dugout shelters; and would be protected by wide belts of barbed-wire entanglements, minefields and tank ditches. Air photography and reconnaissance had given us a fairly accurate picture of how far the works had progressed. We hoped that our advance would be rapid enough to reach the position before they could be completed, and before the German garrisons could be settled down in them ready for a protracted defence. If we could beat the reinforcing German formations to this line, we might "bounce" them out of it through quick thrusts by tanks and infantry. Otherwise, there would have to be a set-piece attack, with an elaborate, co-ordinated plan involving heavy artillery preparation and support.

The advance from the Metauro to the Foglia would be primarily the task of the 1st Division; the 5th Armoured Division would be put into action on the left of the 1st Division just before the Gothic Line was reached, to take part in the breakthrough. After breaking into the Gothic Line, the direction of exploitation would be through Cattolica up the coast road to Rimini. This would pinch out the Polish Corps, whose task would end with the capture of Pesaro.

I was confident in the ability of the corps to accomplish the task that had been set for it; so were the divisional commanders, Vokes and Hoffmeister, and their brigadiers. The time up to the zero hour was occupied in checking all preparations, and trying to see that nothing was left undone, nothing left unforeseen that could contribute to speedy success. There were meetings daily with either the divisional commanders, the commanders of the corps on our flanks, or the Army Command, who approved my proposed plans. In my message to the troops, issued just before D-Day, I pointed out that the enemy, while he had no effective air force, and was short of weapons, ammunition and men, would still fight bravely and skilfully until the final surrender. To compel that surrender, he must be attacked relentlessly with all our strength. Our superiority in weapons must be used ruthlessly until his resistance collapsed. The message ended:

> Let everyone of us go into this battle with the determination to press forward until the enemy is destroyed; to strike and pursue until he can fight no longer. Then, and only then, shall we have

won what we, as Canadians, have been fighting for – security, peace and honour for our country.[6]

In the late afternoon of August 24, after earlier arranging final details of the relief of the Poles on the 1st Division front with Major-General Bohusz-Szyszko,[7] I visited General Vokes and the commanders of the leading brigades, and found that their plans were complete and that they felt everything was going satisfactorily. The day of August 25 was spent partly in final consultations with Generals Anders and Keightley, and then there was nothing to do except wait for the guns to open up at zero hour – 23.59 hours, one minute before midnight. The weather had been good, the ground firm, and the infantry were not going forward to fight mud as well as Germans. Even in the Metauro River the water was low, and the attackers were able to ford it without getting wet much higher than the knees. The attack went strictly according to plan – except that the enemy was not there in the strength expected. A few prisoners of the 71st Infantry Division were captured, and it was learned that the main strength of the division had retired to a position a couple of miles south of the Arzilla River, holding the high ground Monte delle Forche – Mombaroccio – Monte della Matera. This retirement to the "Red Line" had been ordered by the German Tenth Army about a week before. On August 23, General Leese and I had considered whether the enemy might draw back from the Metauro, and he had said that he would instruct the Poles to keep close contact so as to spot such a move. But on a front thinly held by both sides it is not easy to detect a skilfully executed withdrawal by night.

On first receiving this news we feared that the Germans had retired in anticipation of the Eighth Army attack in strength. This could mean he was not surprised, and would be poised to delay our advance sufficiently to enable him to garrison and complete the defences of the Gothic Line. This conclusion was premature, however. One consolation was that the artillery concentrations had caught some of the German rear guards, and inflicted severe casualties on them.

General Vokes, on learning of the enemy withdrawal, and that the first objectives beyond the Metauro were in our hands, ordered the commanders of 1 and 2 Infantry Brigades to press forward as rapidly as they could, always with the purpose of arriving at the Gothic Line before it could be firmly occupied by the enemy.

Late in the evening of August 25, as we were waiting for zero hour, there was a ring on the telephone, and General Leese said he had a visitor at his headquarters who would like to speak to me. Over the line came the unmistakable voice of Prime Minister Churchill. He wanted to wish the Canadians luck in the resumed offensive. Suddenly he inquired: Would the assaulting infantry have a hot meal before zero? This was considered very important in World War I in order to start the attackers off in good heart. Mr. Churchill, who had commanded an infantry battalion in the trenches for a period after he had resigned as First Lord of the Admiralty, would naturally think of this. Well, I had not myself checked whether the men would have their hot stew, and all I could reply, rather weakly, was that I had every confidence the experienced commanders of the 1st Division would not have neglected to see to it.

On the 26th, when the 1st Division brigades were fighting their way up to the line of heights south of the Arzilla, Mr. Churchill went to have a look at the operation. General Alexander, who drove him up front and tried to see he got in no trouble, tells in his memoirs of how nervous he was that something might happen to the irreplaceable Prime Minister. All went well however; Mr. Churchill had a view of the action from a thousand or so yards back. He seemed to enjoy being near the battle, and took obvious pleasure in watching the performance of the tanks named after him, in which the 21st Army Tank Brigade were supporting the advance of the Canadian infantry. The visit of the Prime Minister helped to dissipate the feeling some of the troops had that the Italian campaign – the Spaghetti League – had become a side show, since France had been invaded over the Normandy beaches.

I was sorry not to have the opportunity of seeing the great man himself. After the war, when people asked me if I had met him, I used to answer that I never had, but that I had spoken to him. There would usually be a moment of puzzlement over this statement.

About ten a.m. I went up to join General Vokes in his observation post to have a look at the front. There was not much to be seen. Vokes told me of his instructions to his brigadiers to press on. Until midday the advancing infantry met little opposition, although the supporting tanks had difficulty in keeping up, owing to demolitions and mines. But then a German rearguard was encountered in position around the Convento Beato Sante, and their fire together with mortar and artillery shelling held up the advance until night. The Poles on the right of the Canadian sector and the 46th Division on our left were making good progress, their leading troops were roughly on alignment with the Canadians.

On August 27, the leading brigades of the 1st Division resumed their advance. General Vokes estimated that the very tired 71st Division would fall back to the next position suitable for rearguard action, which was the high ground running southwest to northeast through Monte-Ciccardo. Part of this line, on the right flank towards the boundary with the Poles, was held by the 1st Parachute Division, which after the battles of the early summer had been brought nearly up to strength. They soon showed that they had lost none of their skill and tenacity in defence. Demolitions and skilful rearguard tactics held up the advance, and it was not until the night of August 28-29 that the enemy finally gave ground, and retired across the Foglia.

On August 27 I had flown over the forward area, but little was to be seen of what was happening. I also saw General Vokes and his two brigadiers, J. A. Calder, commanding the 1st Brigade, and T. G. Gibson, commanding the 2nd Brigade. When I spoke to them they felt that the operations had been going pretty well according to plan, with satisfactory co-operation between tanks and infantry in difficult country. Later in the day I had received a visit from General Leese. At that time, and indeed until August 30, we still could not be sure whether we should find the Germans firmly in position in the Gothic Line or whether they would have not had enough time to bring up reinforcing formations and organize the defence properly. Hence we were uncertain whether we should have to pause to organize a set-piece attack with full artillery supporting programme. So far as the Canadian Corps was concerned, plans had been already worked out in considerable detail, including an elaborate artillery programme, which we envisioned being carried out by twelve field regiments (over 200 guns) as well as medium artillery. We still hoped, however, that we might find the Germans off-balance, and would be able to "gate-crash" the line, in General Leese's words.

We should have been much more confident if we could have read the minds of the German commanders at this point of time. Until

August 27 Field-Marshal Kesselring thought the attack in the Adriatic corridor was only a diversion, and would soon peter out. The Canadians had not until then been positively identified on the front of attack. But by August 28, they realized that the Eighth Army offensive could reach the Gothic Line almost simultaneously with the retreating German divisions, and before there was time to reinforce it with fresh formations. Their doubts were finally resolved by the acquisition (in some unexplained manner) of a copy of General Leese's pre-battle message to the troops (which gave the Allied Command's intentions almost in full). The German high command then concluded, as recorded in a telephone conversation between Von Vietinghoff, Commander of the Tenth German Army, and Herr, Commander of the 76th Panzer Corps, ". . . it is now certain that the enemy intends to carry out a big push to the plains of the Po. . . ." So orders were issued on August 28 for the 76th Panzer Corps to withdraw to the Green (Gothic) Line, which was to be held at all costs. On the previous day, orders had been issued for the 26th Panzer and 29th Panzer Grenadier Divisions to move from the central front to the Adriatic side. The tired 71st Division would be reinforced by the 98th Division, from the Ravenna-Cesena area.

On August 28 and 29 I was still discussing details of the previously developed plan for an assault on the Gothic Line with the commanders of the 1st and 5th Divisions, and with General Anders. At five p.m. on the 29th, according to my war diary, I saw General Leese and went over some of these points with him. He agreed with what I proposed to do. However, during the day patrols of the 1st Division had moved down into the valley of the Foglia, and had begun to test the defences, or more exactly, to what extent they were manned. The 5th Armoured Division came into the line, taking over the front on which the 2nd Infantry Brigade had been operating, while the 3rd Infantry Brigade relieved the 1st Infantry Brigade on the right of the 1st Division.

At ten a.m. on August 30, still thinking that probably a set-piece attack would be necessary, I was consulting with General Anders on details. But when I returned to my headquarters, it was reported that the enemy was "remarkably quiet," and later reports indicated that the Gothic Line was very lightly manned. So orders were issued to both divisions to push forward with companies, followed by battalions, to try to effect a lodgement in the line while it was still not fully occupied. General Leese by this time had concluded that it would be possible to gate-crash the defences, and instructed all three corps to drive forward vigorously with this object.

From this point on, it may be said that the battle to get through the Gothic Line and to seize the commanding high ground about two and a half miles beyond it, on which the villages of Monteluro and Tomba di Pesaro stood, was mainly a battalion and regimental commander's battle. By this I do not mean to discount the leadership given by the two divisional commanders, or the brigadiers under them, which was excellent. But the way this gate-crash battle had to be fought laid the responsibility mainly on the lieutenant-colonels, who rose to the occasion and gave notable examples of leadership.

On August 31, my diary records that I visited the 5th Armoured Division and the two brigades which were engaged, and watched the fighting on the divisional front from an observation post. I later saw General Vokes, who was planning to drive north and east from Osteria Nuova with two battalions of the 2nd Brigade.

At five p.m. I attended a conference at Army Headquarters. It was finally decided not to mount a concerted set-piece attack, but to extend the penetration already made in the enemy defences, and then to seize the high ground Monteluro-Tomba di Pesaro, after which the corps would exploit as previously planned.

At first, the battalion attacks in the afternoon of August 30, did not go so well. Two of them were caught in minefields, brought under heavy fire and the troops were unable to get forward. The enemy defences were not so sparsely manned as it had seemed from the earlier reconnaissances. In one important area, west of Montecchio, the German garrison had arrived since it had been reported as vacant. Nevertheless the Perth Regiment, on the right of the 5th Division front, achieved a brilliant success and had the honour of being the first battalion to break into the Gothic Line. They seized the high ground to the northeast of Montecchio (in ruins from the preliminary bombing, as were all the villages in the valley and beyond) and penetrated about half a mile further into the defensive positions before they had to halt for the night.

The Irish Regiment, which had been held in reserve on the left in the 11th Brigade sector, was moved round to the right, and went forward through the gap made by the Perths. After some delays they executed a skilful attack about noon on August 31 on the positions on the high ground west of Montecchio which had repulsed the earlier thrust. The Irish took over 100 prisoners and suffered relatively low casualties themselves. This reflected great credit on Lieutenant-Colonel Clark's tactical leadership.

On the 1st Division front, the Princess Patricia's, after a daunting struggle through the minefields, entered Osteria Nuova during the darkness. When daylight came on August 31 they exploited outwards, and later, supported by the 48th Royal Tank Regiment, fought up to the high ground in rear of the defences in the direction of Pozzo Alto. The battalion captured 231 prisoners during the day.

The 11th Brigade infantry with their supporting tanks had a more spectacular success on the same day. The Perth Regiment with the B. C. Dragoons attacked Point 204 which lay west of Pozzo Alto and on the spur rising to Point 253 and Tomba di Pesaro. Heavy shelling and mortaring stopped the Perths for awhile, but the B. C. Dragoons went on alone, leaving the Perths to take care of a pocket of the paratroopers. Lieutenant-Colonel F.A. Vokes led his regiment with great gallantry to the top of the hill, against heavy anti-tank fire from the west flank (which put many of his tanks out of action). The position was won at a cost of twenty-two killed and twenty-two wounded. Among those who died was Lieutenant-Colonel Vokes. In him the corps lost an exceptionally brave and aggressive tank commander, while General Vokes, Commander of the 1st Division, lost a brother for whom he had a deep affection.

The remainder of the B. C. Dragoons, some eighteen tanks, held Point 204 until nightfall, when the Perths came up supported by the tanks of Lord Strathcona's Horse. Their commander, Lieutenant-Colonel McAvity fought them forward with a drill-book precision of fire and movement. During the night a counterattack by parachutists was beaten off. Lieutenant-Colonel W. W. Reid of the Perths especially distinguished himself by leading an attack which captured two German self-propelled guns, and continued to inspire the defence, although twice wounded. He won the D.S.O. for his fine leadership.

The 5th Division units were now within 1,200 yards of the ridge Monte Luro – Tomba di Pesaro. These peaks dominated the valley and we had seen them as the key to the whole defence ever since we had arrived on the opposite side of the Foglia Valley and viewed the Gothic Line. If we could seize these commanding positions quickly, we could then exploit by driving down towards Cattolica, on Highway 16 close to the sea, and on San Giovanni, towards the Conca River. On the right of the Canadian Corps, the Poles were still being held up by the paratroopers in Pesaro, while on our left the 46th Division of the 5th Corps had also broken into the Gothic Line defences and had captured Mount Grindolfo, about a mile and a half beyond the Foglia.

In accordance with previous orders, the Edmonton Regiment supported by the 12th Royal Tank Regiment, attacked Monte Luro, while the Princess Louise Dragoon Guards, supported by the Lord Strathcona's Horse attacked Point 253. This was the highest ground on the ridge on which Tomba di Pesaro stood — or rather where it lay in ruins. In the early morning of September 1, the breach in the enemy defences on the 1st Division front had been extended by the Royal 22nd Regiment with a company of the Carleton and Yorks under command of Lieutenant-Colonel Jean Allard. They struck to the high ground to the northeast of Borgo Santa Maria. Later in the morning, the Seaforth cleared Pozzo Alto, opening the way for the attack by the Edmontons on Monte Luro.

The attack on Point 253 was the most dramatic of the day. It had been intended that it would be carried out by the Perths supported by the Lord Strathcona's Horse, but that battalion had suffered so many casualties in the last two days of fighting that General Hoffmeister and Brigadier Johnston, the commander of the 11th Brigade, decided that the Princess Louise Dragoon Guards would do it instead. It will be remembered that this unit had been a divisional reconnaissance regiment, trained to operate in armoured fighting vehicles, and had been converted to an infantry battalion only a few weeks before. In their first action they won a most important success. In spite of heavy opposition and more than 100 casualties, forty of the battalion gained the high point. They were led by Lieutenant-Colonel W. W. G. Darling, who, in the words of the citation for his well-earned D.S.O., ". . . visited each company in turn, urging his men on, and by sheer gallantry and personal example led them to the objective." I had known Bill Darling as an R.M.C. cadet when I was an instructor there — a fine football player, and one of the leaders of his class.

Point 253 was taken at about three p.m., and five hours later Monte Luro fell to the Edmonton Regiment and the 12th Royal Tanks. With the high ground captured, the way was open for the planned exploitation. General Vokes had decided that the 21st Army Tank Brigade under Brigadier Dawnay would take the main part in the drive on Cattolica, with the Royal Canadian Dragoons (now the 1st Division Reconnaissance Regiment) and two companies of the Royal 22nd Regiment under command. The 2nd Infantry Brigade would be in support. During the next thirty-six hours this force reached its objectives, and crossed the Conca River, overcoming resistance in several villages still held by the enemy. But in spite of the vigour with which Brigadier Dawnay pressed on the pursuit, we did not succeed in cutting off the retreat of the brigades of the 1st Parachute Division, as we had hoped to do. Their escape was about the only bright spot in the picture for the German Tenth Army commander.

Concurrently with the 1st Division's drive on Cattolica, the Westminster Regiment and the Lanark and Renfrew, supported by the Governor-General's Horse Guards, drove to the northwest to San Giovanni and on towards the Conca River, as ordered by General Hoffmeister. He reported that he intended to direct the 5th Armoured Brigade towards the high ground southwest of Rimini, and the 11th Infantry Brigade was to follow in motor transport. By nightfall on September 2, our advanced troops on the Conca were indeed only nine miles from Rimini, but it was to take three weeks more of hard fighting before we should reach that key objective.

When I went to Eighth Army Tactical Headquarters to report the capture of the high points and the commencement of the exploitation, I found General Alexander with General Leese. They were highly pleased, and, I thought, a little surprised at the speed of the Canadians' advance. I had taken my leave and was twenty or thirty yards away, when General Leese called me back. General Alexander then told me he was recommending me for the D.S.O. I was taken quite by surprise, and after thanking him went off on my next business. I considered the decoration as an honour for the corps whose bravery and sacrifice had won the victory. But I also took it as a sign that the generals had decided that I could handle my command and that confidence had replaced the doubts which had formerly existed.

With the Gothic Line broken, and leading Canadian troops across the Conca River, hopes were high that we should be able to advance rapidly over the remaining nine miles that separated us from Rimini and the Marecchia River. After that we should be on the Romagna plain, the eastern part of the Po Valley. From the maps, supported by air reconnaissance and photos, this looked like even, flat country, with none of the streams with commanding heights on the enemy side which had provided him with so many good defensive positions on which he had stopped the Allied advance up the length of Italy. We thought that once we had broken out onto this plain with room to manoeuvre and seemingly few obstacles, the Allied superiority in tanks, in the air and in artillery would enable us speedily to win the complete victory, to drive the German armies out of Italy or to destroy them.

Time after time the Allies in the advance up the peninsula had driven the enemy from his positions and inflicted heavy loss on him, but the cohesion of his forces never broke down. Somehow he was able to bring his depleted regiments and divisions together, hold off the Allied advance with rearguards, and then take up another position to defend fiercely. General Alexander, in his memoirs, pays the following tribute to the bravery and constancy of the German soldiers against whom we were fighting. I can only echo his views.

> I can understand the German soldier's high morale when Hitler seemed invincible, but I think it very remarkable that they fought their last battles just as toughly and bravely as when they were winning their first – although they must have realized that all was lost. The last battles in Italy were just as bitter as any we had experienced in the Western Desert, or in the earlier stages of the Italian campaign.[8]

As soon as our leading troops moved out beyond the Conca River on the morning of September 3, we were given proof again of the enemy's remarkable power of recovery. From the Palazzo Ceccarini and the village of Santa Maria di Scacciano, on the ridge which ran down from San Clemente to Riccione, their fire held up the advance of the 1st Division. The 5th Division, however, had better success, and by dusk the Westminsters and the Lord Strathconas had taken Misano and moved on up the ridge. The resistance offered by the German rearguards gave time for the 29th Panzer Grenadier Division's leading troops to install themselves on the next ridge to the north, on which the village of Coriano stands. This height dominated the lower ground, about three miles in width, between it and the sea. In the afternoon of September 3, I saw both divisional commanders, and discussed the current situation and the probable intentions of the enemy. We felt he would probably fight delaying actions up to the line Rimini-San Fortunato. We didn't expect to have to mount a strong prepared attack until that position was reached. However, on the next day the enemy resistance continued to hold up the advance elements of both divisions as they moved down the northern slopes of the Misano ridge.

One morning about this time, General Leese called me on the telephone. "How would you like to have some Greeks?" he asked. I asked what Greeks, and was told these were the Greek Mountain Brigade which had recently joined the Eighth Army after a prolonged stay in Egypt. This formation had been somewhat of a legend in the fighting which followed Mussolini's invasion of Greece in 1940, when they had won several engagements against the more numerous invading forces. But the prolonged stay in Egypt had sapped morale, and there had been a mutiny. General Leese warned me to handle them with care; not to commit them to very heavy tasks. As mountain troops they might be usefully deployed in the hills on the corps' left flank. Accordingly, at first I put them under General Hoffmeister's 5th Division.

Before they could become engaged on that flank, however, I thought of another way to employ them. The seacoast from Riccione to Rimini was almost continuously built up with houses and hotels, as it was a popular summer resort for the Italians, with fine beaches as the main attraction. The conglomeration of buildings was not unlike that along most of the south coast of England. I did not want to get the 1st Division tied up in fighting its way through built-up areas. This was always a slow and difficult task against a determined opponent, as indeed the 1st Division had found in its capture of Ortona the previous winter. I intended the advance of both the divisions to be through the open ground between Highway 16 and the hills, where their tanks could operate to advantage. The built-up areas would be outflanked, and their defenders forced to withdraw. So I put the Greek brigade under command of the 1st Division, with instructions that they should be used to face up to the enemy in the continuous towns. Without attacking in strength, they were to keep probing his resistance and infiltrating when opportunity offered. Under its brave and vigorous commander, Colonel Tsakalotos, the Greek brigade did this admirably, capping its operations by the capture of Rimini.

On September 4, the 5th Armoured Brigade, supported by the Westminsters, tried to advance along the spur on which the village of Besanigo stood. But resistance from the vicinity of the hamlet and heavy fire from the Coriano ridge to the north checked the advance after little more than half a mile. On the corps' right, the 1st Division had to fight most of the day to win the Palazzo Ceccarini and Santa Maria. The following day, September 5, also saw little progress, except that the Cape Breton Highlanders and the Irish Regiment captured Besanigo by a flanking attack. It became apparent that it would be difficult for the corps to resume its advance until the Coriano village and ridge were cleared. The village lay within the 5th Corps boundary, and General Keightley directed the 1st Armoured Division (British) against it. This division had only recently moved to the theatre from North Africa, and had not been in action since the spring of 1943. This rustiness showed up in its first offensive operations, which failed to make much headway towards Coriano. To add to the Eighth Army's difficulties, the enemy had greatly increased the weight of his artillery in the Adriatic front, and the first rains serious enough to affect operations fell during the next few days. In the circumstances, General Leese decided to halt the advance briefly, and reorganize prior to resuming the offensive.

I saw General Leese about nine-thirty a.m. on the morning of the 6th of September. He informed me that he would regroup the army for the next phase of the operations, and that the 4th Division (British) together with the 25th Army Tank Brigade (less one regiment) would be placed under my command. It had been intimated some days before that the New Zealand Division would probably come under Canadian Corps command at a later stage. I was impressed with the additional responsibility with which he proposed to entrust me, recalling that after the Liri Valley offensive one of the reasons for withdrawing the corps from the pursuit was his doubts as to our capacity to handle divisions other than the Canadians in open country operations. I felt that our success during the past twelve days had given him confidence in our competence. I was also glad that with the additional divisions it would be possible to withdraw the Canadian formations for rest and reorganization, without halting the offensive.

Later in the morning on the same day, I saw General Hoffmeister and Brigadier Johnston (commander of the 11th Brigade) to discuss the problem of Coriano. At an observation post, the Commander of the 1st Armoured Division joined me and we spoke about how he intended to take the village by advancing down the spur from the south. But he was having difficulties from the enemy who still held the higher ground to his left flank, as the infantry divisions of the 5th Corps had not been able to make much progress.

In the afternoon I attended a conference at Army H.Q., where General Leese announced his decision to make the changes just mentioned. General Keightley, Major-General George Walsh (the Army Chief of Staff) and Major General Ward (Commander of the 4th Division) were also there. General Leese told me I was to work out plans for the ensuing operations, and discuss them with him on the following day.

On September 7 I saw Generals Vokes and Hoffmeister, and went over tentative plans with them, asking them to let me have their views later on how they would carry out the tasks assigned to their formations. Later in the afternoon I saw General Leese again, and told him about the plans I had developed. General Keightley was there, and it was decided that before the Canadian divisions would attack across the Marano River, directed on the Rimini-San Fortunato Line, the 5th Corps would clear the high ground to our flank to the southwest. This included the capture of Coriano.

General Alexander visited the Eighth Army front on September 8, and saw me at my headquarters. He inquired about the condition of the corps, which I was able to assure him still had plenty of offensive power, although the reinforcements for the infantry were being depleted by the casualties suffered during the operations since the Metauro had been crossed. This was beginning to be a worry. General Alexander was convinced that the advance on Rimini could not be resumed until the enemy was driven off the Coriano ridge.

It will be recalled that, according to his strategic plan, when the Eighth Army had drawn off reserves from the front of the Fifth Army, that formation would then commence its drive on the Florence-Bologna axis. He had decided that the time had come, and the Fifth Army was to attack on that day, September 8, but the enemy had just withdrawn to rear positions, leaving the Fifth Army to hit only empty defences.

On September 9, following discussions on the previous day with General Hoffmeister, during which we had considered whether it would not be preferable for his division to take on the capture of Coriano, I went to see General Keightley, and he agreed to my proposal which would involve modification of the boundaries between the sectors of our respective corps. I then saw General Leese at his tactical headquarters and explained the change which Keightley and I had tentatively agreed upon. He viewed the idea favourably and later in the day confirmed his agreement to the change in objectives, and discussed details. I had earlier seen Hoffmeister and Vokes and explained the change in plans to them. We had gone over the operations I intended after the capture of Coriano: to take the corps from the Marano River to the Marecchia, followed by a breakout to the Lombard plain.

The next day a co-ordinating conference was held, and was attended by the Commanders of the 1st Canadian Division (Vokes), 5th Canadian Division (Hoffmeister), 4th Division (Ward) and New Zealand Division (Weir). Major-General Walsh (Army Chief of Staff) called later, and discussed details of the operation. He told me that he had been trying to get the 1st Canadian Armoured Brigade over to the Adriatic front, something which I hoped for very much. Unfortunately General Walsh did not succeed in this.

On this day I issued an operation instruction for the phase to follow the capture of the Coriano ridge. When this feature had been taken the 4th Division would pass through the 5th Canadian Division, and would advance in parallel with the 1st Canadian Division on its right. The plan was rather elaborate, as it was set out in eight phases, but my reasons for this detailed schedule were that our experience after the breakthrough of the Gothic Line showed that we should probably have to fight our way forward against continued and effective enemy opposition. Without careful co-ordination of the moves of the two divisions and clear orders as to the objectives they would have to take, control of the operations and momentum could be lost. Also, study of the map and observation from the air had given me a good idea of the high ground and villages on which enemy resistance would probably be centred. These had to be taken in sequence, by a co-ordinated series of blows by the two divisions, if success was to be ensured.

I did not expect that the operations would necessarily develop exactly as foreseen, but it seemed sounder to have a fairly detailed plan which could be modified if need be. I stuck my neck out to the extent of giving an off-the-record briefing to newspaper correspondents, explaining my intentions. This was on September 12. As it turned out, the operations were carried out with very little divergence from the plan set out. They did, however, take longer than I had hoped for and were carried out at the cost of very hard fighting by the troops of the two divisions. When the operation was completed, some of the correspondents remarked that it was unusual for such a hard-fought and extensive operation to go "according to plan."

On September 11 and 12 there were meetings with all divisional commanders, to go over their operational plans. There were also consultations with Generals Leese and Keightley. I remember particularly discussing Hoffmeister's plan with them. It was simple and complete. He asked for another day for preparation (September 12) — so that "everything could be tidy." I agreed to this without hesitation, for we did not want another failure or partial success before Coriano. The result was good; the taking of Coriano in my estimation was the most effective divisional operation carried out while I was commanding the corps. The importance of the objective (which blocked the corps' further advance), the way the fight developed according to plan, and the final success combined to give it a completeness which was not often attained in the Italian campaign.

As the 5th Corps and the Canadian Corps were preparing to resume the attack on the Coriano ridge and the high ground to the southeast, the Fifth Army had again made contact with the German formations on their front and had begun to penetrate the Gothic Line defences there. In his despatches General Alexander wrote: "This marked the beginning of a week of perhaps the heaviest fighting on both fronts that either Army had yet experienced."

For the several days before the attack, the Canadian Corps artillery kept up a heavy harassing and destructive fire on Coriano village, so as to wear down the defenders and cause as many casualties as possible. Brigadier E. C. ("Johnny") Plow, the Commander of the Corps Artillery, laid on this bombardment most effectively, although he did not have as many 7.2 howitzers and ammunition at his disposal as we should have liked. Any lesser calibre of shell had little effect against the solidly built Italian stone houses.[9]

The fight for Coriano opened by an attack at eleven p.m. on September 12 down the spur, by the lorried infantry (Gurkhas) of the 1st Armoured Division. By midnight they were close to their objectives, which were finally taken on the 13th of September. This success protected the left flank of the 11th Infantry Brigade attack, which was to be made with the Cape Bretons on the right of Coriano, the Perths on its left, with the Irish Regiment having the role of passing through and mopping up when the leading battalions had won their objectives. The infantry would be supported by tanks of the 5th Armoured Brigade. The attack started off from the Besanigo spur which roughly paralleled that of Coriano and had been taken by the 5th Division on the 4th and 5th of September. It was separated from it by the valley of the Besanigo stream, which though narrow was an obstacle across which the engineers had to make tank crossings.

At one a.m. on September 13 the barrages and concentrations came down, and the infantry moved off. By two-thirty a.m. they had attained their objectives on the ridge north and south of Coriano, and at the first light of day supporting tanks got across the obstacle and joined them. The enemy had tanks supporting him also, some of which were in position inside Coriano. He fought desperately to hold off the Irish who had been given the task of cleaning out the village, and it was not until the next morning that Brigadier Johnston was able to report the town finally cleared. The Irish captured sixty prisoners and a tank. However, the Germans who were retreating to the south, having been driven from their positions by the Canadian attack, were taken prisoner in large numbers (789) by the 1st Armoured Division. The 11th Infantry Brigade suffered 210 casualties.

The Desert Air Force had contributed much to the success of the attacks, particularly by hitting reserves and troops forming up for counterattacks. Throughout the series of operations on the Adriatic

Sector, very good tactical co-operation from the air was the rule whenever the weather permitted. The so-called "cab-rank" system was particularly popular with commanders. This was an arrangement under which a flight of fighters, armed with bombs, would rendezvous over the front of a formation, and would then fly in a pattern until called on to attack a target. A forward air control centre, with an air force officer in communication by radio with the flight above, and a gunner officer in touch with the commander, transmitted the latter's requests for action against whatever target needed to be dealt with. The fighters would then peel off their circle in the sky and swoop down, loosing their bombs. This rapid co-operation was a great morale-builder for the attacking infantry, and doubtless was more than depressing for the German defenders who hardly ever saw one of their own aircraft. The capacity to deliver air support in this way was another dividend of the Allied control of the air in the Italian Theatre.

The 5th Division cleared the rest of the Coriano spur to the north, by a follow-up attack by the Westminsters and the Lord Strathconas. Now the 4th (British) Division was to pass through and cross the Marano River. The enemy had been severely handled: the 29th Panzer Grenadier Division had been thrust out of Coriano with heavy losses; the 71st and 98th Infantry Divisions and the 26th Panzer Division were also in bad shape. General von Vietinghoff, Commander of the Tenth Army, told Marshal Kesselring: ". . . all day we have been racking our brains about how to help, but we have nothing left." There was indeed no fresh German division on the immediate front. Although three others were on the way the nearest was still nearly 100 miles distant, while movement in the German rear was not easy because of constant Allied air harassment.

In my war diary for September 12, I noted that the Rt. Hon. L.S. Amery, Secretary of State for India, had visited my headquarters. I remember taking him up to the high ground near Tomba di Pesaro, and showing him from that vantage point how the Gothic Line had been broken through. He was a former soldier, and I think enjoyed the interlude with the corps.

I don't find anything in my diary about a short visit I had from another political gentleman – the Rt. Hon. Harold Macmillan; yet he did come and see me. He was at that time the representative of the British Cabinet – resident Minister – in the Mediterranean.

# Rimini and the Lombard Plain

Tough as the fighting had been to break through the Gothic Line and to capture Coriano, the battle that lasted through the eight days between the 14th and the 22nd of September was to be the hardest and costliest in casualties that the Canadians fought during the whole Italian campaign. The key of the operation would be to take the San Fortunato ridge which lay behind the Ausa River, and controlled the corridor between the mountains and the Adriatic. Before it could be attacked the enemy had to be driven off the outpost positions, the ridge on which the hamlets of St.-Martino and San Lorenzo-in-Correggiano stood, and the San Patrigiano-Cerasola feature.

On the morning of September 14 the 1st Division began its advance across the Marano with the Royal Canadian Dragoons and the Greek Mountain Brigade on the right. Their task would be to contain the enemy in the built up area along the coast and to capture some lightly held "casas," or large farmhouses, with their adjunct buildings. These lay about two miles west of Riccione, south of the Marano. Co-operating with the Greeks was a squadron of New Zealand tanks and the mortars and machine guns of the Saskatchewan Light Infantry, the support battalion of the 1st Division. In their first action the Greeks did well, and captured several of the farms despite stiff casualties.

The 3rd Brigade, next in line to the west, had a difficult day. The West Novas, in spite of heavy artillery fire and resistance from some pockets of the enemy south of the Marano, succeeded towards noon in seizing a bridge that the enemy had not had time to blow, and established themselves on the left bank of the stream. In the afternoon they advanced on San Lorenzo-in-Correggiano, accompanied by British tanks. However, the 29th Panzer Grenadiers were solidly established in the village and the enemy gunners had excellent observation over the battlefield from the Fortunato ridge. The West Novas, with their supporting tanks destroyed, and under the heaviest artillery and machine-gun fire, were brought to a halt about half a mile short of their objective.

The Royal 22nd Regiment, the right hand battalion of the 3rd Brigade, after a hard struggle succeeded in crossing the Marano during the morning. In the afternoon it moved forward to the attack of San Martino, which lay north of San Lorenzo on the ridge. Repeated efforts of the battalion to advance, supported by the 12th Royal Tanks, failed in the face of the stalwart defence of the paratroops and the flanking fire from San Lorenzo on the left. After suffering nearly 100 casualties, the 22nd had to dig in, having advanced only half of the way from the river to the ridge.

The day had gone better with the 4th Division in the left sector. It had fought its way across the Ripabianca ridge, and finally had won a bridgehead over the Marano at Ospedaletto. During the night it prepared to cross the stream and attack San Patrignano on the heights on the other side. The 1st Armoured and 56th Divisions in the 5th Corps sector were gaining ground, and promised continued pressure on the enemy. This would make the 4th Division's continued advance easier. The enemy, however, was busy reinforcing his threatened line with elements of the 356th and 20th Air Force Divisions, and closing up his front so as to concentrate the defence on the most threatened points.

At eight-thirty a.m. on September 15 the West Novas began the advance on the 1st Division front, supported by a fresh squadron of the 12th Royal Tanks. It took the battalion the rest of the morning to get into San Lorenzo, and after a long day's fighting they finally cleared and held it firmly by six-thirty p.m.

At two-thirty p.m. the Royal 22nd Regiment on the right of the brigade sector drove forward, accompanied by a squadron of the 48th Royal Tanks, with strong artillery support. In the face of heavy fire from the enemy infantry and tanks, they rushed across the open ground to the foot of the ridge, climbed it, and stormed the Palazzo des Vergers, a huge warren of 700 rooms with deep cellars for shelter and a roof which commanded all the country round. Then the battalion turned to the right and attacked along the ridge towards San Martino. Part of one company together with some tanks occupied this village later in the afternoon.

One of those unfortunate setbacks which are common enough when soldiers and officers are worn out after days of battle occurred during the night of the 15th-16th of September. General Vokes had ordered the 2nd Brigade to form up behind the 3rd Brigade battalions on the San Martino-San Lorenzo ridge, for the attack on the San Fortunato feature. But there was confusion and misunderstanding between the company of the Royal 22nd Regiment holding San Martino and the company of the Seaforths which was to relieve them. As a result, the part of San Martino which the Royal 22nd had held was left ungarrisoned, and the stout fighters of the 1st Parachute Division reoccupied it. This unlucky slip-up was the principal cause of several day's delay in attacking the Fortunato ridge, the key to the hoped-for break-out into the Romagna plain. It was obviously impossible for the 2nd Brigade to attack towards Fortunato, leaving enemy-held San Martino in their rear to rake them with fire from the high ground on which the hamlet stood.

The enemy on San Fortunato were in a similar position to check the advance of the 4th Division from its right flank. On September 15, after the 28th Brigade had taken San Patrignano, their further advance was held up, both on that day and on September 16, mainly by fire directed from Cerasolo, which commanded the division's intended line of advance from the left flank.

In discussing the operation which the 4th Division had been ordered to undertake beyond the Marano, I had warned General Ward that he might well have to protect his left flank by attacking enemy positions on the higher ground. In the higher and more broken terrain which the divisions of the 5th Corps had to traverse, topographical conditions made attack more difficult and defence stronger than on the front where the Canadian Corps was operating. This factor made the task of the 5th Corps more difficult, and explained why it sometimes lagged a little behind the advance of the Canadian Corps. On the other hand, the strongest German divisions were concentrated to oppose the Canadians. The situation at Cerasolo reproduced more or less what had happened at Coriano.

On September 16 about three p.m., General Ward phoned me that he considered it would be necessary for his division to attack Cerasolo, if they were to continue their advance. I accordingly consulted General Keightley, and it was agreed that the inter-corps boundary would be adjusted to permit the 4th Division attack on Cerasolo. The Army Commander later approved this arrangement, and the 28th Brigade captured Cerasolo at first light on the 17th of September. Enemy positions on the spur that ran down from the village, roughly parallel to the Ausa, took the rest of the day to clear out, and the forward troops of the division did not reach the line of the river until midnight of the 17th-18th of September.

During September 16, the situation around San Martino remained confused. This threw the plans of the 2nd Brigade out of joint, for they were based on the assumption that this area would be cleared of the enemy and that their attack on the San Fortunato feature could start off from the line of the railway running from the Republic of San Marino to Rimini. An attempt by the Seaforth to drive the paratroopers out of San Marino broke down. The Royal 22nd, however, had better fortune, and with detachments of the 48th Royal Tanks succeeded in capturing the Belvedere spur, which ran down from the main ridge towards the Ausa. They held on to the ground against counterattacks during the night and most of the next day. Further on the right, the 1st Brigade was unable to advance more than a few hundred yards in the face of heavy shelling and mortaring from San Marino and the positions on the airfield on their right.

On September 17, little progress could be made on the front of the 1st Division. A combined effort by the 1st Brigade to continue its advance and by the Seaforth supported by four troops of tanks to capture San Martino failed to get the objective, and resulted in heavy losses to the attacking infantry and tanks. In the afternoon, I saw Generals Vokes and Ward, and the plans of both divisions for crossing the Ausa on the following day were discussed and coordinated. The 4th Division would try to get two battalions across during the night, while General Vokes felt he had to clear up the ground between his troops and the Ausa River in daylight. The 5th Corps were to attack on our left, which should help our advance. A strong artillery programme, of which a principal feature was the use of smoke to blind the enemy's observation from the high ground, was laid on. (The smoke screening was largely successful, judging from complaints about it by the German command which post-war study of their records revealed.) After seeing the divisional commanders I visited Eighth Army Tactical Headquarters and explained the plans to the Army Commander. He found them satisfactory.

When I had talked with General Vokes, before we joined General Ward, we had discussed the state of the 1st Division troops, which had suffered heavy casualties during the fighting since they had jumped off to cross the Marano. I suggested that if he had doubts about the continued offensive power of his battalions, the New Zealand Division could relieve. The plans for the further advance, once the bridgeheads over the Marecchia had been gained by the 1st Canadian and the 4th (British) divisions, were that the New Zealand Division (which was so strong in armour that it could practically rate as an armoured division) on the right and the 5th Canadian Armoured Division on the left should pass through the 1st Canadian and 4th British divisions, and take up what we had hoped would be a pursuit of the disorganized enemy. The New Zealand Division, which had recently come under Canadian Corps command, was in position to pass through the 1st Canadian Division the next day, if need be. However, General Vokes was very positive that his men were still able to carry out the tasks assigned to them. Later he spoke personally to groups of the infantry battalions which had been engaged. What he said to them is not recorded, but it must have been effective, as in the ensuing days, the division, battered as it had been, won its most dramatic success of the campaign. (If Generals Rain and Mud had not intervened, it might have opened the way to a decisive victory.)

The dominating San Fortunato ridge rose some 470 feet above the plain across which the 1st Division brigades would have to advance. The feature was some two miles long, with the hamlet of San Fortunato at the highest point, running down to the northeast to the other hamlet of Le Grazie, only a mile from the southwestern outskirts of Rimini. On the top and slopes of the ridge was a crisscross of roads and tracks. In places these were sunk many feet below the surface of the adjoining fields, which was to be of help in the 2nd Brigade's infiltration of the position. To the southwest of the main feature, the ground dipped to a saddle on which the little villages of Sant'Aquilina and Casa Brioli stood. They were in the sector allotted to the 4th Division.

The attacks of the 1st Canadian Division and the 4th Division from the 18th to the 20th of September had very powerful support from the guns of the four divisions under corps command, plus the corps medium artillery. All were directed by the Commander Royal Artillery of the 1st Division, Brigadier W.S. Ziegler. This central control, plus good observation from the air and generally effective communication between the attacking infantry and the supporting artillery, ensured great flexibility and concentration of fire. But the enemy had reinforced his artillery, and with the observation provided by the high ground he held, its fire had played a great part in checking the attacks of both divisions. What the enemy did not have, and which we were fortunate in having, was the air support by the Desert and Tactical Air Forces, as well as medium bombers from more distant bases. These hit and destroyed German tanks and infantry moving up to concentration areas for counterattacks, and either by bombing attack or by directing counter-battery fire, did much to break down the power of the enemy artillery. General von Vietinghoff, of the Tenth Army, complained: "If the reserves are kept near the front they are decimated by the preparatory fire; if held further back they are dispersed by attacks from the air."

The very important role played by the air support in the successful battles from the Metauro to the Marecchia was realized when the bad weather with rain and low cloud which was to soon come down on the Romagna plain prevented tactical air operations, and thus greatly reduced the Eighth Army's offensive power.

When the attacks were carried forward on the night of September 17-18, for the first time in the Italian Theatre the device of "artificial moonlight" was employed. This was the illumination of parts of the battlefield by searchlights from far in the rear. The searchlights had been originally intended for anti-aircraft defence at night, but since German bombing had practically ceased they were no longer required for this. The artificial moonlight technique had been used in Normandy about a month before, and, in fact had been used in World War I in Italy. A night attack enabled the assaulting troops to close with the enemy positions without coming under his observed fire, but *total* darkness made it very difficult for even well-trained troops to keep direction. So that the favourite period for attacking had been when there was a full moon. The "artificial moonlight" could reproduce this once-monthly natural condition when desired. In addition to helping the attackers find their way, it showed up the defenders' movements, and often dazzled them, making it all the more difficult to bring the attackers under fire. German commanders reported that this newly introduced technique had a most depressing effect on their men.

During the night of September 17-18 the 4th Division succeeded in crossing the Ausa, and captured the hamlets of Casa Brioli and Sant' Antimo, about 1,000 yards short of the crest. Neither the 1st Canadian Division on their right, nor the 1st Armoured Division on their left had been able to advance. There was also strong opposition from the enemy directly ahead of them, so General Ward's troops were unable to get farther forward this day.

General Vokes' plan was that the 1st Brigade would continue to press forward east of San Martino to keep the enemy occupied on that front, while the 2nd and 3rd Brigades attacked the San Fortunato ridge, with the railway and Rimini-San Marino highway as first objective. But the attack, starting off before dawn on September 18, broke down through the continued resistance of the paratroopers in San Martino and the heavy fire from the San Fortunato side. Companies of the Princess Patricia's and the Carleton and Yorks reached the first objective, greatly reduced in strength, and with most of their supporting tanks knocked out. The enemy's defence had been successful that day.

I saw Generals Vokes and Ward after the check to the operations became clear, and a revised plan was made. The 3rd Canadian Infantry Brigade, reinforced by the Hastings and Prince Edward Regiment, would attack San Fortunato, while the 4th Division would push ahead from their bridgehead and take the enemy positions on the top of the ridge.

The 19th of September was a day of hard fighting, with some advances. On the 4th Division front, the 10th Brigade succeeded in capturing the village of Sant' Aquilina by noon, taking many prisoners, while on the 5th Corps front the 1st Armoured Division was waging a fluctuating struggle for Monte dell' Arboreta. This pressure on the left helped to loosen the German hold on the main feature of San Fortunato.

The 3rd Canadian Infantry Brigade won its bridgehead over the Ausa, during the night of September 18-19, and before daylight the Hastings and Prince Edward Regiment and the West Novas began to fight their way up the heights. After a day of trying to advance in the face of heavy small-arms and artillery fire from an enemy in prepared positions on the crest, supported by tanks and self-propelled guns, they had to fall back on their first objective, Highway 72. The H.P.E.R. on the right fared a little better, in reaching a road parallel to the highway and some hundreds of yards farther up the hill.

The 76th Panzer Corps had packed no less than eight battalions onto the San Fortunato ridge, from four separate divisions, two of which, fortunately for us, were inexperienced in battle. Even taking this weakness into account the two brigades of the 1st Division had a formidable force of infantry to overcome.

Almost the only favourable event for us in the fighting on September 19 was that the paratroopers in San Martino who had been holding up the advance of the 1st Division's centre had withdrawn. They saw the 3rd Brigade advancing across the fields to the west and feared that they would be cut off. The 48th Highlanders, who had found the hamlet empty, advanced for about a mile towards Rimini during the afternoon.

General Vokes conferred with his brigade commanders, and it was decided to make another attempt on the Fortunato feature during the hours of darkness. The 3rd Brigade was ordered to press on where the Hasty P's had gained ground, while the 2nd Brigade was to infiltrate during the night over the northern part of the feature. They were to get behind the enemy's main line of resistance and thereafter seize San Lorenzo-in-Monte and Le Grazie. Later I explained these plans to General Leese, and he agreed to them.

The Royal 22nd had come up on the left of the West Novas, and attacked at last light, supported by elements of the 145th Royal Tanks. These, however, had difficulty in keeping up with the infantry during the night. The "Vandoos" under the gallant leadership of Lieutenant-Colonel Jean Allard, who was with the forward companies and platoons most of the time, seized the Villa Belvedere, a very large building on the crest, before midnight, and took numerous prisoners. By nine a.m. the next morning one of the Royal 22nd companies was pursuing the retiring enemy to the westward.

The infiltration attack of the 2nd Brigade was spectacularly successful. The Edmontons, under command of Lieutenant-Colonel H.P. Bell-Irving, were in the lead, and began moving uphill at nine p.m. They penetrated between San Fortunato and the Palazzo Paradiso, another large building farther up the hill from the Villa Belvedere. Advancing further to a crossroads about 1,000 yards to the northwest, which had been chosen as an intermediate objective, some of the units lost cohesion, but a platoon did reach the crossroads. Shortly thereafter one of the reserve companies passed through, and at four-thirty a.m. occupied San Lorenzo-in-Monte, which they found empty. On the way this company had destroyed an enemy tank and an accompanying patrol, and now took by surprise a unit of the enemy coming up to take over the village, mowing down many of them with light machine-gun fire. A subsequent German counter-attack was beaten off with the aid of artillery fire called down by the company commander, Captain Dougan, whose brave leadership won him a bar to a previously-earned Military Cross.

The Seaforth followed the route taken by the Edmontons, still in darkness, and wheeled right behind San Fortunato village. By six a.m. on September 20, they were fighting for Le Grazie and the crossroads locality about 300 yards to the south. The Hastings and Prince Edward Regiment advanced to help, and the two battalions between them captured 326 prisoners. Further south the West Novas had come up alongside the Vandoos, and had captured Palazzo Paradiso. By noon the whole of the ridge was in the hands of the gallant attackers — every battalion of whom had suffered repulse and heavy casualties in the actions against San Martino and in the plain they now looked back upon.

About one-thirty p.m., Brigadier Gibson (Commander 2nd Brigade) ordered the Princess Pats supported by a squadron of the 48th Royal Tanks, to drive ahead to the Marecchia. The enemy were retiring across the several miles of flat ground to the river; the German higher command at last had had to give the order to withdraw. One group of the 29th Panzer Grenadier Division, with several Tiger tanks, made a stand at Monticello, and held off the Patricia's advance. Heavy rain came down and made the going very difficult. However, two reserve companies of the Princess Patricia's bypassed Monticello, and reached the Marecchia by midnight. One company crossed before ten a.m. on September 21, and by noon the whole battalion was across.

With the San Fortunato ridge gone the enemy could not stay in Rimini, and withdrawal had been ordered. The 48th Highlanders on the right of the 1st Division front reached the Marecchia during the morning of September 21, and later came into contact with a German rearguard at Celle.

Meanwhile the Greek brigade had entered and occupied Rimini.

This triumph was richly deserved, for they had fought most stoutly during the preceding weeks, and their small force had suffered 314 casualties. In a despatch General Alexander wrote later, "I was very glad . . . that a new victory in Italy should be added to the fame won in the mountains of Albania."

On September 21, the 4th Division had reached the Marecchia, although its tanks could not accompany it owing to the heavy rains which had made the ground too soft to bear their tracks. On the next day two battalions crossed the river and occupied San Giustina on Highway 9 — the road leading from Rimini to Bologna. On the following morning the division was relieved by the 5th Canadian Armoured Division. The New Zealand Division took over on September 22 from the 1st Canadian Division, as had been planned, and was ready for the next phase. We hoped this would be a rapid pursuit of the defeated enemy over ground favourable to the action of armoured forces. The advance of the 5th Corps had been favoured by the capture of the San Fortunato ridge, and the 1st Armoured Division was across the Marecchia.

Meanwhile, the Fifth Army's two-pronged offensive in the Apennines, directed on Bologna and Imola, had penetrated the Gothic Line defences after fierce fighting and heavy casualties.

The Canadian Corps, including the 4th British Division and the 21st Army Tank Brigade which had served so bravely and effectively with it, could be proud of what it had accomplished since it crossed the Metauro four weeks before. The eight-phased Canadian Corps plan had been carried out substantially as foreseen. But the plan would have been nothing without the bravery, endurance and determination of the men in the fighting units who had made Rimini-San Fortunato a lustrous addition to the roll of hard-won Canadian victories.

General Leese sent me a generous message of congratulation to the Corps:

> You have won a great victory. By the bitterest fighting since El Alamein and Cassino you have beaten eleven German divisions and broken through into the Po Valley. The greater part of the German armies in Italy were massed against us and they have been terribly mauled. I congratulate and thank you all. We must now hit hard day and night and force them back over the Po.

The cost in casualties to the Eighth Army had been heavy — more than 14,000. Of these, the 1st Canadian Division had suffered 2,511, 626 of them fatal. The 5th Canadian Armoured Division had lost 1,385 officers and men, including 390 killed. But the corps had taken 2,500 prisoners of war during the period up to the 22nd of September. The 76th Panzer Corps had suffered 14,604 casualties from the beginning of the Eighth Army's offensive and the 15th of September — and must have lost many more before withdrawing across the Marecchia. The German battalions in the Tenth Army by September 25 had an average strength of only 250.

But the losses suffered by the British infantry were so heavy that all infantry battalions had to be cut to three companies instead of four, and several brigades had to be disbanded. We Canadians were feeling the manpower pinch also; reinforcements for the infantry in the theatre were drying up, in spite of the energetic measures that had been taken by Brigadier E.G. Weeks (Officer in Charge of the Canadian base, near Naples) in remustering the surplus reinforcements for other arms into the infantry. The heavy drain on reinforcements caused by the fighting in the Normandy bridgehead and the break-out had obliged Canadian Military Headquarters in England to reduce the numbers sent to Italy. All this, while disturbing at the time of the battle for the Rimini Line, did not make its full impact until some weeks later.

The stern struggle to break the Gothic Line, and then against the concentrated German divisions from the Conca to the Marecchia, had all been seen as opening the way to a decisive series of blows against the defeated and retreating enemy. This would be possible in open country with the Eighth Army's superiority in armour and air support. It was not long before we began to realize that this hope was based on a too superficial inspection of the maps and air photos, without taking into account the real character of the terrain in the Romagna, the eastern part of the Lombard plain. A great part of this area was reclaimed marsh, with a network of drainage canals banked high on the sides — and ditches, most of which became tank obstacles when it had rained. And it did rain — earlier and more heavily than could have been forecast from the meteorological records, according to General Alexander's despatches. The soil was a light clay, made slippery by even a light shower. When there was much rain it became so soft that wheeled vehicles and even tanks sank deeply into it and could not move. The only practicable routes for movement of vehicles were the few and indifferently paved roads — and of course, the enemy could readily build a strong defence against armour which was confined to the roads. General Mud had assumed a dominating role in the campaign, multiplying the power of the German defenders, decimated, but brave and dogged as ever.

Besides the watercourses and the soft, rainsoaked ground, the cultivation, mainly vineyards, made another obstacle. It prevented observation from any distance, and made control of infantry-tank attacks and their artillery support difficult. The landscape was dotted with farmhouse aggregations and clumps of orchards or orange groves, all of which made good positions for the Germans to use in the delaying and defensive tactics in which they were so adept.

Another factor, perhaps the most important, which caused the offensive to lag once the Marecchia had been crossed, was the incidence of the casualties which had been suffered in the preceding four weeks' battles. The nearly 4,000 casualties of the 1st and 5th Canadian Divisions had been almost all among the leading attacking troops, infantry and tanks. In a good analogy, General Chris Vokes used to say, "The cutting edge has been blunted." That meant that the losses had been heaviest among the leaders of sections, platoons and companies, trained and experienced on the battlefield. Reinforcements could replace these leaders physically, but could not replace their battle-craft, their knowledge of what could be done, and how it could be done in the conditions of close combat. So although the ranks of the formations could be filled with some difficulty, neither of the divisions had the same offensive power they had when they crossed the Metauro. This had a depressing effect on everybody's spirits. As the month of October dragged on, with all these dispiriting circumstances, the bright expectations that had been entertained of finishing the war in Italy in 1944 vanished, and the reality, contrasted with the hope, could not but be discouraging.

Before September 4, General Leese had given me the general axis of advance for the Corps after the Romagna plain was entered. This lay along Highway 16, the ancient Via Adriatica, through Ravenna to Ferrara. The 5th Corps would move on the axis of Highway 9, the Via Emilia. On September 17, I had issued an operation instruction after discussions with Generals Hoffmeister and Weir and the Army Commander, which gave the New Zealand Division the Via Adriatica as its axis, while the 5th Armoured Division would move ahead roughly along a line bisecting the angle between the two main highways, 16 and 9. The first two bounds were set on the lines of the Fiumicino and Savio Rivers — reflecting a hoped-for rate of advance which in fact we would be far from attaining.

The higher command began to realize that decisive victory over the German Armies in Italy would not be won that year. General Alexander reported his view to F.M. Wilson on September 26:

> The trouble is that my forces are too weak relative to the enemy to force a break-through and so close the two pincers. The advance of both Armies is too slow to achieve decisive results unless the Germans break, and there is no sign of that.[1]

He was later to write in his memoirs:

> . . . the 'rushing streams of summer' were to become the raging torrents of an 'abominable autumn'; and although by mid-October both the Fifth and the Eighth Armies were within a day or so's march of their goals—Bologna and Ravenna—it was shortly obvious that final destruction of the German armies in Italy would have to be postponed until the spring of 1945.[2]

The New Zealand Division began moving forward on September 22, but with stiffening German resistance could only get as far that day as a small canal about two miles beyond the Marecchia.

The 5th Armoured Division had considerable difficulty in moving up over the bad roads and did not pass through the 4th Division bridgehead until the morning of the 23rd. During September 23rd and 24th, the 12th Brigade became entangled in fighting for the villages of Casale, Variano and San Vito, to the east of the Uso stream. The operation was made difficult for them by the character of the terrain. However, the brigade fought doggedly and closed up on the Uso River by the evening of the 24th. The next day they crossed successfully on a front of over two miles.

The New Zealand Division had also crossed the Uso, near the Adriatic, and had encountered similar German resistance and physical obstacles. The 5th Corps, to the left of Highway 9, had captured

Santarcangelo on September 25, while the 56th Division were not far short of the Fiumicino at Savignano.

There was considerable uncertainty as to how the operations on the Eighth Army front would develop. General Leese told me on September 24 that if the enemy held on to his positions, it would be necessary to put in a co-ordinated attack, after some regrouping. This would mean that the Canadian Corps would close up to the 5th Corps, towards Highway 9 presumably. But the directive to advance on Ravenna was not cancelled. On September 26 I was informed that it was intended to move the Polish Corps into the coastal sector, which would enable the New Zealand Division to be brought into reserve.

In view of the losses of the German troops, Field-Marshal Kesselring had recommended withdrawal behind the Po River, as we had expected he might do. But Hitler thought otherwise, and told Kesselring that he must hold on to the Apennine position and northern Italy ". . . not only until late autumn, but indefinitely."[3] And the word went down to the subordinate commanders that they were "not to relinquish one foot of soil to the enemy without inflicting heavy casualties."[4] So the stubborn German infantry and tankmen did their best to carry out these orders, helped by the weather, the spates which filled the watercourses and the sodden Romagna soil.

On September 27, General Hoffmeister passed the 11th Brigade through the 12th, and it advanced during the day to reach the Fiumicino. One company of the Irish crossed and advanced some hundreds of yards farther west, but they were badly cut up on the morning of September 28 by a counterattack supported by tanks. With no anti-tank weapons, a number of the company were taken prisoner. During the day, Brigadier Johnston sent the Cape Bretons and the Perths forward to the right and left of the Irish, to try to seize a crossing, but heavy rain hampered the operations and obliged the Brigadier to cancel the night-crossing he had planned.

> By the morning of the following day mud and washed-out bridges and culverts had made most of the roads in the rear impassable. None of the fords across the Marecchia and Uso could be used, and at the former river the only bridge to survive the floods was the time-tested Ponte di Tiberio [on Highway 16, just north of Rimini]. In a few hours the Fiumicino grew from a

> shallow stream to a muddy torrent, 30 feet wide, which no patrols could pass.[5]

The New Zealand Division had also reached the line of the Fiumicino, but there both divisions were halted for the next ten days while the rains continued to pelt down, forcing the cancellation of various plans for resuming the advance.

On September 29 after visiting the 11th Brigade and the Irish Regiment in the forward area, I called at Army Tactical Headquarters and learned that General Leese was relinquishing command. He was going to become Commander-in-Chief, Allied Land Forces, South-East Asia, and was succeeded by Lieutenant-General Sir Richard L. McCreery, until then Commander of the 10th Corps. The plan for putting the Polish Corps in on the Canadian Corps' right was altered by the new Army Commander, owing largely to the extensive flooding of the coastal area.

On September 28 Colonel The Hon. J.L. Ralston, Minister of National Defence, arrived at corps headquarters. He spent the next three days seeing as many of the troops as he could; holding informal talks with them and asking if they had any problems, or if there was anything he could get for them. Most of the points brought up concerned home leave for those who had been three years or more away, return home for those three times wounded, and an improved supply of Canadian beer. (This was sent to the theatre in good quantity, but none reached the Canadians. A soldier of the Royal 22nd Regiment, I recall, rather took the Minister aback by a demand for cigars. This must have been a surprise to the man who had commanded the 85th Battalion in World War I. But our boys had seen the Americans smoking cigars in the theatre, so why shouldn't they have them too?) Colonel Ralston insisted on visiting — at some risk — the Cape Breton Highlanders on the Fiumicino. We were very glad to see him emerge safely from the armoured car we provided for him.

The Minister and I had several conversations about the prospects of the operations and the state of mind of the troops. The impending shortage of reinforcements was my principal concern. Brigadier Weeks, who had come up from the base with the Minister, informed us that if casualties continued at the same rate as during the previous weeks, the reinforcement pool would run dry by the 10th of

October. This might necessitate reducing the number of companies in the battalions, as the British had had to do, or reduce some formations to cadre strength. Neither of these were pleasing alternatives. With regard to morale, I told the Minister that I felt that the main sore point with the men in the ranks was that they knew reinforcements were running low and many of the units were under strength, yet there were many thousands of the men called up under the National Resources Mobilization Act who had refused to volunteer for service outside Canada. The general servicemen contemptuously called them "Zombies."

> . . . I advised him that in my opinion the troops would not feel that the government and the country was supporting them wholeheartedly if, while it possessed the power to send these potential reinforcements overseas by order-in-council, it allowed them to sit safely and comfortably in Canada, seeming to defy the general will.[6]

Colonel Ralston, on his return to Ottawa, urged the Cabinet, headed by the Rt. Hon. Mackenzie King, to pass the required order-in-council; but the result was that he was forced to resign — only to see, some months later, the measure he had advocated put into effect.

Before leaving the theatre the Minister sent me a handwritten personal note, wishing good luck and success to the corps and expressing his full confidence in me as Commander.

On October 8, General McCreery visited me at my headquarters, and talked over a proposed regrouping, in order to get better ground for attack when the weather conditions improved. The 1st Canadian Division would relieve the 56th Division along Highway 9, and the New Zealand Division would side-slip to the left, relieving the 5th Canadian Armoured Division. On the next day there was a conference at which orders for the regrouping were given out. Generals Vokes, Hoffmeister and Weir were present, and according to my diary:

> All divisional commanders pointed out the very bad going, and expressed the opinion that we might be drifting into the carrying on of an offensive in similar conditions to those of last

> autumn and winter, where the hard fighting and numerous casualties resulted in no great gain.
> I pointed out that the general situation required the offensive action of this corps, and that other troops in Italy and on the Western Front were attacking despite bad weather conditions and mud. I later informed General McCreery of the divisional commanders' views.

On October 10 General McCreery told me that he had decided on a changed plan of operation. Considering the bad ground over which the Canadian Corps would have to operate, its role would be restricted to protecting the right flank of the 5th Corps, which would be making the main offensive effort. We were to follow up the Germans if they withdrew, opening up Highway 9, and to be prepared, if the weather improved, to put in a secondary attack on the German positions. After giving me this information, he held a conference at which Generals Vokes, Hoffmeister and Weir were present, explaining this plan and the situation in Italy and the European Theatre generally, and how the projected operations of the Eighth Army would fit in with them.

The next day I saw the commanders of the 1st Canadian and the New Zealand Divisions at their tactical headquarters, as the reliefs ordered on October 8 had been carried out. The enemy was withdrawing along most of the corps front. During the day the Hastings and Prince Edward Regiment advancing astride Highway 9 got as far as the Scola Rigossa canal. On October 14 the 1st Brigade ejected the rearguard of the 90th Panzer Grenadier Division from the hamlet of Bulgaria. A further adjustment of sectors followed, with the 1st Division taking over more frontage from the New Zealand Division. Lieutenant-General Freyberg had resumed command of the New Zealanders, having recovered from injuries received in an aeroplane crash. The Division had been commanded until then by acting Major-General C.E. ("Steve") Weir, an excellent officer whose regular appointment was the command of the divisional artillery. General Freyberg, however, held a special position:

> He was, in effect, a law unto himself. Responsible only to his own government for his activities, he represented to Alexander and Clark a major problem in diplomacy. On paper he could be commanded, in practice he was only asked, and therefore he had almost the status of an autonomous ally.[7]

If the Commanders of the Allied Armies in Italy and of the Fifth Army had a delicate problem, it can be imagined that it might have been even more difficult for me to have as a subordinate a divisional commander of the same rank as myself. Not to mention that he was also a veteran of the victorious campaign in the Western Desert, and a legendary hero of World War I. Nevertheless, we got on very well. As I mentioned earlier, General Freyberg, in spite of his extreme personal bravery, was not a great "thruster"; he tended to take a less than optimistic view of some of the operations planned by the higher command. But during the time he was under my command (So to speak!) there was never any trouble about his carrying out the plans decided upon. He certainly remembered the difficulties the New Zealanders had had the previous winter at Cassino, and did not relish the prospect of again battling rain and mud, as well as Germans.

The next watercourse that had to be crossed was the Pisciatello; about six miles along Highway 9 towards Cesena, and about a mile short of that town. This was one of the several streams locally known by the name of Rubicon — famous because Julius Caesar crossed it with his legions against the prohibition of the Roman laws.

During the night of October 17-18 the Edmontons, under command of Lieutenant-Colonel J.R. Stone, began the crossing of the Pisciatello south of Ponte della Pietra, in pouring rain. For some time the next morning the fight to enlarge the bridgehead was inconclusive, but shortly after noon some tanks of the 12th Regiment got across the obstacle. With this support, and thanks to a brilliant feat by Corporal G.E. Kingston (who led his platoon to capture several machine guns and farm buildings), the situation was made safe, and the battalion advanced another half mile before night. Corporal Kingston received an immediate Distinguished Conduct Medal.

The New Zealand Division had seized a fairly extensive bridgehead over the Pisciatello on the 1st Division's right. The 5th Corps was advancing well on the high ground to the south of Highway 9, while the 46th was the right-hand division approaching Cesena. The German high command debated for a while whether (or rather when) to retire behind the Savio, the next river obstacle, and finally in the afternoon of October 18 Kesselring gave the order to do so.

Following the retiring Germans, the 1st Canadian and New Zealand Divisions advanced towards the Savio on October 19, while the Carleton and Yorks entered Cesena simultaneously with the 46th Division. By the evening of October 20, both divisions were lined up along the river.

When the weight of the corps had been shifted to the left, on to Highway 9 and north of it, it had been necessary to form a force to act as flank guard protecting the advance of the corps from any interference from the Germans echeloned back along Highway 16, about Cesenatico and beyond. The bulk of the 5th Armoured Division had to be withdrawn for rest and recuperation, but a composite force was made up under command of Brigadier I.H. Cumberland (normally Commander of the 5th Canadian Armoured Brigade). At various times it included the Greek Mountain Brigade, New Zealand armoured and artillery units, Canadian artillery and Engineers, and later the Governor-General's Horse Guards, the 27th Lancers and the B. C. Dragoons. The composition of this force did not allow it to carry on a strong offensive, but it kept in touch with the enemy, followed up his withdrawal to the line of the Savio, and occupied the town of Cesenatico.

> The Savio River . . . was a strong natural military barrier, at all times a tank obstacle and when in flood virtually impassable to infantry. The normal water gap was about 50 feet at Cesena, but the sudden spates caused by heavy rains falling over the extensive river basin could quickly produce a torrent threatening to overtop the great earthen dykes, whose crests were 300 feet apart. Allied bombing and German demolitions had put out of action all the high-level bridges on the west side of the town, as well as the crossing at Mensa, six miles to the north; between these points the soft banks and seasonal floodings through the years had defied all civilian attempts to span the river.[8]

On the morning of October 20, I saw General Vokes and told him to get a bridgehead over the Savio. The corps had been given no tasks beyond this except possibly to follow up with light reconnaissance forces to a limited distance. The New Zealand Division were also to cross the river if the opposition was not too heavy.

An attack by the Princess Pats the same afternoon was held up on the western bank of the canal; only a few men were able to cross and maintain their position. A new attack for the next day was planned, with two battalions supported by a much stronger artillery fire plan. The Seaforth and Edmontons moved off at eight p.m. in pouring rain, to struggle against the swift current of the Savio. Two companies of the Seaforth reached Pieve Sestina and a road junction to the south, which was to be the scene of one of the most brilliant examples of heroism of the campaign. Private "Smoky" Smith, the PIAT[9] team leader of a newly-organized Seaforth "Tank-hunting" platoon, came under fire by approaching enemy tanks, but making good use of cover got close enough to disable one Mark V tank. Ten Germans jumped off the rear of this tank and charged Smith, but he shot down four of them with his tommy gun, and the others did not stay longer. A second tank opened fire from a greater distance, and more German infantrymen tried to close with the Seaforth man, but he fought them off with his sub-machine gun, protecting his wounded comrade in the ditch until they finally withdrew. For this action he was awarded the Victoria Cross.

With this epic of an infantryman's bravery, my narrative practically comes to an end. The situation looked unpromising; 1st Division headquarters had warning of strong German counterattacks supported by tanks, and the engineers had been unable to bridge the rapidly rising Savio, or find any means of getting our tanks or anti-tank guns across to support the infantry companies. I remember a midnight telephone conversation with Vokes. He was worried, and wanted my decision whether he should try to hang on, or withdraw the unsupported infantry. I told him to hang on, as it seemed to me that the Germans really would not have the power to throw us back, and the engineers might have better luck next day. So General Vokes acted with vigour, and threw in one attack during the night of October 22-23, which did not succeed. He was preparing for a further crossing when word came from the Army Commander not to make further attempts to win bridgeheads; the operations of the 4th Division to the south of Cesena and by other divisions to the south-west promised to make the Germans retire from the line of the river without further costly assaults. This was indeed what happened. The pressure by the 5th Corps and by the Fifth Army obliged the troops facing the Canadian Corps to retire on the 24th of October. The 1st Division and the 11th Brigade of the 5th Armoured Division (which had relieved the New Zealanders) on the night of October 22-23 followed up with practically no opposition, and reached the

Ronco River on the 26th of October. Shortly after that the corps was withdrawn into reserve.

My war diary ends with the entry for October 24. I do not know whether it was on that date, or a day or so later that General McCreery called me to his headquarters and informed me that he was not satisfied with me as corps Commander, and had recommended that I be replaced. I was surprised; I had thought that after the victories of the corps in the Adriatic offensive the higher command had revised its previously unfavourable opinion of my ability. Giving me command of divisions other than Canadian had seemed to confirm this. I argued with General McCreery along these lines, but he also made a little speech, to the effect that during the offensive of the previous winter, when he commanded the 10th Corps in the operations to cross the Garigliano River, weather conditions had been very bad and he did not like the prospects at all. Nevertheless, when he had been ordered by General Clark to cross the river and seize a bridgehead, he had driven ahead ruthlessly and accomplished his purpose.[10] This homily implied that he did not believe I had the determination to drive the Canadian Corps ahead with similar ruthlessness, in the bad conditions we had been meeting and would meet in the Romagna plain.

It was the intention of the higher command to pursue a winter campaign.

> In spite of the unprofitable struggle against an enemy aided on one flank by the barriers of river and waterlogged plain, and on the other by strong mountain fortresses on which the snows of winter were already falling fighting was to continue without abatement. This policy followed General Eisenhower's decision to wage a winter campaign on the western front, in the hope of bringing about a German collapse either directly, or by the attrition it caused, in the spring. In keeping with the role of the Italian campaign to supplement the Allied offensive in Western Europe, the Allied Armies in Italy were called upon to assist the operations about to be launched in that theatre.[11]

One of the three courses proposed by General Alexander to carry out this role was "... to continue the offensive on the Italian front at full stretch to the limits set by exhaustion and material shortage."[12] This was the alternative which General Eisenhower chose, and which General Alexander tried to put into effect.

The decision to continue the offensive in Italy under the unfavourable conditions that all commanders were aware of was therefore neither General McCreery's, nor General Alexander's but that of General Eisenhower, Supreme Commander of the Allied Armies in Western Europe. Or perhaps it was a decision of the combined Chiefs of Staff, in Washington. Whether continuing the offensive during the winter on all the Allied fronts in Western Europe was the best strategy to follow in the circumstances has not, so far as I know, been analyzed by strategic specialists. The question to be asked remains: By carrying on the offensive through the winter of 1944-5 did the Allies bring about the collapse of the Nazi Reich more quickly and with less loss to themselves in manpower than if, for example, offensive operations had been suspended from mid-November to mid-March, except when the local conditions favoured limited attacks?

However, in October 1944, the decision to continue the offensive was taken, and General Alexander and those under him had no choice but to try to carry out the orders, to the extent that their resources permitted.

With this task facing the Eighth Army, it is not surprising that General McCreery would want to replace any of his subordinate commanders who he considered would not be fully effective in the hard, forbidding operations which apparently lay ahead. From what has been written throughout this book, the reader will be able to judge that I did not believe it would be sound policy to continue an all-out offensive, and to incur further heavy casualties under the conditions in the Romagna, where the prospects for decisive victory during the winter months of rain, snow and mud appeared negligible.

No one can be an impartial judge in his own case. I felt, however, that in judging fitness for command the proof of the pudding should be in the eating; that is, a commander should be judged on the results which his command achieves. As I reported to General Crerar when I left the theatre, during the period of my command the corps had taken:

> . . . all objectives assigned to it, inflicting heavy losses on the enemy, which comprised the best divisions in Italy. Though progress was not always as rapid as desirable, nevertheless, during our period of action, we went farther and faster than any other corps.

At the time I was very resentful of the way in which my service in the Italian Theatre had been terminated. Now I can look at it in a more philosophical way. It had the result, after the war was over, of setting my life on another course, which permitted me to serve the country in ways in which I may have been more useful than I could have been if I had gone on until the end of the war as commander of the 1st Canadian Corps.

In the two weeks or so before the crossing of the Savio, I had gone round to each of the brigades and spoken to as many of the officers as could be assembled. I was sensible of the feeling of letdown and tried to do something to counteract it. I felt that some of the discouragement came from the realization that the promises of victory in 1944 and a speedy return home could not be fulfilled. So I talked to my audiences about the events of the last hundred days of the war in 1918. I said that then, too, it seemed the war would never end. We would drive the Germans from one line of defence after another, but always they would reorganize and meet us on another position, fighting as fiercely as ever. But finally, when few of us expected it, came the word — an armistice and the end of fighting. I said that was the way it would be this time. No one could predict when, but given the situation into which the Nazi Reich had been driven, it was inevitable.

I have been told that this made some impression. At any rate I did not try to "kid the troops." And in seven months the war indeed ended, for the forces in Europe.

Although the action of the Canadian Corps in Italy after I had left does not properly form part of my memoirs, a brief account may be appreciated by the general reader who has probably either not heard of, or forgotten this part of the history of the Canadian forces in World War II.[13]

Shortly after reaching the line of the Ronco River, the corps was withdrawn into reserve, in the area from Cervia through Rimini and the coastal towns, and further to the south. It remained there resting and training for about a month.

During this period the higher command had been assessing how much longer the offensive could go on, within the general strategy laid down by the Supreme Command. In view of the weather and ground conditions and the fact that he did not have sufficient superiority in force over the enemy in the theatre, Field-Marshal Alexander (whose promotion to that rank had been announced late in November) had decided that the final drive to destroy the enemy armies in Italy would have to be postponed until better weather in the spring of 1945. The Allied Chiefs of Staff concurred. Nevertheless, the pressure on the enemy was to be kept up as long as possible, even during the unfavourable season.

In November, the Eighth Army was to continue its drive on the axis of Highway 9 towards Bologna, while at the same time advancing on Ravenna. The Fifth Army would have to suspend operations to rest and refit during November. Both armies would take the offensive during the first half of December, but all operations should cease by December 15, in order to leave time to prepare for the 1945 spring campaign.

Lieutenant-General Charles Foulkes took over command of the corps during its period in reserve. Major-General Harry Foster took over the 1st Canadian Division, while Major-General Chris Vokes went to the Western European front to lead the 4th Canadian Armoured Division (which had been previously under Foster).

The Canadian Corps reentered the line, and commenced the planned offensive on the 2nd of December. The corps front ran from near Highway 9 to the Adriatic – a stretch of about fifteen miles. However, the Germans had inundated the greater part of the seaward sector, and this required only watching by light forces until the operation to take Ravenna began. Ravenna was a secondary objective of the corps, while the main objective was to reach the line of the Santerno River and to seize bridgeheads across it. This required an advance of about twelve miles. The Santerno had been picked out by the higher command as a desirable start line for the decisive operations in the spring.

To carry out this task the Canadians would have to cross no less than seven watercourses, each of which constituted, in the weather conditions obtaining, a more or less serious obstacle. The engineers met the greatest difficulties in getting bridges which could take tanks or even anti-tank guns across these swollen streams or overflowing canals. The result was the ". . . all too familiar pattern of infantry unsupported by armour engaged in costly effort against strong enemy positions."[14]

On several occasions the troops that had reached the other side of the rivers or canals were counterattacked and lost prisoners. For this neither the units concerned nor the Canadian command could be blamed. It was the conditions under which they were ordered to fight.

A bright spot was the capture of Ravenna with very few casualties, by the Princess Louise Dragoon Guards and the B.C. Dragoons, operating on the right flank of the 5th Canadian Armoured Division. Ravenna, a provincial centre with a population of 30,000, was once the seat of the imperial court of the Western Roman Empire, and contained many ancient buildings. It was the most important place captured by the Canadians in Italy. Participating in the 5th Division's success had been "Porterforce," a mobile mixed formation under Brigadier Cumberland which had been watching the portion of the front towards the Adriatic, and a considerable number of Italian partisans. The partisans had been increasingly active as the Allies pushed northwards. They harassed the enemy in his rear areas, sabotaged whatever they could, and provided useful intelligence.

By the end of December, Field Marshal Alexander had decided to suspend the offensive. A combination of factors led to this decision: a German attack on the western flank of the Fifth Army which struck a weak and inexperienced division and gained such initial success that two divisions had to be diverted from the offensive to contain it, the bad conditions of weather and terrain on both the armies' fronts, and the depletion of stocks of artillery ammunition, both British and American.

The Canadians closed the chapter with a brilliant success. Between the 2nd and 6th of January, 1945, the 5th Armoured Division cleared the enemy from the area between Ravenna and the Valli di Comacchio – a large lagoon about two miles wide, extending from close to the sea about ten miles north of Ravenna for some twenty miles to the west. This further improved the position for the start of the final spring offensive. Field-Marshal Alexander's despatch covering the period says:

> The Canadian Corps began an attack . . . on 2nd January in bright weather with a hard frost. This meant that we were able, for almost the first time in the Romagna, to use tanks and air support on a large scale.

The results showed the difference which the better weather and ground conditions made.

> General Hoffmeister . . . in five days had gained all his objectives, taken 600 prisoners and killed and wounded a great many more – 300 enemy dead were counted in the area. Total Canadian casualties numbered less than 200.[15]

In his Christmas message to the troops, General Foulkes summarized what the corps had accomplished from December 2 until the Senio was reached. It had liberated 145 square miles of Italian territory, including the city of Ravenna, four other towns and thirty villages; had forced three strongly defended water lines, obliging the enemy to bring in a division from another part of the front; and had captured 1,670 enemy officers and soldiers.[16] But the Canadian casualties had been heavy: 2,556 in all, with the ratio of killed to other casualties being one to four.

In February and March of 1945 the 1st Canadian Corps and other Canadian units and establishments left Italy and joined the First Canadian Army on the western front. The Canadian Government had intimated in a note in November 1944 that the reunion was desired. The matter was discussed back and forth between governments and staffs for a while, and finally at the beginning of February the decision was taken. Within a week the Canadian formations were on the move from Italy to Holland, in what was called "Operation Goldflake." This transport operation was most efficiently carried out. For example, the 5th Division, less its tanks which had preceded it by rail and tank-landing ship, began embarking at Leghorn on February 15 and reentered the line south of Arnhem on the last day of the month. The last brigade of the 1st Division left the line on the Senio on the 27th of February. After a brief period under 2 Corps in the Reichswald Forest, the 1st Division reverted to General Foulkes' command, and together with the rest of the 1st Corps it took part in the final operation of clearing Western Holland. So the war ended for them, with victory and the gratitude of a liberated population.

When the Canadians left, and it was planned to move other formations to the western front, the task of the Allied armies left in Italy had been cut down to holding the existing front, and containing the enemy formations facing them. However, Field-Marshal Alexander and General Mark Clark (who had succeeded to command of the 15th Army Group) decided that the remaining forces could do more than carry on an active defence. They received authority from the Joint Chiefs of Staff that when the time was ripe they should put into effect the plan made in December for the destruction of the German Armies in Italy. The plan was slightly modified, and now called for the Eighth Army to drive on Ferrara, while the Fifth struck past Bologna for Ostiglia. This would constitute a pincers movement, which it was hoped would entrap the bulk of the German forces between the Apennines and the Po River.

On April 9 the Eighth Army offensive started, followed by that of the Fifth Army on April 14. The staggering of dates was to allow concentration of air force bombing in the initial phase of each prong of the general offensive. The operations succeeded better than had been hoped. The German divisions which were not trapped and destroyed between the converging arms of the Allied offensive lost most of their equipment and many of their men in trying to cross the Po River under heavy air attack. By the evening of April 25 nearly 50,000 German front-line troops were prisoners of war. The American formations drove for Lake Garda and the Brenner Pass; the British for Venice and Trieste. Negotiations for an armistice had been under way in Switzerland for some weeks, and the announcement of Hitler's death on May 1 led Field-Marshal Kesselring to agree to what was in truth a surrender.

The Italian campaign ended in complete victory. The Canadians, advancing from the beaches of Sicily to the Santerno in the Lom-

bard plain, and winning many hard-fought battles, had made a contribution to that victory more than proportionate to their numbers. Canada should not forget the valour of the men who fought there, nor the sacrifice of those who lie beneath soldiers' headstones in the Italian cemeteries.

# Notes

CHAPTER I *First days at the front*

1 Verdun is located near the German border, 150 miles almost due east of Paris.
2 St. Eloi was three miles due south of Ypres.
3 See Chapter V, *Canadian Expeditionary Force, 1914-1919,* Colonel G.W.L. Nicholson, C.D. (Ottawa: Queen's Printer, 1964).
4 *C.E.F.*, p. 153.
5 *Ibid.*, p. 154.
6 Bruce Bairnsfather's cartoons of life in the trenches with *Bystander* magazine captured the humour of the British soldier.
7 Dickebusch was about a mile west of St. Eloi.
8 These were high explosive howitzer shells of 15 cm. (5.9-inch) calibre.
9 *The Memoirs of Field-Marshal Montgomery* (London: Fontana, 1960), p. 35.
10 *Ibid.*, p. 111.

CHAPTER II *The Somme*

1 *Memoirs of an Infantry Officer,* Siegfried Sassoon (London: Faber & Faber, 1930), p. 161.
2 King's Own Yorkshire Light Infantry.
3 *The Fighting Newfoundlander,* Colonel G.W.L. Nicholson (St. John's: Government of Newfoundland, 1964), p. 259.
4 Anyone who has been through several campaigns knows that the most essential quality of a soldier is to be able to keep a stout heart in spite of privations.
5 *World Crisis,* Winston Churchill (New York: Scribners, 1931), p. 739.
6 About four miles northeast of Albert, on the road to Bapaume.
7 *The Private Papers of Douglas Haig, 1914-1919* (London: Eyre and Spotteswood, 1952).
8 *C.E.F.*, p. 189.
9 Six miles northeast of Albert.
10 Meat and vegetable ration.
11 The successive attacks on Regina Trench were part of what was called The Battle of Ancre Heights, which turned out to be the last stage of the British effort on the Somme. At the time the attacks were planned, "The British Commander-in-Chief was opposed to any relaxation of the offensive. He felt the enemy might be close enough to the breaking-point for the Allies to achieve a success that would 'afford full compensation for all that has been done to achieve it.' " (From the Commander-in-Chief's report to the Chief of the Imperial General Staff, October 7, 1916. Quoted in *C.E.F.*, p. 187.)
12 *C.E.F.*, p. 193.
13 John Swettenham, "The Battle of the Somme," *The Legionary* (September 1966).
14 *C.E.F.*, p. 200.

CHAPTER III *Vimy Ridge*

1 For a fuller account of the situation on the western front and the setting of the Battle of Arras, see *C.E.F.*, Chapters IX and X.

2 Three miles northwest of Lens.

3 *Goodbye to All That,* Robert Graves (London: Jonathan Cape, 1929).

4 From *Soldiers and Politicians,* Lieutenant-General M.A. Pope (Toronto: University of Toronto Press, 1962), p. 41: "In Canada . . . we had known some man-power troubles but these were mainly political in significance and in terms of numbers minor compared to those of the British Army. When we resorted to conscription in 1918, we were required only to call on our young unmarried men under the age of thirty. In the United Kingdom the authorities found themselves obliged to draw on their reserves of married men up to the age of forty or thereabouts. Our field divisions rarely, if ever, found themselves seriously under strength. Indeed, at all times reinforcements equal to our anticipated casualties in a forthcoming battle were already available to us in advance of railhead. On the other hand, in the British Army not a few divisions were so weak in numbers that they could not be employed offensively."

5 "Jumping-off" trenches were rather shallow and straight, without traverses, and were dug by working parties immediately before an attack. They were located in advance of the forward positions occupied by our troops. Their purpose was twofold. First, they afforded some shelter from enemy fire, and, by putting the attackers ahead of our established front line, avoided the defensive barrage which the enemy would bring down on it when he thought an attack was beginning. Second, they were laid out on a line perpendicular to the line of advance of the attack. Experience had shown that without such a means of aligning the attackers there was great danger of the units losing direction right at the outset of their attack, and driving off to one flank or another, leading to failure to reach the objectives. Jumping-off trenches were a tactical expedient in use only during the 1916-17 phase of the war.

6 The operation has been described in the television documentary on Vimy Ridge, produced by the C.B.C. in 1965, as part of the "Flanders Field" series. It is also found in Herbert Wood's book, *Vimy.*

7 It was one of those unofficial local truces which occasionally occurred on the western front—especially at Christmas—when Germans and British met in no man's land, and saw each other as human beings, not just as targets for bullet or bomb. But after these short truces the war went on as before and the Germans were still the dangerous and obdurate foe.

8 The power buzzer worked—or was supposed to work—by transmitting Morse signals through the earth to the receiving station, where they would be picked up by induction and amplified.

9 The following account of my experience on the first day of the Vimy battle was published in *The American Mercury* (August 1927).

10 This reluctance or inability to use the rifle, the infantryman's primary weapon, may seem astonishing to the civilian reader, or indeed to any military reader who was not familiar with the quality of the reinforcements who came to the front-line units to replace casualties during World War I. Lack of rifle training was due in part to the conception of the role of the infantry in attack which

was prevalent at this period of the war — perhaps from 1915 through 1917. The artillery was to conquer by fire; the infantry to occupy.

There were, of course, specialists who made excellent use of the rifle — the "snipers" who were on the establishment of every battalion. These men were selected from those who were good shots, and perhaps had some experience of hunting game. They had telescopic sights for their rifles, and would lie up in a carefully camouflaged hideout from which they would survey the enemy undetected, ready to knock out any unwary German who exposed himself. The sniper usually played his part during "normal" trench warfare, but did not really affect the events of a full-scale attack, as on the Somme, and at Vimy. Snipers, the German prisoners said after the attack, inspired more fear than artillery fire, mortars or machine guns. German snipers inspired equal fear and respect among our front-line troops.

11 *C.E.F.*, p. 259.

12 *Ibid.*, p. 244.

13 *Ibid.*, p. 267.

CHAPTER IV *Vimy to Passchendaele*

1 Arleux was about four miles east of Vimy.

2 *C.E.F.*, p. 278.

3 About three miles north of Vimy.

4 *C.E.F.*, p. 281.

5 *Ibid.*

6 Six and a half miles northeast of Ypres.

7 Perhaps the most complete description of the battle is given by Leon Wolff in his book *In Flanders Fields*, published in 1959. Mr. Wolff, an American, was not himself a witness to the battle, being too young for World War I. But many of those who were there have praised his book for its objectivity and complete presentation of the background of the offensive, how it was carried out, and the horror it became for all engaged in it.

8 That is, the controversy carried on by military critics. The British and Canadian publics have long ago given their verdict.

9 *The Fifth Army*, General Sir Hubert Gough (London: Hodden & Stoughton, 1931), p. 205.

10 This figure was arrived at by adding up the casualties given for the four successive operations in *C.E.F.*, pp. 320, 323, 325, 326. But on p. 327 it is stated, "During its stay in the north, the Canadian Corps had suffered 15, 654 battle casualties." (The 8,134 casualties were those suffered in actual days in battle.)

CHAPTER V *1918 and victory*

1 After World War II, George Pearkes retired from the Army as a Major-General, entered politics as a Conservative, became Minister of National Defence in the Diefenbaker government, and ended his distinguished career of public service as Lieutenant-Governor of British Columbia.

2 Compare *C.E.F.*, pp. 379-81.

3 See *C.E.F.*, Chapter XII.
4 *C.E.F.*, p. 407.
5 Adjutant and Quartermaster-General's Branch.
6 *C.E.F.*, pp. 434, 435.
7 See footnote to *C.E.F.*, p. 482; also *To Seize the Victory*, John Swettenham (Toronto: Ryerson Press, 1965).
8 *The Long, Long Trail*, John Brophy and Eric Partridge (London: André Deutsch, 1965), p. 26.

CHAPTER VI *Between the wars*

1 *Megamurder* (Toronto: Clarke, Irwin & Company Limited, 1966).

CHAPTER VII *1939 to 1943*

1 Although the division was a formation containing all the elements of arms and services which it would need to conduct operations independently, more frequently than not the tactical situations would be such that it would need additional support, in artillery, engineers, or certain specialized fighting and administrative units. Such support was provided by the units of "corps troops" or "army troops" which could be allotted to work with divisions as required.
2 For continuity and convenience I use the title "Canadian Army," although in 1939 it was still the "Canadian Active Militia," and when the government decided to send troops overseas the first name of the force formed for the purpose was the "Canadian Active Service Force."
3 Leaving his civil post as President of the National Research Council, he had been appointed, in the rank of Major-General, to command the 1st Canadian Division and other troops of the Canadian Active Service Force overseas.
4 This is described in Chapter IX of *Six Years of War*, Vol. I, Official History of the Canadian Army in the Second World War, Colonel C.B. Stacey (Ottawa: Queen's Printer, 1955).
5 The Chief of the General Staff was *primus inter pares* of the military members of the Militia Council. This body, presided over by the Minister of National Defence, included the C.G.S., the Adjutant-General (responsible for discipline and all personnel questions); the Quartermaster-General (responsible for feeding, quartering and transporting the troops); the Master-General of the Ordnance (responsible for provisions of weapons, ammunition and fighting equipment); and the Deputy Minister (responsible for civilian administration, including finance). The General Staff was responsible for intelligence, planning, operations and general military policy. All these high officers had the status of principal military advisers to the Minister of National Defence, and through him to the Cabinet.
6 The process is fully described in Chapters III and IV of *Six Years of War*.
7 Reproduced in part in *Six Years of War*, p. 89.
8 The British used this designation for a type which was faster and less heavily armoured than the "infantry" tank.
9 Russia and the U.S.A. were not yet in the war.

10 *Six Years of War*, pp. 88-9.
11 *Ibid.*, p. 245.
12 *The Memoirs of Field-Marshal Montgomery* (London: Fontana, 1960), p. 76.
13 *Six Years of War*, p. 253.
14 *Ibid.*, p. 542.

CHAPTER VIII *To Italy*

1 For a full account see *The Canadians in Italy, 1943-1945*, Vol. II., Official History of the Canadian Army in the Second World War, Lieutenant-Colonel G.W.L. Nicholson (Ottawa: Queen's Printer, 1956), Chapter XII.
2 *C. in I.*, p. 344.
3 *Ibid.*
4 *Six Years of War*, p. 252.
5 I had known for a long time (since I had been instructor at R.M.C. when he was a cadet in the senior class) that Guy Simonds had an excellent brain. He had proved himself a very capable commander in the Sicily campaign, and subsequently on the Italian mainland. He was later to add to his reputation by leading the 2nd Canadian Corps in the 1944-5 campaign in Northwest Europe. The high point in his war career came when he was acting in command of the 1st Canadian Army (during General Crerar's absence through illness) and directed the brilliant operations which led to the fall of Antwerp. (*The Victory Campaign*, Vol. III, Official History of the Canadian Army in the Second World War, Colonel C.P. Stacey (Ottawa: Queen's Printer, 1960), Chapters XV, XVI).
6 *C. in I.* gives a detailed account of the operations, pp. 364-72.
7 The "Gustav" Line ran from the Adriatic roughly south along the Foro River, thence through the Apennines to in front of Cassino, and behind the Rapido-Garigliano River to the Tyrrhenian Sea.
8 *C. in I.*, p. 306.
9 *Ibid.*, p. 338.
10 *Memoirs of Field-Marshal Montgomery*, p. 203.
11 *C. in I.*, p. 380. Generally less than a quarter of the fighting strength of infantry would be in the most forward defensive localities.
12 General Vokes was acting Commander of the 1st Division, while General Simonds was ill with jaundice.

CHAPTER IX *The Liri Valley and the Hitler Line*

1 The Gari River, also called the "Rapido," flowed down from the mountains to the east of Cassino and joined the Liri farther south to form the Garigliano River.
2 *C. in I.*, p. 405.
3 Field Reinforcement Battalion.
4 *C. in I.*, p. 413.
5 *Ibid.*
6 *Ibid.*, p. 414.
7 For a complete account of the day's action, see *The Canadians in Italy*, pp. 417-26.

8 The divisional reconnaissance regiment was a tank unit with an establishment different to those of other armoured regiments in the division.
9 88-millimetre, dual purpose, self-propelled, anti-aircraft and anti-tank gun.
10 *C. in I.*, p. 451.
11 *A Full Life,* Lieutenant-General Sir Brian Horrocks (London: Collins, 1960), p. 140.
12 *C. in I.*, p. 442.

CHAPTER X *1st Canadian Corps in reserve: June — July 1944*

1 *C. in I.*, p. 451.
2 In General Crerar's personal opinion the views held by Generals Alexander and Leese regarding the 1st Canadian Corps were influenced by some degree of national bias as well as by "the military inconvenience, if nothing else, of restrictions on the complete interchangeability of formations, units, etc., under a higher command. . . . In practice, this means that no Canadian, American or other national commander, unless possessing quite phenomenal qualities, is ever rated quite as high as an equivalent Britisher. It also means that, to a British Army Commander, such as Leese, the Canadian cohesiveness created by the existence of a Canadian higher formation, such as a Corps, is a distinctly troublesome factor." (*C. In I.*, p. 451).
3 *C. in I.*, p. 479.
4 *Canadian Defence Quarterly* (April and October, 1938).
5 *C. in I.*, pp. 469-70.
6 *Ibid.*

CHAPTER XI *From the Metauro to Coriano*

1 *C. in I.*, p. 491.
2 One feature of this successful strategic move was the construction of an alternate route for the tanks and other tracked vehicles of the force by the Corps Royal Canadian Engineers, under Brigadier Colin Campbell. In five days the 120-mile long route, using existing secondary roads where possible, but involving the construction of many culverts and diversions, was completed — a most creditable piece of work.
3 After the war, General Keightley held a number of important appointments in the British Army. One which was not so fortunate was that of Commander-in-Chief of the Anglo-French Expeditionary Force which landed at Port Said in November 1956. As Commander of the U.N. Emergency Force, I met him again there, and found him friendly as ever. See *Between Arab and Israeli,* Lieutenant-General E.L.M. Burns (Toronto: Clarke, Irwin & Company Limited, 1962), pp. 195, 211.
4 The Metauro was the ancient Metaurus River, where in a famous decisive battle in 207 B.C. the Carthaginian General Hasdrubal had been defeated. It was generally supposed that the site of the battle lay somewhere within our frontage of attack.
5 *An Army in Exile,* Lieutenant-General W. Anders, C.B. (London: Macmillan, 1949).

6 *C. in I.*, p. 504.

7 Major-General Bohusz-Szyszko was acting as second in command to General Anders, and was a brave, robust soldier. We were told that while his name was written as above, in speech the order was reversed, to make "Szyszko-Bohusz." The British immediately nicknamed him "Whisky-Soda," which he good-naturedly accepted, having no aversion to the beverage.

8 *The Memoirs of Field-Marshal Earl Alexander of Tunis, 1940-45*, Ed. by John Norton (London: Cassell, 1962), p. 156.

9 During all the battles in Italy, the bombardment by air force and artillery of the towns and villages which the Germans were defending was an inescapable necessity. We pitied the Italian inhabitants who cannot have wanted the war into which Mussolini had plunged them. But the Hague and Geneva conventions for the protection of civilians in war admit the legitimacy of bombarding cities and towns which are being defended. The Italians usually fled from their homes when the fighting drew near.

CHAPTER XII *Rimini and the Lombard Plain*

1 *C. in I.*, p. 570.

2 *Memoirs of Field-Marshal Alexander*, p. 137.

3 *C. in I.*, p. 571.

4 *Ibid.*

5 *Ibid.*, p. 573.

6 *Manpower in the Canadian Army, 1939-1945*, Major-General E.L.M. Burns (Toronto: Clarke, Irwin & Company Limited, 1956).

7 *Rome Fell Today*, Adleman and Walton (Boston: Little, Brown, 1969), p. 2.

8 *C. in I.*, p. 585.

9 Projector Infantry Anti-Tank.

10 "The British X Corps had gained an important bridgehead on the Allied left flank, near the coast, but had lost almost four thousand men among its three divisions before being stopped by the rugged terrain and the apparently immovable defensive position held by four German Divisions." (*Rome Fell Today*, p. 175.) It must be remembered, however, that the bridgehead, won at such cost, was the base from which the U.S. 2nd Corps and the French Expeditionary Corps began their drive in the battle for Rome.

11 *C. in I.*, p. 595.

12 *Ibid.*

13 For a full account see *C. in I.*, pp. 607-82.

14 *C. in I.*, p. 638.

15 *C. in I.*, p. 651.

16 The prisoners taken in the Comacchio operation were included in this total.

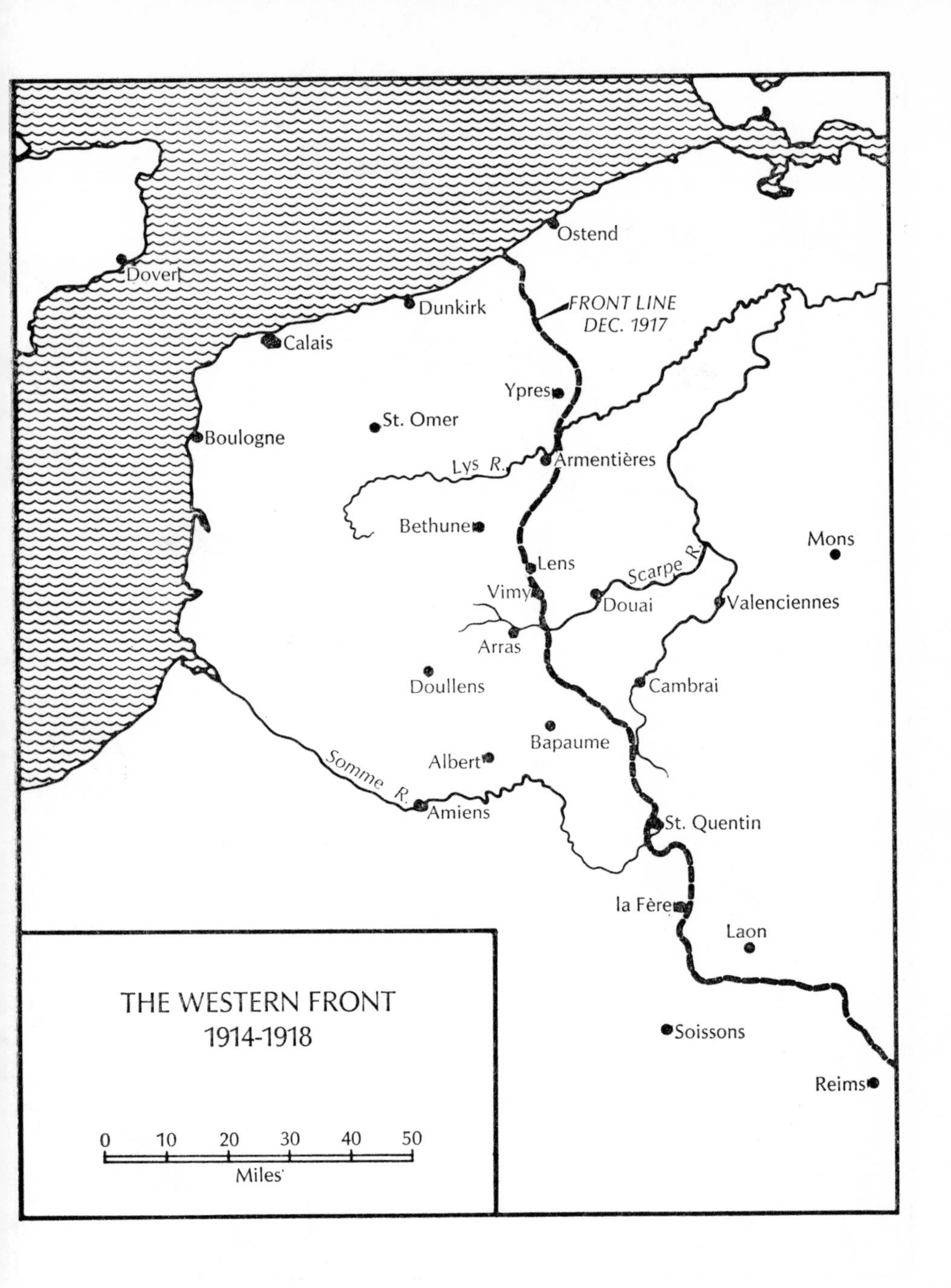
Ostend
Dover
Dunkirk
FRONT LINE
DEC. 1917
Calais
Ypres
St. Omer
Boulogne
Lys R.
Armentières
Bethune
Mons
Lens
Scarpe R.
Vimy
Douai
Valenciennes
Arras
Doullens
Cambrai
Bapaume
Albert
Somme R.
Amiens
St. Quentin
la Fère
Laon
THE WESTERN FRONT
1914-1918
Soissons
Reims
0
10
20
30
40
50
Miles

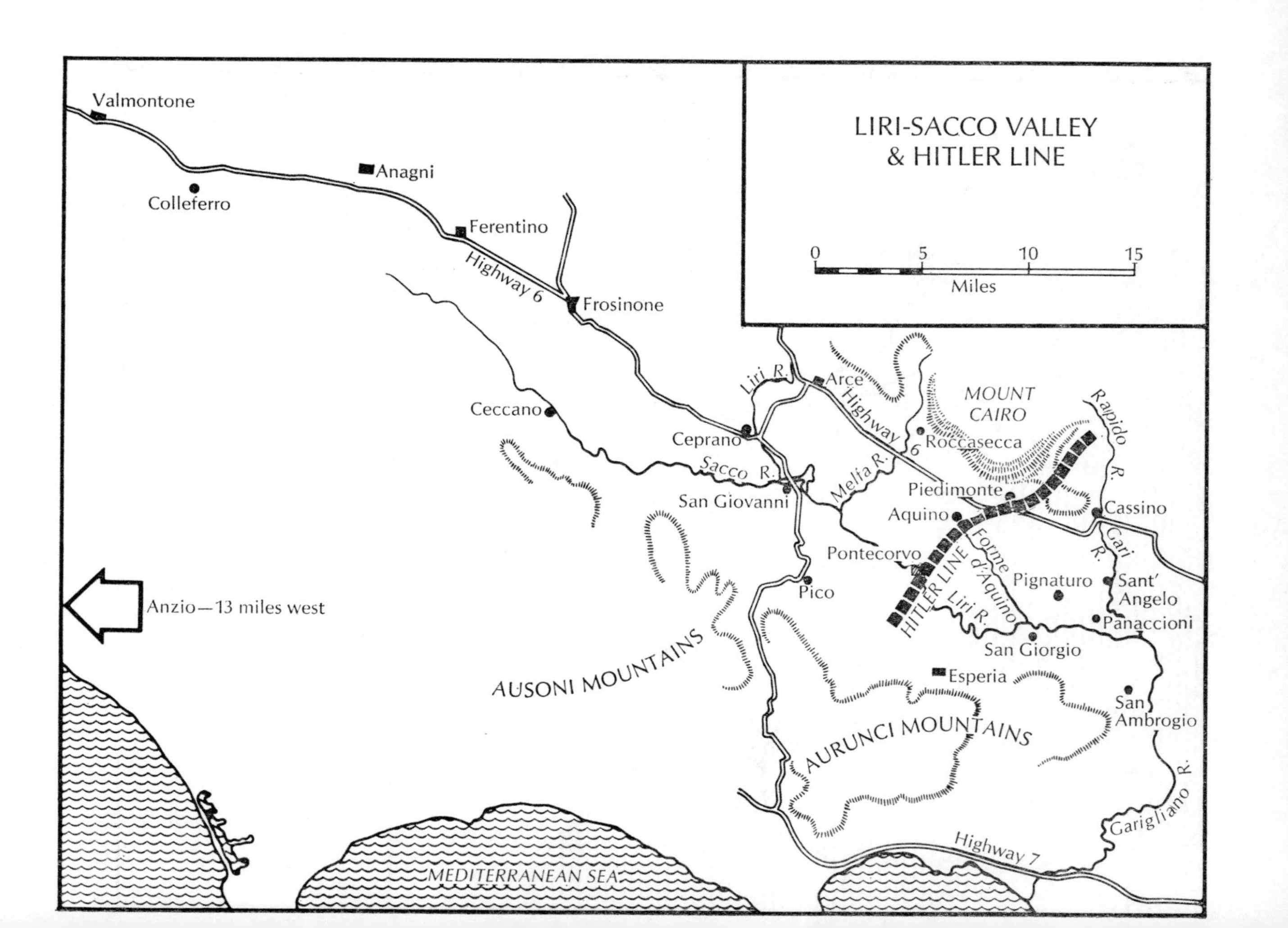

LIRI-SACCO VALLEY
& HITLER LINE
0
5
10
15
Miles
Valmontone
Anagni
Colleferro
Ferentino
Highway 6
Frosinone
Ceccano
Liri R.
Arce
Highway 6
Ceprano
Sacco R.
San Giovanni
Melfa R.
MOUNT CAIRO
Roccasecca
Rapido R.
Piedimonte
Aquino
Cassino
Gari R.
Pontecorvo
HITLER LINE
Forme d'Aquino
Liri R.
Pico
Pignaturo
Sant' Angelo
Panaccioni
San Giorgio
Esperia
Anzio—13 miles west
AUSONI MOUNTAINS
AURUNCI MOUNTAINS
San Ambrogio
Garigliano R.
Highway 7
MEDITERRANEAN SEA

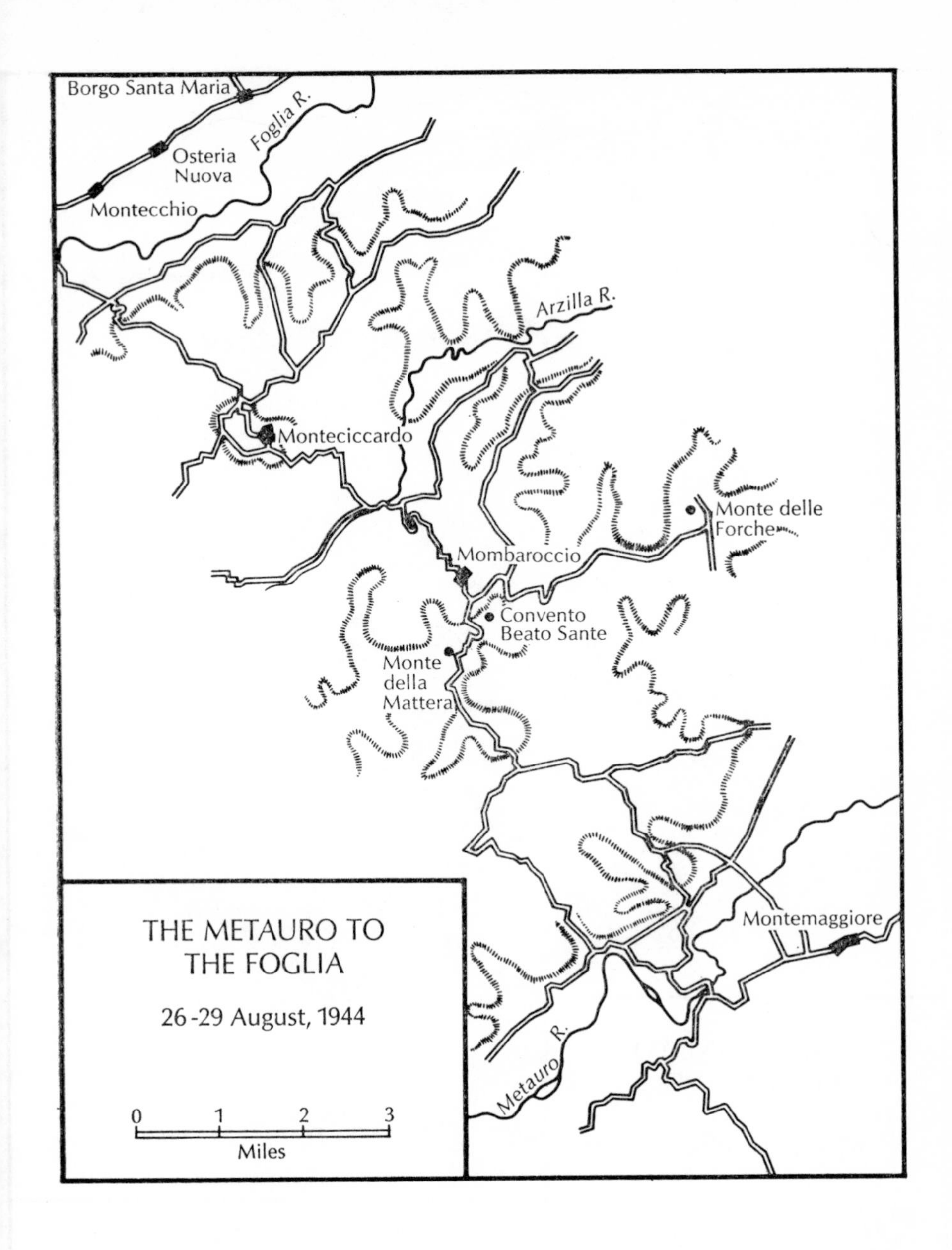
Borgo Santa Maria
Foglia R.
Osteria
Nuova
Montecchio
Arzilla R.
Monteciccardo
Monte delle
Forche
Mombaroccio
Convento
Beato Sante
Monte
della
Mattera
Montemaggiore
Metauro
R.
THE METAURO TO
THE FOGLIA
26-29 August, 1944
0
1
2
3
Miles

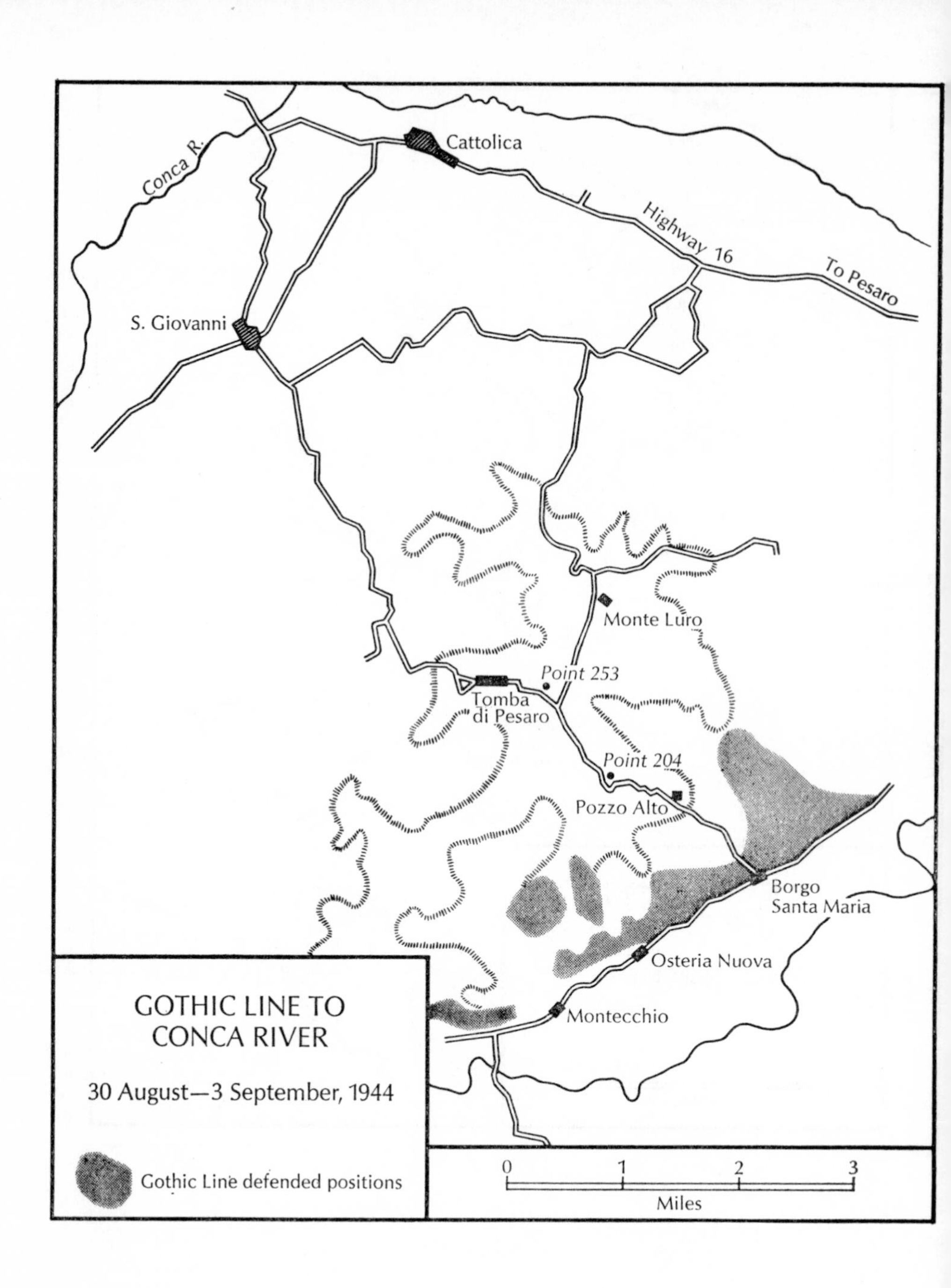
Cattolica
Conca R.
Highway 16
To Pesaro
S. Giovanni
Monte Luro
Point 253
Tomba di Pesaro
Point 204
Pozzo Alto
Borgo Santa Maria
Osteria Nuova
Montecchio
GOTHIC LINE TO CONCA RIVER
30 August—3 September, 1944
Gothic Line defended positions
0
1
2
3
Miles

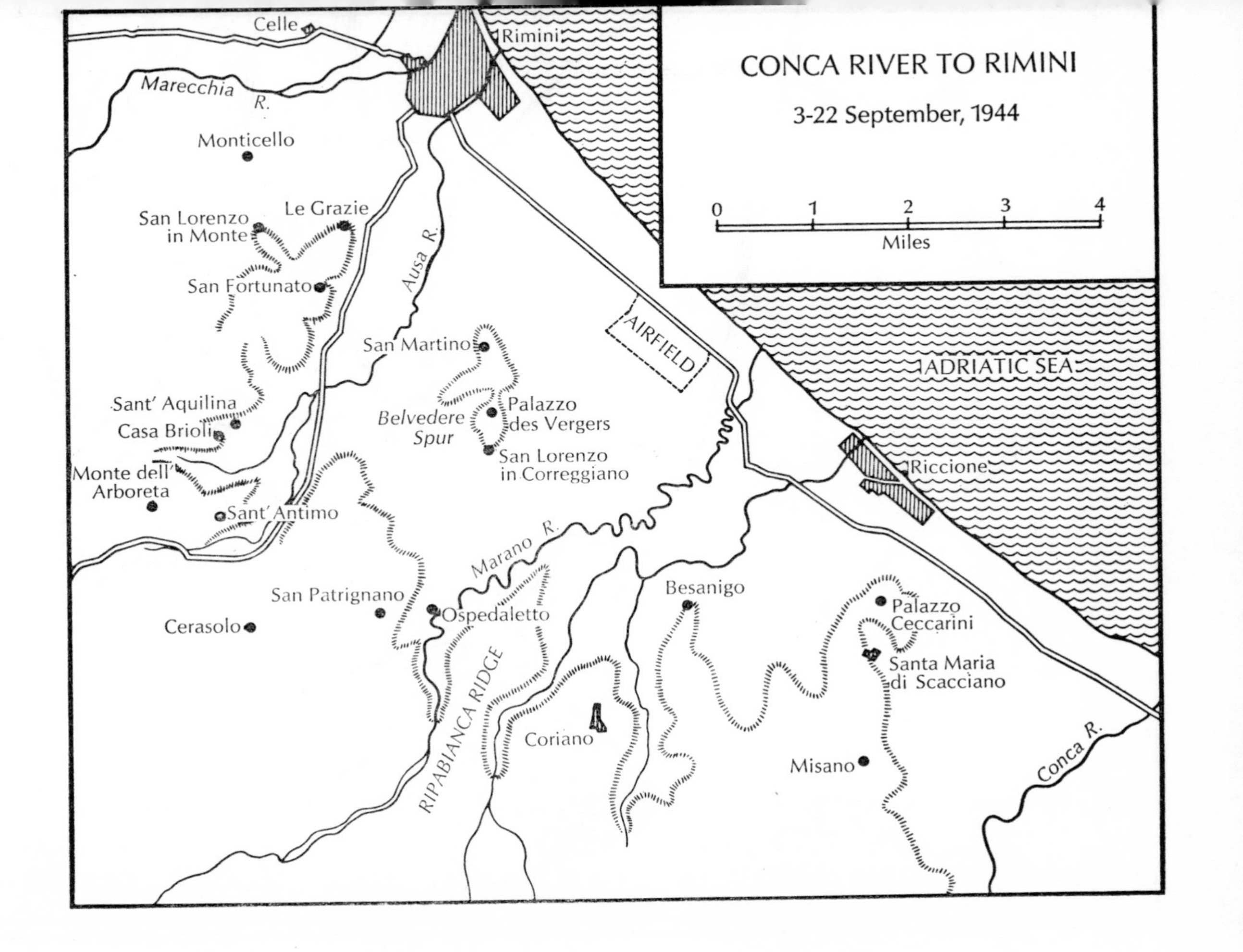
CONCA RIVER TO RIMINI
3-22 September, 1944
0
1
2
3
4
Miles
Celle
Rimini
Marecchia R.
Monticello
San Lorenzo in Monte
Le Grazie
San Fortunato
Ausa R.
San Martino
AIRFIELD
ADRIATIC SEA
Sant' Aquilina
Casa Brioli
Belvedere Spur
Palazzo des Vergers
San Lorenzo in Correggiano
Monte dell' Arboreta
Sant' Antimo
Riccione
Marano R.
San Patrignano
Ospedaletto
Cerasolo
Besanigo
Palazzo Ceccarini
Santa Maria di Scacciano
RIPABIANCA RIDGE
Coriano
Misano
Conca R.

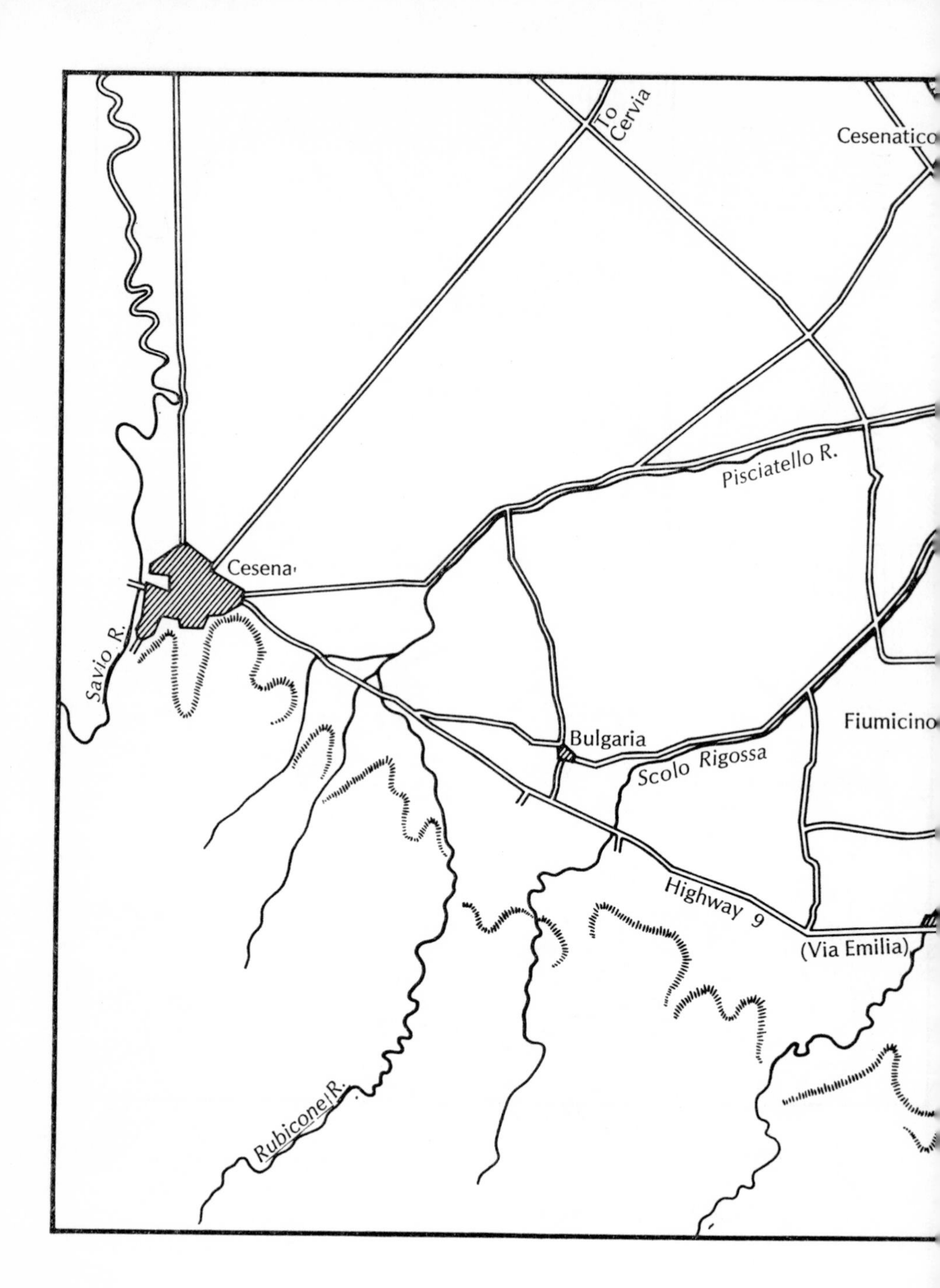
To Cervia
Cesenatico
Pisciatello R.
Cesena
Savio R.
Bulgaria
Scolo Rigossa
Fiumicino
Highway 9
(Via Emilia)
Rubicone R.

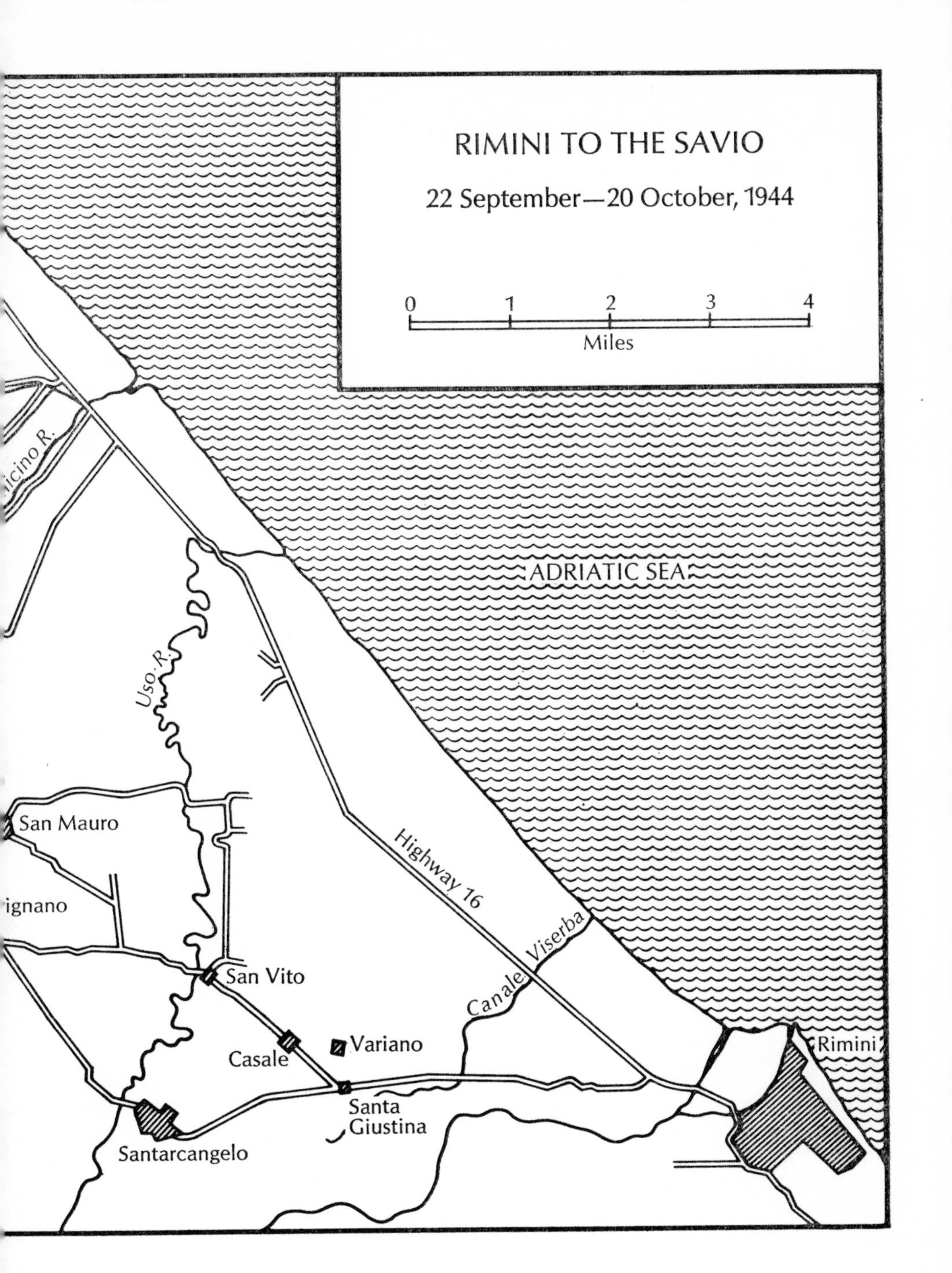
RIMINI TO THE SAVIO
22 September—20 October, 1944
0
1
2
3
4
Miles
ADRIATIC SEA
Uso R.
Highway 16
Canale Viserba
San Mauro
ignano
San Vito
Casale
Variano
Santa Giustina
Santarcangelo
Rimini

# Index

The rank shown against officers' names is usually the highest attained; not necessarily that held during the period covered by the narrative. The following abbreviations are used occasionally in the index: Armd.—Armoured; Bde.—Brigade; Bn.—Battalion; Cav.—Cavalry; Cdn.—Canadian; C.E.F.—Corps Expéditionnaire Français; Div.—Division; Inf.—Infantry; Regt.—Regiment.

PART I: PERSONS AND PLACES

## PART II: FORMATIONS AND UNITS